Junior Master Gardener®
Teacher/Leader Guide

Level 1

Published by:
Texas Agricultural Extension Service
Agricultural Communications
107 Reed McDonald Building
Texas A&M University
College Station, Texas 77843-2112
http://texaserc.tamu.edu

Copies may be ordered from:
JMG Kids℠
4066 State Hwy 6 South
College Station, TX 77845
1-888-JMG-KIDS
fax (979) 690-7547

ISBN 0-9672990-1-2

Junior Master Gardener,® JMG,℠ and associated logos are registered service marks and terms Golden Ray Series℠ and Operation Thistle℠ service marks of Texas Cooperative Extension, The Texas A&M University System.

CONTENTS

INTRODUCTION TO THE JMG® – JUNIOR MASTER GARDENER® PROGRAM

Welcome to the JMG Junior Master Gardener program. The JMG program is a new and innovative 4-H youth gardening project. Level One of the JMG^{SM} program is designed for children in grades 3 to 5. It is modeled after the highly successful Master Gardener program and offers horticultural and environmental science education, and leadership and life skills development through fun and creative activities. This program is committed to helping young people become good gardeners and good citizens so they can make a positive contribution to their community, school and family.

The JMG program incorporates group and individual activities, and is supported by a JMG youth handbook and a teacher/leader guide. Group activities can be held with a school class, JMG club, after-school program, home school or any group of interested young gardeners. Individual activities allow the youth gardener to pursue self-directed learning at home. Flexibility is a key component of the JMG program. Most of the activities presented allow the JMG leader and youth gardeners to customize the JMG program to meet their needs and interests.

Youths can become certified JMG Junior Master Gardeners by completing one group and one individual activity for each teaching concept in the eight chapters of the JMG Junior Master Gardener Handbook, and by participating in one leadership/service learning project per chapter.

More information about participating in the JMG program or other 4-H activities can be obtained from the county Extension agent. Look in the telephone book under "COUNTY" to locate your county Extension office. Call the main county telephone number if you have difficulty in contacting the county office.

Another information source is the National JMG Headquarters, JMG Web Site, and JMG Kids^{SM} Distribution.

Junior Master Gardener Program
225 Horticulture/Forestry Building
Texas A&M University
College Station, Texas 77843-2134
Phone (979) 845-8565
Fax (979) 845-8906

JMG Kids^{SM}
4066 State Hwy 6 South
College Station, TX 77845
1-888-JMG-KIDS
fax (979) 690-7547

Web address: *www.jmgkids.org*

An exciting adventure is just waiting for you and your gardeners in the JMG program. Make plantable greeting cards. . .discover the wonderful world of worms. . .make big suckers. . .create your own spider web. . .grow your own vegetables. . .make yummy dishes for you and your family and so much more!

The JMG program began more than 4 years ago as a dream of a few avid Master Gardeners, teachers, children and Extension faculty. These few planted the initial seed that has now germinated into a premier children's gardening program. A team of more than 600 children and adults contributed to the development, writing, layout, art and piloting of this curriculum. They have shaped and molded this program into a handbook and teacher/leader guide that will be fun, educational and exciting for everyone. We hope that by using this guide and teaching materials, each of you will use horticulture as a tool to cultivate children and communities. So come on and "Get Jammin' with JMG!"

"Bloom Where You Are Planted and Happy Gardening,"

Lisa A. Whittlesey
Extension Program Specialist
JMG Junior Master Gardener Coordinator

Randy L. Seagraves
JMG Junior Master Gardener Curriculum Coordinator

Douglas F. Welsh
Texas Master Gardener Coordinator

Gayle W. Hall
Texas 4-H and Youth Development Specialist

JMG® PROGRAM AND MANAGEMENT GUIDELINES

Who administers the JMG Junior Master Gardener program?
The JMG Junior Master Gardener program is administered by the Texas Agricultural Extension Service of The Texas A&M University System in College Station, Texas.

Locally, administration of JMG groups is flexible. They may be administered by county Extension offices or by other local educational organizations with support from Extension. For example, a school district can organize a JMG group in its after-school child care program, with horticultural and youth development expertise and support provided by the local Extension office.

Who can start a JMG Junior Master Gardener group?
Any organization with a mission of youth development and education can register a JMG Junior Master Gardener group, including:
- ✓ 4-H clubs
- ✓ Schools (i.e., classroom, after-school child care and home schools)
- ✓ Community/neighborhood youth programs (i.e., Master Gardener projects, scouting/church groups, Boys and Girls Clubs, camps, arboreta/botanical gardens, garden clubs)

To register as a JMG Junior Master Gardener group:
- ✓ A minimum of five youths must be members of the group;
- ✓ The group must have one or more adult leaders/teachers;
- ✓ Suitable meeting facilities (i.e., classroom, garden area) must be provided; and
- ✓ A registration package must be properly submitted and approved.

How to Enroll a Group in the JMG Junior Master Gardener Program
A group can enroll in the JMG Junior Master Gardener program by completing the JMG Registration Packet, which can be obtained from:
- ✓ The county Extension office
- ✓ The JMG headquarters at (979) 845-8565
- ✓ The appendix of a JMG Teacher/Leader Guide
- ✓ The JMG web site at *www.jmgkids.org*

The JMG Registration Packet includes the four forms needed to organize a JMG group:
- ✓ *JMG Junior Master Gardener Registration Agreement Form*
- ✓ *JMG Junior Master Gardener Member Group Enrollment Form*
- ✓ *JMG Publication Order Form*
- ✓ *Leader/Teacher Registration Form*

Once you have received the JMG Registration Packet, complete each form carefully. Mail the completed JMG^{SM} Publication Order Form, plus your check or money order for the publications, to JMG Distribution. All other forms in the JMG Registration Packet should be mailed to the Junior Master Gardener headquarters.

JMG Junior Master Gardener Headquarters
225 Horticulture/Forestry Science Building
Texas A&M University
College Station, Texas 77843-2134
(979) 845-8565
FAX: (979) 845-8906
E-mail: jmg@tamu.edu

JMG Distribution
4066 State Hwy 6 South
College Station, TX 77845
1-888-JMG-KIDS

JMG Headquarters will send an official letter of registration for your group, plus the publications ordered. A copy of your registration packet will be sent to your nearest Extension office for its records. Your group of young gardeners will then be ready to begin the JMG Junior Master Gardener experience.

After members of your group complete the JMG Junior Master Gardener curriculum requirements, you can order JMG Junior Master Gardener Certificates by completing the *JMG Completion Form* and mailing it to the JMG Headquarters at Texas A&M University. Certificates will be promptly returned for presentation to the newest JMG Junior Master Gardeners!

Upon starting each new JMG Junior Master Gardener group, the sponsoring organization/group must provide the state JMG headquarters with a completed registration packet.

JMG Junior Master Gardener Program Policies and Guidelines
The JMG Junior Master Gardener program is flexible; a successful JMG group can be managed in many ways. There are a few policies that have been established and must be adhered to by all JMG groups. These policies have been established to ensure that the objectives of the JMG Junior Master Gardener program are met, and to protect the credibility of the JMG Junior Master Gardener program as a youth development and education program of the Cooperative Extension Service.

Service marks, copyright and logos: The terms Junior Master Gardener, JMG, Golden Ray Series and associated logos are service marks of the Texas Agricultural Extension Service, College Station, Texas. Permission to use the terms and logos is granted solely by the Texas Agricultural Extension Service. The terms and logos are to be used for noncommercial, educational purposes by Cooperative Extension Services of Land Grant universities and other youth organizations. Permission to use the Junior Master Gardener and JMG service marks, logos and curriculum is granted to registered JMG groups of the Texas Agricultural Extension Service.

The 4-H name and emblem are copyrighted and governed by the Secretary of Agriculture, United States Department of Agriculture. Registered JMG groups are authorized to use the 4-H name and emblem in association with their JMG group and activities.

The JMG Junior Master Gardener Teacher/Leader Guide and the JMG Junior Master Gardener Handbook are copyrighted and may not be copied or duplicated without written permission from the JMG headquarters. However, any document in the appendices of the JMG Junior Master Gardener Teacher/Leader Guide may be duplicated.

Commercialism: The JMG Junior Master Gardener program is intended to be a noncommercial youth educational program. No individual associated with a JMG group or 4-H project may enter into a contract or relationship of a commercial nature involving the JMG program unless authorized by the JMG headquarters and state 4-H office of the Texas Agricultural Extension Service.

No local JMG group or 4-H project may enter into a contract or business relationship with a business, corporation or individual that may be construed as using the JMG or 4-H programs and/or their service marks, logos, names or emblems to conduct, sell or give endorsement for commercial purposes. This policy is not intended to interfere with any JMG or 4-H group conducting fund-raising activities to support its local project.

Certificates and badges: JMG Junior Master Gardener certificates and badges are to be used only by the groups and participants of the JMG Junior Master Gardener program. No alterations, modifications or additions to the JMG certificates and badges can be made without written permission of the JMG headquarters of the Texas Agricultural Extension Service.

Equal opportunity statement: The JMG Junior Master Gardener program of the Texas Agricultural Extension Service is open to all people without regard to race, color, sex, disability, religion, age or national origin.

Financial issues: Regarding financial matters (i.e., fund-raising, accounting, banking), JMG Junior Master Gardener groups are encouraged to follow the guidelines set forth by the sponsoring organization or by the Texas 4-H Club Management Guide (4-H 1-5.0128).

Insurance: All youth groups are encouraged to secure insurance against liability and accident. Follow the procedures of the sponsoring organization or refer to the Texas 4-H Club Management Guide (4-H 1-5.0128) for insurance guidelines and policies.

PROGRAM INFORMATION FOR THE JMG® TEACHER/LEADER

Your role as a JMG leader
As a JMG Teacher/Leader you should:
- ✓ Participate in training as needed
- ✓ Submit the JMG Registration Packet to the JMG Headquarters
- ✓ Request handbooks and remit payment
- ✓ Serve as instructor or coordinator
- ✓ Distribute information to JMG participants and parents
- ✓ Participate in evaluation and reporting of JMG activities
- ✓ Provide recognition for JMG participants

The JMG headquarters will develop and coordinate the JMG Junior Master Gardener program, including:
- ✓ Curriculum and program development
- ✓ Program management
- ✓ Assistance in securing financial resources
- ✓ Interpretation and evaluation
- ✓ Recognition

About the JMG Junior Master Gardener Teacher/Leader Guide and JMG Junior Master Gardener Handbook
A strength of the JMG Junior Master Gardener program is its comprehensive curriculum composed of a teacher/leader guide and a youth handbook.

The JMG Junior Master Gardener Teacher/Leader Guide is designed to accompany and correspond to the youth handbook. The JMG Junior Master Gardener curriculum has eight instructional chapters, each with teaching concepts or categories that have corresponding activities. The teacher/leader guide contains a smorgasbord of group activities for each teaching concept. As a JMG leader, you and your young gardeners may select which group activity to complete for each teaching concept.

Included in each chapter of the teacher/leader guide is an overview page that lists all the teaching concepts and corresponding group and individual activities included in the teacher/leader guide and the youth handbook. This can help you see at a glance the choices available for you and your group.

The teacher/leader guide also contains helpful appendices including the Registration Packet, Rhythms, Working with Young People, 4-H Basic Facts, and Work Sheets. For schoolteachers, there are special sections that include activity correlation to academic standards, and reading passages with corresponding questions written in a standardized testing format.

About the JMG Junior Master Gardener Handbook
The youth handbook, called the JMG Junior Master Gardener Handbook, contains individual activities designed to enhance the group activities for each chapter. For certification, each youth must complete one individual and one group activity for each teaching concept in the curriculum. Also, at the end of

each chapter is a section entitled "Leadership/Service Learning Projects." These are projects and activities the young gardeners can do to share their new knowledge with their families, friends and community. To be certified as a Junior Master Gardener, each youth must participate in one of these leadership/service learning projects.

Each youth is encouraged to have his or her own JMG Junior Master Gardener Handbook. The handbook has places for the young gardener to write, draw and circle the activities completed. This is a good way for each child to see progress and to have a record of the many adventures in the JMG program.

Both the JMG Junior Master Gardener Teacher/Leader Guide and JMG Junior Master Gardener Handbook have eight chapters. Here is a brief description of each chapter:

Chapter 1. Plant Growth and Development
Participants will learn how plants grow and make our world a better place.

Chapter 2. Soils and Water
Participants will get their hands dirty and learn how soil and water are important to plants and all living things.

Chapter 3. Ecology and Environmental Horticulture
Participants will get the big picture of how people, plants and animals all depend upon each other and how they can help to take care of our environment.

Chapter 4. Insects and Diseases
Participants will find out what's bugging them and their plants by exploring the world of insects and plant diseases.

Chapter 5. Landscape Horticulture
Participants will learn how to create and take care of beautiful gardens, and how to attract birds, insects and other creatures to their backyards or neighborhoods.

Chapter 6. Fruits and Nuts
Participants will learn about many different kinds of fruits and nuts, and make fruit smoothies, raisins and even peanut butter!

Chapter 7. Vegetables and Herbs
Participants will learn to grow many different kinds of vegetables and herbs and how to cook them in some yummy dishes.

Chapter 8. Life Skills and Career Exploration
Participants will learn more about themselves, their friends and their school, and discover how to make plans for the future.

"What is Service Learning?"
Service-learning combines service to the community with student learning in a way that improves both the student and the community. According to the National and Community Service Trust Act of 1993:

Service-Learning
- Is a method whereby students learn and develop through active participation in thoughtfully organized service that is conducted in and meets the needs of communities;
- Is coordinated with an elementary school, secondary school, institution of higher education, or community service program and the community.
- Helps foster civic responsibility;
- Is integrated into and enhances the academic curriculum of the students, or the education components of the community service program in which the participants are enrolled;
- Provides structured time for students or participants to reflect on the service experience."

"Golden Ray Series℠ Curriculum"
Completing a Golden Ray Series is a good way to recognize youths completing a small portion of the JMG program. Youths can receive Golden Ray Series certification in any of the eight chapters of the Level 1 curriculum and/or one of the stand-alone Golden Ray Series curricula such as *Health and Nutrition from the Garden or Wildlife Gardener℠."*
Other Golden Ray Series related to a variety of topics will be available in the future from the JMG headquarters.

Requirements for Golden Ray Series Certification are:
- Complete any combination of 12 activities in a single chapter (from teacher guide, youth handbook or a combination of both) or from other Golden Ray Series curricula
- Complete 1 Life Skill/Career Exploration activity
- Participate in 1 Community Service project

Individual Activities of the JMG Curriculum: Schoolteachers, 4-H leaders, Master Gardeners and others may choose to use individual activities found in the JMG Junior Master Gardener Handbook or JMG Junior Master Gardener Teacher/Leader Guide to enhance any youth educational program or class. The handbook and teacher/leader guide are comprehensive educational resources for horticultural and environmental sciences, youth life skills and leadership development, and community service.

Next in the JMG Junior Master Gardener Program: After being certified as a JMG Junior Master Gardener – Level I, young gardeners may continue in the JMG program by participating in Level II (sixth through eighth grades) and Level III (ninth through twelfth grades). New JMG'ers can use their knowledge and leadership skills to teach their peers and younger children the art and science of gardening.

JMG'ers may also continue expanding their expertise and involvement with the JMG program by completing a Golden Ray Series curriculum. JMG'ers are also eligible to participate in the 4-H program through a variety of activities and projects at the county, district and state levels.

About the 4-H program
As a participant in the JMG Junior Master Gardener program, youths may be new to the 4-H program. There are many ways to participate in 4-H. They can become members of a 4-H club or interest group. They may attend 4-H camps or local, district and state 4-H activities, and share what they have learned with friends and the community.

The motto of the 4-H program is "To Make the Best Better." Through the Junior Master Gardener program, horticulture is used as a tool to cultivate youths and communities.

For a child to be certified as a Junior Master Gardener, one individual and one group activity should be completed for each section/teaching concept in this chapter. Your JMG group should also select one leadership/service learning project for this chapter to complete.

Importance and Uses of Plants

GROUP ACTIVITIES
Hamburger Plant (p. 3)
Benefits Mobile (p. 4)
Know & Show Sombrero (p. 4)
The Choo-Choo Song (p. 5)
The Medicine Plant (p. 6)

INDIVIDUAL ACTIVITIES
Plant Product Collage
Plant Press Sandwich
Journal

Plant Classification

GROUP ACTIVITIES
Leaf-and-Seed-Sort Information Chart (p. 7)

INDIVIDUAL ACTIVITIES
Leaf Rubbing Rainbow
Can You Be-Leaf It?
JMG Web

Plant Parts

GROUP ACTIVITIES
Plant Parts Rap (p. 8)
Touch and Tell (p. 9)
Plant Parts We Eat (p. 9)
Seed Science (p. 10)
Flower Dissection (p. 11)

INDIVIDUAL ACTIVITIES
Fantastical Plants
JMG Rap Performance
Uncover and Discover
Happy Birthday Dear Tree

Plant Needs

GROUP ACTIVITIES
P.L.A.N.T. Needs (p. 11)
What's Not the Same? (p. 12)
Plant People (p. 12)
Picture Yourself a Plant (p. 13)

INDIVIDUAL ACTIVITIES
Variable Menu
2-liter Terrarium

Plant Growth

GROUP ACTIVITIES
Coconut Float (p. 13)
Plant Performance (p. 15)
Topiary Design (p. 16)
Power Seeds (p. 16)

INDIVIDUAL ACTIVITIES
Pinwheel Plants
Pinto Plant Parts
Seed Sock Search
See the Seed Flee

Plant Processes

GROUP ACTIVITIES
Oxygen Factory (p. 17)
Gas Gobblers (p. 18)
Spinning Seeds (p. 19)

INDIVIDUAL ACTIVITIES
Initial Leaves
Plant Maze
Upside Down Seed
Patriotic Plant
Smothering Stomata

Propagation

GROUP ACTIVITIES
Paper Pots (p. 20)
Gallon Greenhouse (p. 21)
Propagation Demonstration (p. 21)

INDIVIDUAL ACTIVITIES
Stick and Grow
Seed Sponges
Time to Transplant
Grow Your Own Pineapple
JMG Web
Journal

Leadership/Service Learning Projects

Gifts for Others (p. 24)
Variable Day Demonstration (p. 24)
Adopt-a-Spot (p. 24)
Share What You Know (p. 24)
Create Your Own (p. 24)

Plant Growth and Development

Importance and Uses of Plants

Plants are a vital part of Planet Earth. They are the beginning of the food chain, providing nourishment for both animals and people. They also make our world beautiful: Trees give shade during the summer and protect us from the wind in winter; shrubs, vines and flowers beautify our homes and provide a place for wildlife, such as birds, squirrels and insects, to live.

Plants are also used to make clothing, medicine and shelter for people. Some clothes are made from plants, and our ancestors used plants to dye their clothing. Long ago, people treated common illnesses with medicines not from the pharmacy or grocery store, but from plants. And our homes are made and furnished with wood and many other plant-based materials.

Plants also enhance the very air we breathe, by producing the oxygen our bodies need. Without plants, we could not live.

ACTIVITIES

✿ Hamburger Plant

Objective: To learn that we depend on plants as the original source of most food.
Time: 30 minutes.
Materials: Paper, crayons or colored pencils, chalkboard or poster.

Ask the junior gardeners if they know that hamburgers come from plants. Have them imagine what a hamburger plant might look like. Ask volunteers to describe it for you. Assign them to draw what they think a hamburger plant looks like.

Explain that hamburgers really do come from plants, but there is no such thing as a real hamburger plant. Have the gardeners call out the ingredients found in hamburgers, and write the ingredients on a chalkboard or poster.

Tell them you will circle any word that names a plant. Go through each ingredient on the list that is not a plant and ask them where it comes from. Beside the ingredient, write where it originates until you find a link to plants.

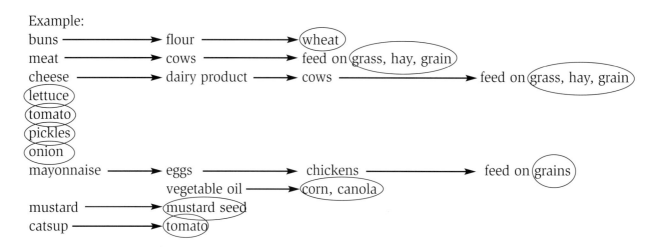

Chapter 1

Example:

buns ⟶ flour ⟶ (wheat)

meat ⟶ cows ⟶ feed on (grass, hay, grain)

cheese ⟶ dairy product ⟶ cows ⟶ feed on (grass, hay, grain)

(lettuce)
(tomato)
(pickles)
(onion)

mayonnaise ⟶ eggs ⟶ chickens ⟶ feed on (grains)

vegetable oil ⟶ (corn, canola)

mustard ⟶ (mustard seed)

catsup ⟶ (tomato)

❧ Benefits Mobile

Objective: To understand that all people depend on plants.
Time: 45 minutes.
Materials: Construction paper, glue, string, scissors, crayons or colored pencils, sticks and twigs.

Ask the junior gardeners what the world would be like without plants. Explain that we couldn't live without the food that plants provide for us and for the animals that people eat. Ask them if they can think of what else plants give us. As the gardeners offer correct responses, list them on the chalkboard or a poster titled "The Benefits of Plants." Be sure to include that plants give us food, clothing, shelter, fresh air, food, food for other living things, as well as add beauty to our world. Go outdoors and collect sticks and twigs and other plant parts for a mobile.

Have the gardeners use art supplies and be creative in building a mobile that displays all the benefits plants provide for our world. Ask them to interpret how their mobiles represent the plants' benefits to humans.

❧ Know & Show Sombrero

Objective: To make wearable works of art that show an understanding of the benefits of plants to people.
Time: 1 hour.
Materials: 2-inch clear tape, newspaper, miscellaneous art supplies (markers, yarn, glitter, pipe cleaners, tissue, etc.).

The junior gardeners will create pieces of wearable art: decorated newspaper hats. Help each individually or have the gardeners choose partners to help make a hat for each member of the JMG group.

Place the middle of two large, square sheets of newspaper on the top of a student's head. Lay the rest of the paper flat against the student's head. Tape around the newspaper starting right over the gardener's ear and continue wrapping until the tape goes all the way around the student's head.

Chapter 1

Curl up the edges of the newspaper to form the brim of the hat. Have the gardeners decorate their hats with different art supplies to show what they have learned about the benefits that plants provide us. Have the gardeners be creative—for example, a pair of jeans might be cut out of construction paper and hung to the brim of the hat to show that some plants provide us with clothing.

When all the gardeners are finished, have them show the group their creations and discuss what each decoration means. You may want to have hooks for the gardeners to hang their hats on for storage when they are finished. This is a good activity for students to show they understand the concept. As gardeners learn more concepts in the Plant Growth and Development section, they could add them to their hats.

This activity is listed as a project competition at the end of this section.

🌾 The Choo-Choo Song

Objective:	To associate a variety of plants with their food products by learning a rhythm.
Time:	15 minutes.
Materials:	Rhythm sheets (in the Appendix and JMG Handbook).

Read the verse first so the gardeners can pick up its rhythm. Have them join in. Challenge them to create additional verses. The group could plan to perform the rhythm for a younger group of gardeners.

The Choo-Choo Song
Tomato sat on the railroad track,
Thought he was the boss,
Along came the choo-choo train, (clap)
Tomato sauce.

Avocado sat on the railroad track,
All jolly and rolly,
Along came the choo-choo train, (clap)
Guacamole.

Cucumber sat on the railroad track,
For this there is no excuse,
Along came the choo-choo train, (clap)
Pickle juice.

Other Verses:
Blueberry, huffin' and puffin', (clap) Blueberry muffin

Apple, playing with a spider, (clap) Apple cider
Lemon, where he often stayed, (clap) Lemonade
Strawberry, being such a ham, (clap) Strawberry jam
Orange, silly as a goose, (clap) Orange juice
Grape, Sunning his fat belly, (clap) Grape jelly
Onion, Doing his own thing, (clap) Onion ring
Potato, Wishing he could fly, (clap) French fry

The Medicine Plant

Objective: To recognize the medicinal properties of the aloe vera plant.
Time: 40 minutes.
Materials: Aloe vera plant, aloe vera products (examples: lotion, gel, shampoo), unscented lotion, colander or juicer, baby food jars, Popsicle® sticks, knife.

Show the gardeners a real aloe vera plant. Ask them if they know what is special about it. Share with them that the aloe vera plant is used to treat burns. Tell them that one-half of all of the medicines in the world come from plants. Tell the group that people all over the world use aloe vera for its medicinal value. Show them some aloe vera products they may have seen.

Cut off an aloe vera leaf, then cut it lengthwise to expose the fleshy gel inside the leaf. Tell the gardeners that products are made from the juice from the leaves and that they will make their own jar of aloe lotion. Explain that the aloe vera plant can heal itself when leaves are cut.

Cut and split several leaves. Crush the leaves with juicer, and use the colander to extract juice from the leaves. The gel can also be scraped away from the "skin" of the leaf. Allow the gardeners to touch and smell the juice. Give each one a paper plate and spoon. Pour a small amount of lotion onto each plate along with a few teaspoons of aloe juice. Allow them to mix the ingredients with their Popsicle® sticks. Each student can spoon the mixture into a baby food jar. Have them create labels for their jars.

Show the gardeners that the aloe plant produces young plants, called "pups," at the base. Explain that these pups are exactly like the parent plants. As the pups sprout, pull them up and transplant them so the gardeners can take home their own medicine plants.

Plant Classification

Without a classification system, identifying the millions of plants in the world would be difficult. Tell the gardeners that if they took all the clothes from their rooms and threw them on the floor, it would be hard to find anything. But if they organize their clothes so that socks are together, shirts are together, and pants are together, it is easy to find the clothes they want.

Scientists have ways of organizing plants. They look at different plant parts, such as flowers, leaves, stems and fruits, and group together the plants that are similar. For example, some plants produce flowers; others produce cones. Plants are also grouped according to where and how they grow. Some plants, such as trees, live for many years. Others, such as radishes, live for only one season before they die. Take the gardeners outside to see all the many different plants in the neighborhood. Have them take a minute to look closely at one plant and imagine what other plants might be related to it.

ACTIVITIES

❀ Leaf-and-Seed-Sort Information Chart

Objective: To be able to classify leaves and seeds as monocots or dicots.
Time: 25 minutes.
Materials: Corn seed, peanuts, leaf with parallel veins, leaf with netted veins, construction
            paper, crayons.

Ask the gardeners if they have a certain place in their room where they keep their socks, shirts or toys. Have them think about a kitchen drawer full of knives, forks, spoons, etc. The drawer is organized so that each utensil has its own place. Tell them that the reason they are organized that way is to make them easier to find and use. Explain that scientists who study plants do the same thing: They organize or classify plants into different categories so they are easier to learn about and use.

Explain that scientists divide plants into two main groups: monocots and dicots. The veins in monocot leaves all go the same direction, or parallel; veins in dicot leaves go different directions, and are called netted. Hold up the two leaves and see if gardeners can tell which is a monocot and which is a dicot. Show them how to lay a sheet of paper over the leaf and rub over it with the edge of a crayon to show the veins of the leaf on the paper.

Monocot	Dicot

Another way to differentiate a monocot seed from a dicot seed is that a monocot seed is in one piece, whereas a dicot comes in more than one piece. Show them the corn and peanut seeds and ask which is which.

Have each gardener fold a large (11- by 17-inch) sheet of construction paper in half three times to make a sheet with eight sections or boxes. The gardeners should turn the papers so that they make two long columns up and down. Have them label the first box with the word MONOCOT in large letters. In the box below that, they should make a rubbing of a monocot leaf. They should glue the monocot leaf below the rubbing, and a monocot seed in the box under the leaf.

Have them complete the second half of the box the same way using the dicot information.

In the classroom

Folding paper is a good opportunity to reinforce fraction skills. When you fold the construction paper in half, show the students that the paper is folded into two parts. Tell them that each part is called one-half and write $\frac{1}{2}$ on the board. Ask them how many halves are on the page. Since there are two, explain that there are two halves on the page. Write $\frac{2}{2}$ on the board. Do the same thing each time you fold the paper in half again—you can introduce one-fourth ($\frac{1}{4}$), four-fourths ($\frac{4}{4}$), one-eighth ($\frac{1}{8}$) and eight-eighths ($\frac{8}{8}$).

Plant Parts

A plant has many different parts that work together just as a person's body parts work together. The plant roots, found in the soil, carry water and nutrients to the plant. The stem supports and carries water and food throughout the plant. Leaves use sunlight to make food for the plant. Explain that flowers are usually the bright, colorful part of the plant; when they are pollinated by insects or wind, they produce seeds, which are sometimes stored in fruit. A seed can make a new plant.

ACTIVITIES

✿ Plant Parts Rap

Objective:	To learn the main parts of a plant and their roles.
Time:	15 minutes.
Materials:	Rhythm sheets (in the Appendix and JMG Handbook), Plant Parts Page (Appendix).

Say the rap to the gardeners so they can learn its rhythm. As you do, build a plant by attaching parts to the poster as you rap about them. Have the gardeners use their rhythm sheets and do the Plant Parts Rap as a group.

Plant Parts Rap

Plants are our friends, we give them special care.
They feed, they shelter, they give us fresh air.

Without plants in our world, we simply could not live,
Because of all of the awesome gifts that they give.

The tiny plant begins as a seed that germinates.
And from this moment on, here's the journey that it takes.

The roots are in the dirt to help the plant grow
And hold it in place when the winds blow.

Just like a soda straw, they suck up H_2O.
And when the plant gets water, stand back and watch it grow.

Stems hold the plant up, they carry water to
The leaves, flowers, fruit and seeds. . .that's what the stems do.

Leaves grow from the stem. They soak up lots of sun.
When they change it into food, then their job is done.

The food is for the plant—it gives it strength and power.
It helps it to grow and make a nice flower.

Wind, birds, and bees. . .these are a flower's friend.
They help the life cycle to start once again.

The flower makes a fruit with a seed deep inside.
Some are eaten, some are blown, or some just hitch a ride.

Once a fruit is dried and a little seed comes out,
The seed will find the dirt and a new plant will sprout.

❀ Touch and Tell

Objective: To use the information learned about plant parts to identify them by touch.
Time: 15 minutes.
Materials: Several cardboard boxes, various plant parts from different plants.

Ask the gardeners to name the main parts of a plant. Review each one and ask them to say what each part does for the plant.

Go out and collect several plant parts—you may need to search outdoors and find parts of weedy plants so that you do not destroy wanted plants. Make several blind, touch and feel boxes by cutting two hand holes in one side of each box. Place a different plant part in each box and number the boxes. Have the gardeners number a sheet of paper, go to each plant box and guess each part by feeling only, and write their guesses on their papers by the corresponding box numbers. After the whole group has completed guessing, unveil each part and review its purpose for the plant.

❀ Plant Parts We Eat

Objective: To identify the various plant parts used for food.
Time: 40 minutes.
Materials: Poster, markers, "Tops and Bottoms" by Janet Stevens, Sequencing Tops and Bottoms page (in the Appendix), plant parts that are food items.

Have the gardeners recall the six basic plant parts. Ask them which plant parts are eaten by people. Show them the items you brought and have them guess from what part of the plant they originated. Explain that we eat all kinds of plant parts.

With the gardeners, create a plant parts food web. In the middle of a poster board, write the words PLANT PARTS. As the students call out the names of each plant part, write them on the poster and connect them. Have the gardeners complete the web by thinking of examples of each type of food. They can write those words and connect them to each of the plant parts.

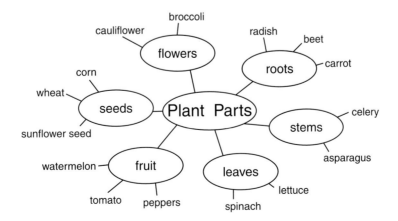

In the classroom

Read the book, "Tops and Bottoms," by Janet Stevens. On a sheet of poster board, create three columns labeled TOPS, BOTTOMS and MIDDLES. Have the gardeners categorize where to find the items you brought.

Have the gardeners complete the Tops and Bottoms sequencing page.

Seed Science

Objective: To use the scientific method to determine the effect on plant growth of removing the cotyledons from seeds.

Time: 30 minutes.

Observation: 1 week.

Materials: Sealable plastic bags, stapler, pinto beans, paper towels, Seed Science Experiment Page (Appendix).

Soak a bag of pinto beans in water overnight to prepare for this activity.

Have the students recall the differences between monocot and dicot plants. Review that monocot seeds are made up of a single whole while the dicot seed is made up of pieces. Hold up a dry bean seed and ask gardeners to identify if it is a monocot or dicot. Show them a seed that has been soaking and show them the different parts to reveal that it is a seed from a dicot plant.

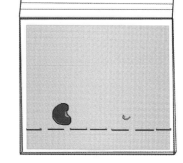

Give each gardener a bean. Have each gardener peel off the seed coat. Each student should take the seed and gently pull it apart to reveal the two halves called cotyledons. Have them look inside the seed for the baby plant, called the embryo.

Tell them that cotyledons are the seed's "lunch box." They feed the seed until it can grow its leaves and make its own food. Tell them that they will conduct an experiment to see how well seeds grow without their food supply.

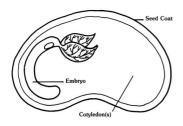

Seed Coat

Embryo

Cotyledon(s)

Fold a paper towel to fit inside a plastic bag. Punch a row of staples across and 1 inch from the bottom of the bag. Have the gardeners place one whole seed in the bag. Beside the seed, place an embryo plant that has been removed from the food-storing cotyledons. Wet the paper towel to moisten the seeds. Observe the growth. Have the students complete the Seed Science Experiment Page.

❧ Flower Dissection

Objective: To identify the different parts of a flower.
Time: 30 minutes.
Materials: Large, simple flowers such as lilies (contact a florist for free, wilted or unsaleable flowers), tape, construction paper, flower parts diagram (Plant Parts Diagram in the Appendix).

Allow each gardener to have his or her own flower. Show the gardeners the diagram of flower parts. Tell them that as you discuss each part, you want them to carefully remove that part from their flowers and neatly tape it to their construction paper.

First have them title their construction paper FLOWER PARTS. Explain that sepals protect the flower. Have them remove the sepal and tape it on their paper under the heading, "Sepal—protects flower." Tell them that petals also help protect the flower and attract pollinators. Again, have them carefully remove the petals and tape them under a heading that tells what the part is and what it does. Help them complete the flower dissection and label the pistil and stamen (both help create a seed) the same way.

Take the gardeners on a search outdoors to find a flower with parts they can identify.

Plant Needs

Plants need sunlight to make food. They make their own food in a process called photosynthesis, which occurs mainly in leaves. Plants combine carbon dioxide from the air, green pigment (chlorophyll) from the leaves, and sunlight to produce food. When plants make their own food through photosynthesis, they give off oxygen. People need oxygen to breathe.

ACTIVITIES
❧ P.L.A.N.T. Needs

Objective: To become familiar with plants' needs.
Time: 20 minutes.
Materials: Poster, markers, handbook.

Start a discussion of what people need to be able to live. On a poster, make a list of the five basic needs all people share: food, water, air, shelter and clothing. Ask a student to circle the items that the group thinks plants must have to live. Ask if plants need anything that people do not. On the left side of a poster write the word PLANT and tell the gardeners that everything a plant needs is in that word. Complete the chart as shown below and challenge the gardeners to recall the list of plant needs without looking at the list.

P	Place	In a container or garden.
L	Light	Sun or artificial light.
A	Air	Oxygen and carbon dioxide.
N	Nutrients	Nitrogen, phosphorus, potassium.
T	Thirsty	Plants, like all living things, need water.
S	Soil	Or other material (sand, gravel, water) to grow roots in.

❧ What's Not the Same?

Objective: To become familiar with variables and constants.
Time: 40 minutes.
Observation: 1 week.
Materials: Three small containers for planting, soil, nine pinto beans, Light Variable Lab Sheet (in the Appendix).

Tell the gardeners they will conduct a science experiment, but that it will be a "fair" experiment. Remind them that plants need light to live. Tell them that this experiment will test how light helps plants grow. This experiment will be "fair" because you will treat each plant the same in almost every way. Each container will be the same size. The containers will start with the same number of seeds and have the same amount of soil, water, etc. These are all called constants. The only thing that will be different about the experiment will be what is being tested.

Assign a gardener to measure the same amount of soil for each container, plant three beans in each and make sure each plant has the same amount of water to keep the soil moist. Place one container under an artificial light source, one in a spot that receives natural light (but not a hot area) and the last in a dark location. The part of the experiment that is different for each plant is called a variable. Have the gardeners complete the Light Variable Lab Sheet except for the Results, which will be added 1 or 2 weeks after planting.

❧ Plant People

Objective: To show through creative arts an understanding of plant needs.
Time: 30 minutes.
Materials: Nylon stockings, grass seed, potting soil, soda can, plastic eyes, miscellaneous art supplies.

Ask the gardeners to recall what plants need. Ask them where plants grow. Point out that plants can grow in many places—in the ground, a pot and even a crack in the sidewalk. Tell them they will make plant people. Explain that plant people are growing, living things that will need to be cared for. Show the group all the materials. Demonstrate how to create one, then help the students make their own.

Pour 1 to 2 tablespoons of grass seed into the stocking toe (Note: If the section of stocking does not have a toe, tie a knot at one end and turn the stocking inside out. Each section of stocking should be about 10 inches long). Pour soil on top of the seeds and tie a knot to hold in the dirt. Add enough soil to form a baseball-sized shape.

The seeds will grow from the end to form the hair of the plant person. Glue eyes to the "head" of the person. Once the glue has dried, submerge the head in water to allow water to penetrate the soil.

Set the head aside. Use various art supplies to decorate an empty soda can to be the plant person's body. It can be wrapped in a strip of construction paper. The gardeners can add paper or pipe cleaner arms and legs to complete the effect. Fill the decorated can with water and set the head on the can top. Push the excess stocking into the can opening to help wick water to the soil of the plant person.

Within several days, the plant peoples' hair will sprout. Have the gardeners keep the plant people in a well-lit location and make sure they stay moist. Before long, the gardeners will need to clip the grass to give their plant people haircuts!

❧ Picture Yourself a Plant

Objective: To show an understanding of plant needs through creative arts.
Time: 30 minutes.
Materials: Paper, colored pencils.

Have the gardeners draw a picture of a plant with personality. Tell them that their plant should look healthy and should include eyes and a smiling mouth to show that it is happy, healthy and strong.

On another sheet of paper, ask the students to illustrate the same plant, only depicting it as getting too little water because of a drought or because someone forgot to water it. On the next page have them illustrate their plant getting no fresh air because of pollution or a forest fire. The next page could show their plant getting too much sunlight or living in a container that is too small. The gardeners could role-play these same situations.

After the pictures are complete, have each gardener name the plant and write a story about it and the problems it has had. After the stories are written, allow volunteers to read them to the group.

Plant Growth

Plants have special needs, just as people do. When plants receive the proper light, water and nutrients, they grow and thrive. Most plants start as seeds and develop during their life cycles. The following activities demonstrate how plants grow.

ACTIVITIES

❧ Coconut Float

Objective: To illustrate the different ways seeds are dispersed.
Time: 15 minutes.
Materials: 10-gallon aquarium or large plastic tub, coconut, pinto bean, Coconut Float rhythm sheets (in the Appendix and JMG Handbook).

Have the gardeners recall the main parts of the plant they have already learned. Ask them what seeds do for a plant. Ask where they think seeds go once a plant creates them—do they all just fall down to the base of the plant?

Ask the group to imagine what it would be like if they had to stay in the same room together for the rest of their lives AND they had enough food for only one person and had to share it with everyone AND there was enough water for only one person to drink and that, too, would have to be shared with everyone. Ask them if they think they could live very long that way.

Tell them that plants do poorly if they live too close together, because they have to share and compete for water and light. Explain that plants have many ways of dispersing their seeds so the new, young plants can grow well on their own.

Have the gardeners share with you some creative ideas on how a seed might leave its parent plant, because it can't just get up and walk away. Tell them that seeds get away from the mother plant in many ways. Have them try to learn the verse:

"Some hitch-hike, some hide, some float away,
Some are buried, some are blown and some just have to stay."

Fill a tub or aquarium with water and hold up the coconut and bean. Ask the gardeners to predict which seed might leave its mother plant by floating away. Have a student drop both seeds in the tub to discover which floats.

To review different ways seeds are dispersed, read the "Coconut Float" poem to the group. Afterward, give volunteers a few minutes to practice and have them perform it for the group.

Coconut Float

Once a young seed said to its big Mother plant,
"I want to stay with you!" She said, "I'm sorry, seed—you can't."

"You need your own piece of earth, a place where you can grow."
Then the trees began to rustle and strong winds began to blow.

The seed was pulled far away and carried by the winds.
It fell lonely to the ground, but soon it made some friends.

A squirrel scampered by with some seeds in his cheeks.
It buried seeds all over, to hide them for a week.

The squirrel forgot about them and they began to sprout.
Those plants were growing strong when they heard a bird call out.

That bird squawked, "Watch out!"—earlier he'd been eating berries,
And now the bird was dropping droppings his body could no longer carry.

The droppings landed with a "SPLAT" in the open field.
From the seeds in that pile sprouted a plant that grows there still.

Soon a cat trotted by with stickers in its tail.
It stopped and scratched to get them out and on the ground they fell.

Those stickers were seeds that sprouted, now a huge bush grows there.
So if you walk in that area, be sure to take great care.

Another young plant that came nearby traveled far and at slow speed.
A coconut tree dropped a nut on the beach. Yes, a coconut is a seed.

The coconut did not grow on that beach, it got washed out to the ocean.
It traveled across great distances just by riding on wave motion.

The seed was splashing along when it bumped into a boat.
The captain looked up as the nut passed by and said, "Look a coconut float!"

The coconut finally landed on an island; it could no longer wait.
Once it found a good sandy spot, it began to germinate.

Now remember, plants need many things like water, air and light.
If they grow too close together, for those things they have to fight.

If seeds did not travel, they couldn't last very long.
But since they are carried, plants can grow to be healthy and strong.

Plant Performance

Objective: To develop an understanding of plant needs through creative writing.
Time: 40 minutes.
Materials: Pencil, paper.

Have the students imagine what plants would say if they could talk. Ask them what they think might make a plant happy, or sad or afraid.

Have the gardeners try to guess the mystery plant described in this riddle:

I'm a plant that you probably see every day.
You walk on me, run on me—on me you like to play.
I make the ground softer, and greener and pretty.
I grow well in parks, the country, even in the city.

Have them describe what their neighborhood would be like without grass. Tell the following story about a stormy day. Have the gardeners listen closely. After you finish reading, each one should write about the same day, but from the perspective of the grass!

This morning I woke up and it was pouring down rain! I looked out the window and saw that my yard was completely flooded under water. I dressed, grabbed my umbrella and went outside. It was cold and windy, and it even began to hail. Suddenly a really big wind blew the umbrella out of my hand. I had to run onto that sopping wet grass to get it. The yard was so wet that I sank down to my ankles and got mud and grass all over my shoes. Later that day, the rain finally stopped and the sun came out. It warmed up and things began to dry out.

After you finish reading, give the students several minutes to describe the day from the grass's point of view. To encourage them to write more freely, you should write while the gardeners are writing. Share your writing first by reading expressively, then ask for volunteers.

❧ Topiary Design

Objective: To create living, growing works of art.
Time: Initial activity, 45 minutes.
Materials: 1-gallon plastic plant pots (from a nursery), ivy, gravel, soil, wire coat hangers, sphagnum moss, fishing line, paper clips (opened and broken to make two U-shaped pieces).

Ivy plants are needed for this activity. You may either buy them or begin this activity after the propagation section of this unit and get the needed ivy from a single plant.

Have the gardeners fill a container or pot one-fourth full with gravel or rocks and plant the ivy in it.

Straighten the coat hanger hook (this end will serve as a spike to anchor the topiary into the pot.) Have the students bend the coat hanger into any form they like. The gardeners should work as partners to wet the sphagnum moss and bunch it around the wire. As the moss is being attached to the wire, begin looping the fishing line around the moss to secure it. Cover the entire coat hanger except for the spike.

Insert the spike into the soil next to the plant. Keep the soil and moss moist. As the ivy grows, attach it to the moss with the paper clip halves.

Mature topiaries can be used as gifts, fund-raising items or opportunities for gardeners to express themselves artistically while beautifying their surroundings.

❧ Power Seeds

Objective: To observe the force seeds exhibit in the germination process.
Time: 15 minutes.
Observation: 3 days.
Materials: Plaster, can, bean seeds.

To prepare for this activity, you will need a seed that has just germinated.

If the gardeners were asked to describe a young plant that is sprouting, they might say it is very young and fragile. Show them a plant that has just broken the surface of the dirt. Ask them if they think the young seedling is powerful enough to flip a coin. Hold up a quarter and tell them that seeds are powerful and the force they use to sprout and grow is quite strong. Lay the quarter on top of the sprout and have the students observe the seedling over the next few days.

Show them a hardened piece of plaster and ask the gardeners if they think sprouts are powerful enough to break through rock. Mix some plaster in a can and plant the seeds in the wet plaster. After the plaster has completely dried, have a student water the can daily to keep the plaster and seeds moist. Have the gardeners make predictions on whether the seeds can germinate.

Plant Processes

Plants need sunlight to make food. They make their own food in a process called photosynthesis, which occurs mainly in the leaves. Plants combine carbon dioxide from the air, green pigment (chlorophyll) from the leaves, and sunlight to produce food. When plants make their own food through photosynthesis, they give off oxygen, which people need to breathe.

ACTIVITIES

❧ Oxygen Factory

Objective: To illustrate the process of photosynthesis.
Time: 25 minutes.
Materials: Oxygen Factory illustration page (in the Appendix), crayons.

Distribute the Oxygen Factory illustration page. Tell the gardeners that plants are the only living things in the world that don't need to find food to eat. Tell them that plants make their own food within the leaves, in a process called PHOTOSYNTHESIS.

Explain that just as when we use different ingredients to follow a recipe, plants need different ingredients to make their food. We use ovens to bake our food to change it into something we can eat; plants use sunlight to change their ingredients into food they can use. Plants use three ingredients to make food: CHLOROPHYLL, WATER and CARBON DIOXIDE.

Explain that the green in the leaves comes from CHLOROPHYLL. Have them lightly color the leaf green. Remind them that the roots bring water to the plant from the ground. The water is carried to the leaves through the stems and veins. Have the gardeners color the stem and veins of the leaf blue. Tell them to take a deep breath and let it out slowly. When they breathe out, remind them that they are breathing out CARBON DIOXIDE—the last ingredient plants use to make their food. Have them color the bubbles of carbon dioxide gray.

Ask the students to remember what plants use to change their ingredients to food. Tell them that the leaves soak up sunlight; they should color the arrows labeled SUNLIGHT bright yellow.

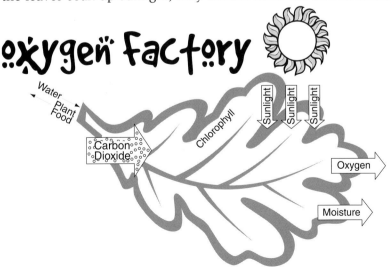

Tell them that the plant sends the food it makes to the stem for the rest of the plant. Have the gardeners take a breath again and tell them that the best part about the plant making its food is that it has leftovers that it does not need. Explain that in this process OXYGEN is made and the plants do not use it, so they send it into the air. Have them color the OXYGEN arrow red. Moisture is also released. Color the MOISTURE arrow blue.

Gas Gobblers

Objective: To demonstrate the interdependence people and animals share with plants through the exchange of oxygen and carbon dioxide.

Time: 20 minutes.

Materials: Four bottles of blow bubbles, construction paper (red, green), red and blue arm bands.

Ask the gardeners to recall some of the benefits we receive from plants. Explain that plants help people and animals breathe. Tell them that people inhale air and use the oxygen in it to live, and that we exhale carbon dioxide. Ask them why they think people have not used up all of the oxygen in the world yet. Explain that plants breathe the carbon dioxide we exhale and they breathe out the oxygen for us to use.

Game 1

Ask your group how many gardeners would be in each group if the whole group were divided in half. Then have half the class wear green arm bands to represent the plant group and the remaining gardeners wear blue arm bands to represent the people/animal group. Choose two people from each group to be bubble blowers. Have those students spread out to make a square with the remaining gardeners in the middle.

Remind the gardeners that people, animals and plants rely on each other to survive. Tell them that when you call out "OXYGEN," the plant bubble blowers should begin blowing bubbles while the people/animal group begin popping the bubbles to represent breathing them. After several seconds, call out "CARBON DIOXIDE" and have the other group pop bubbles blown by the people/animal group. Remind the gardeners that plants and people need each other for both to survive.

Game 2

Choose four bubble blowers to represent plants of the rain forest. The rest of the students represent the people and animals of the world. Explain that the largest concentration of plants in the world is in the rain forest.

Have the gardeners try to hold their breath for 30 seconds. Have the gardeners describe the feeling that tells them it's time to start breathing again. Tell all those who represent the people/animals that they need oxygen to survive. In this game, they must be able to "breathe" (or touch) 10 bubbles before you say "stop," or they are out of the game.

Call out the word "BREATHE." The "plants" should begin blowing. Allow enough time for all the gardeners to grab the needed bubbles. Explain that much of the rain forest is being removed through deforestation. Have one of the plant bubble blowers stop blowing and again tell the students they need 10 bubbles to survive before you say "STOP." Call out the word "BREATHE." Allow the same time as you did before, but point out that fewer gardeners were able to get the oxygen they needed. Remove another blower (plant) and continue playing this way until you have removed all plants, and the people can no longer survive.

Have the gardeners tell you what this game teaches them.

❦ Spinning Seeds

Objective: To determine the effect of geotropism on plants.
Time: 20 minutes.
Observation: 1 week.
Materials: Two aluminum pie plates, soil, grass seed, record player, bean seed.

Ask the gardeners to explain what gravity is. Drop an object, let it fall and ask in which way gravity pulls objects (to the ground). Place the bean on the record player and turn it on, allowing the bean to fly off the turntable. Have the students guess why they think gravity did not keep the bean seed down on the turntable. Explain that the spinning record player makes a force that pulls objects to the side. Ask them what they think a plant would do if you tried to grow it on a record player.

Fill two pie plates up with soil and level it off. Sprinkle grass seed heavily over both plates, and then sprinkle a layer of soil over the seed. Moisten the soil on both plates. Place one plate on the record player and one on a flat surface beside the record player. Have the gardeners make predictions about what will happen.

Turn the record player on and allow the seeds to germinate and grow. Allow the record player to run continuously; it can be turned off at night. The seedlings will start to grow toward the center of the plate and will start to make a pyramid shape.

Once the seeds have sprouted and grown to about 3 inches tall, ask the gardeners if any of them have completed the Upside Down Seed experiment in the handbook. Have them share the results of their experiment.

Explain that plants always grow in two directions: The roots grow with the pull of gravity, and the plant grows against the pull of gravity. This effect is called geotropism.

Propagation

Propagation means making new plants from older ones. Most plants reproduce by producing seeds. Seeds need water, oxygen and the right temperature to start growing. Some seeds germinate and form new plants quickly. Other seeds take a long time to form new plants.

For some kinds of plants, it is easier to start new plants by cutting off part of the parent plant. Your gardeners can use stems, leaves and roots to start new plants. These pieces are called cuttings. Cuttings must have plenty of moisture to form new roots.

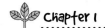

ACTIVITIES

❧ Paper Pot

Objective: To create recyclable pots, and to propagate plants by seed.
Time: Day 1: 20 minutes; Day 2: 15 minutes; Day 3: 10 minutes.
Materials: Newspapers, plastic tub, plastic cups, pencil, soil, seed.

For this activity, the gardeners need to shred several newspapers into small pieces (about the size of business cards) and allow them to soak in a tub of water overnight before the activity.

Here are the steps the gardeners should take in making a paper pot: Blend the paper mixture for several minutes by hand—wiggling fingers and tearing pieces. Take a handful of the mixture and drop it into a plastic cup. Form the mixture against the inside bottom and sides of the plastic cup. Create a layer over the entire interior of the cup. Tilt the cup to drain the water as it is pressed out of the mixture. Use a pencil to push apart an empty space in the middle to create a drainage hole for the pot. It is also a good idea to push a second cup into the first to create a thinner layer. Allow a few days of drying time in a warm place such as outdoors or in a window sill. Then pop the paper pots out of the plastic cups. (The plastic cups can be used again.)

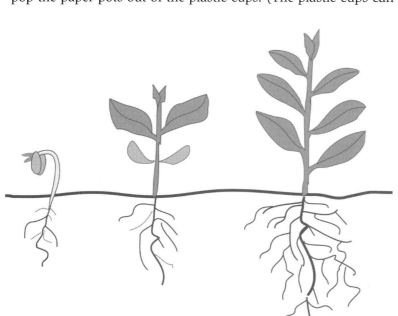

Explain that some plants propagate best by seed. Decide which plants the gardeners will plant in their chosen area and have them plant those seeds in the cups. After the seedlings have sprouted, have the students keep watch for the plant to produce its second set of leaves. These TRUE LEAVES are the signal that they are ready for transplant.

When these young plants are ready to be transplanted, the entire plant and paper cup can be transplanted directly into the ground.

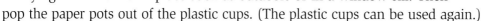

Young plants accustomed to being indoors need to be hardened off before being transplanted outdoors. A few days before planting them in the ground, take them outside each day to spend a few hours in their original pots.

🌿 Gallon Greenhouse

Objective:	To show an understanding of the environment needed to propagate plants.
Time:	30 minutes.
Materials:	Gallon plastic jugs, soil, twigs, gallon plastic bags, plant cuttings (see next activity).

Have the gardeners save gallon jugs for 2 weeks before beginning this activity.

Remind them that in order for plants to propagate, a moist environment is needed. Tell them that they will create a miniature greenhouse that will preserve moisture in the soil and air and help keep the plants warm.

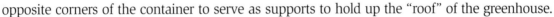

Rinse the jugs and have the gardeners cut the bottom halves off with scissors. You may need to begin the initial cut with a razor or sharp scissors. They should poke two or three small holes in the bottom of the container and fill it with soil. Stick two small twigs in opposite corners of the container to serve as supports to hold up the "roof" of the greenhouse.

The gardeners can use their gallon greenhouse to propagate plants in the Propagation Demonstration activity. Once cuttings are taken, moisten the soil and plant the cuttings. Cover the entire cutting with a plastic bag and place it in a well-lit area. Make sure that the light is not direct, because it is likely to cause too much heat to build up in the gallon greenhouse.

🌿 Propagation Demonstration

Objective:	To propagate plants by direct seeding, stem cuttings, leaf cuttings, root cuttings, division and layering.
Time:	40 minutes.
Materials:	Sharp knife or hand pruners, potting soil, 1-gallon greenhouse or other container to hold cuttings, paper pots or other containers, rooting hormone (for harder to root plants), clear plastic bag, favorite flower or vegetable seed (be sure to check the package for the plant's best growing season), stock plants to propagate (see next page).

This activity demonstrates to students the many ways plants can reproduce. Fill one of the hand-made paper pots or a cup with potting soil and show the gardeners how to plant a seed.

Ask them how deep to plant a seed. Remind the gardeners that the depth depends on the size of the seed. The larger the seed, the deeper it can be planted. A good rule of thumb is to plant seeds at a depth of two to three times the width of the seed. Once the seed is planted, water it thoroughly. Encourage the students to name all the things seeds need to grow, such as water, light, air, nutrients and a place to grow. You can use this activity to start transplants for a fall or spring vegetable garden or for transplants for a flower or container garden.

Some plants do not grow well from seed. Many can reproduce when part of the parent plant is cut off. The part removed is called a cutting. When it grows and develops, it will look just like the parent plant. Show the gardeners how to start new plants using each of the following techniques.

Use a sharp knife or pruning shears to make cuttings or divisions. When making cuttings, always remove any flowers or flower buds. They will compete with the food the plant will need to make new roots. Also, the large leaves of some of the plants, such as a rubber plant, may need to be cut in half so that the cutting will not dry out as quickly. Generally a 4- to 6-inch cutting is enough for most plants.

Remind the gardeners of the proper safety techniques for using this equipment. Place the cuttings in the damp potting soil in your gallon greenhouse, which should be able to hold all the cuttings until they have formed their own roots.

Plants propagated by division can often be put in their own containers, because they already have roots. Cover the cuttings and the gallon greenhouse with a clear plastic bag. Make sure that the cuttings do not dry out. Place them in a warm, well-lit location, but not in direct sunlight. Check for roots after about 5 days by gently pulling the cuttings out of the soil and examining them for roots. If there are no roots, simply put them back into the greenhouse.

Stem cuttings

Arrange single eye cutting so that dashed lines are inserted into in moist soil. Arrange double eye cutting so that bottom portion of stem is in moist soil.

Single eye   Double eye

Ficus, pothos ivy, wandering Jew, English ivy, geranium, arrowhead ivy, rosemary.

Leaf cuttings

Make small cut along veins and pin leaf down so that veins are in contact with moist soil.

Arrange leaf so that the petiole (base of the leaf's stem) is inserted into moist soil.

Cut sections of a leaf around veins and lay leaf sections flat so they are in contact with moist soil.

Begonia, African violet, kalanchoe.

Root cuttings

Root division

Aloe vera, mother-in-law's tongue, liriope, daylily, mint.

Layering
Blackberry, philodendron, pothos ivy.

As the plants start to form their own roots, place each one in its own individual pot. Remember: These cuttings have been growing in an ideal environment. Gradually move them to their new location. Often, removing the plastic covering several days before transplanting allows the plant to adjust to a new environment. Some techniques root plants quickly; others (leaf type) are much slower.

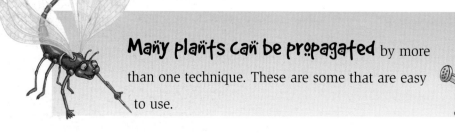

Many plants can be propagated by more than one technique. These are some that are easy to use.

LEADERSHIP AND SERVICE LEARNING PROJECTS

❀ Gifts for Others

Your group can participate in a community service project to give of their time and talents. Have the group press plants and flowers between the pages of a book, then carefully glue them to heavy paper to create bookmarks or note cards. Then establish a time when the JMG group can personally give them as gifts to a hospital or nursing home. Or, give them to volunteers at your school or to JMG volunteers.

❀ Variable Day Demonstration

In this chapter, your JMG'ers may have learned about and experimented with variables. Have each person in the JMG group choose a variable for testing plant growth. It must be something you have not already experimented with. Encourage creativity. They could test freezing seeds, colored light, how plants grow with music—anything they want! Have a special day for the gardeners to show their experiments to the rest of the group or even their school.

❀ Adopt-a-Spot

Topiaries are beautiful, growing works of art. Have the group create a large topiary for the entrance of your school or some other location. Decide ahead of time how the topiary will be maintained.

❀ Share What You Know

One of the best ways for gardeners to learn is for them to be taught by their peers. Have your group choose an activity they completed in this section and teach it to a group of younger children. They should practice teaching with others in their JMG group before doing it for the first time for others.

❀ Create Your Own

Your JMG group can have fun creating your own unique leadership/service learning project.

For a child to be certified as a Junior Master Gardener, one individual and one group activity should be completed for each section/teaching concept in this chapter. Your JMG group should also select one leadership/service learning project for this chapter to complete.

Soils and Water

Soil Color, Texture and Structure

Living things as diverse as cows, beetles, sunflowers and people all depend on soil. Cows and other animals feed on plants growing in the soil. Beetles burrow and live in the soil during their life cycle. Sunflowers and other plants grow in soil, which anchors them and holds the water and nutrients they need to grow. And people depend on soil for food to eat, clothes to wear, wood to build houses, and even for sweet treats such as ice cream and chewing gum to enjoy.

Soil is a building block for all life. It is composed of many materials, just as a favorite cookie recipe contains many ingredients. The main ingredient in soil is rock that has been broken into tiny particles over time. It also contains decomposing plants and animals, such as the leaves that have fallen from trees, or grass clippings after mowing. These are broken down by another soil ingredient, microorganisms, which are creatures living in the soil that are too small to see without a microscope. Finally, the soil also contains water and nutrients.

ACTIVITIES

❧ Touchy Feely

Objective:	To understand soil texture and the properties of different soil types and soil particles.
Time:	35 minutes.
Materials:	Three balls (three different sizes, basketball, baseball, nickel-sized rubber ball or BB), flour, sugar or sand, water, poster, marker.

Have the gardeners tell you some of the things they have learned about plant needs. Ask them what they think would happen if the roots were always dry or always sopping wet. Tell them that for a plant to stay healthy, its roots must have good soil. Display a sheet of poster board titled "SOIL—What's In It?" Have the gardeners call out what they think they would find in soil if they started digging.

When the list is complete, tell them that part of the soil is different little pieces called particles. Tell them that soil has three main kinds of different-sized particles: sand, silt and clay. If they could look at soil particles under a microscope, sand would look the biggest. Show them the largest ball. This ball represents sand, which is the largest soil particle. Show them the medium-sized ball. This ball represents the next smaller particle, silt; it is very small. The smallest particle, clay, is very tiny. Show them the smallest ball and tell them that clay particles would even be much smaller than this ball—so small they could not see it with their eyes only.

Tell them that plants grow poorly in soil containing much sand, because it dries out quickly and doesn't allow roots to get enough water. Have each child feel the sugar, salt or sand and describe it to you. Sand usually feels gritty.

Allow the gardeners to rub dry flour between their fingers to feel the silky, powdery texture of silt.

Tell them that the fine clay particles clump together and become sticky. Explain that plants grow poorly in some soil with too much clay, because it keeps the roots too wet. Let them feel some flour with a little water mixed in. Explain that the best soil is usually a mixture of all of these soil types, but with only a small amount of clay.

Add the three soil types to the poster list if they are not already included.

Mud Pies

Objective: To determine soil texture by feel.
Time: 20 minutes.
Materials: Water, soil.

Have the children recall the three types of particles in soil that determine its texture. Remind them that the best soil texture is a mixture of all three types.

Ask the gardeners if they have ever made mud pies. Tell them they can make mud pies to determine if a soil has a good texture. Have them help you dig a hole large enough for everyone to get a handful of soil. Add a little water to the soil and squeeze it together. (Add just enough water to get the soil to stick together. It should not ooze through your fingers but should make a good mud ball.)

Have the gardeners determine the soil's texture. If it's crumbly and fails to keep its shape, it is a sandy-textured soil. If it's sticky, glistens and stays the shape it is squeezed to, it is a clay-textured soil. If the soil is loose and clumps together but is not sticky, the soil is called loam.

Tell the gardeners that later they will learn the ways to make the soil texture better for plants.

Shake, Rattle and Roll

Objective: To identify the amounts of soil particles that make up a soil's texture.
Time: 20 minutes.
Materials: Jar, soil, water, permanent marker.

Explain to the gardeners that when they take a soil sample, they should not just scrape soil off the top, but should dig about 6 inches into the soil and take the sample from there. Briefly discuss how to safely use a garden tool such as a shovel or trowel. Tell them they will test the soil to find out how much sand, silt and clay are in it.

Take a soil sample from an outdoor play area. Fill a large jar half-full with soil from the soil sample and the rest of the way with water. Have the gardeners take turns shaking the jar for several minutes until the larger clumps are broken apart. Let the jar sit for 1 minute and use a permanent marker to draw a line to mark what has settled. Tell the gardeners that sand makes up the heaviest particles, which sink more quickly to the bottom. Allow 24 hours without moving the jar for the mixture to settle further. The top layer will be clay, which includes the smallest, lightest particles. The middle layer will be silt, and the bottom, sand. Have the gardeners decide which layer is the thickest to determine the soil's texture.

Point out that any material floating on the water surface is organic matter. Explain that organic matter contains nutrients and makes any kind of soil texture even better. Tell the group they'll learn more about organic matter in the next section.

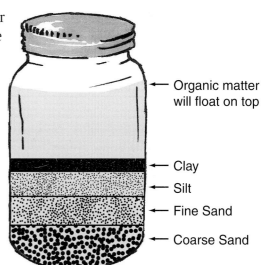

Organic matter will float on top ←

Clay ←

Silt ←

Fine Sand ←

Coarse Sand ←

Chapter 2

In the Classroom
Have the children graph in centimeters the height of the separate layers. Then break the gardeners into small groups and have them duplicate the activity with soils from different areas and graph those results. The groups should then present their findings to the rest of the JMG class. Ask the gardeners if they think this activity might influence where they might place a garden.

❧ Candy Aggregate

Objective: To create an edible model illustrating that soil is made up of many different components.

Time: 15 minutes.

Materials: Paper plates, spoons, peanut butter, M&M's®, pretzel sticks, marshmallows, brown sugar, gummy worms (these ingredients are suggestions—any snack and candy bits of varying sizes will do).

Tell the gardeners that soil is just dirt. Ask if anyone disagrees. If they disagree, ask them to prove it by listing all the things they can think of that are in soil. Tell them they will make a model showing that soil is made up of many things. Tell them that a mixture of many different things is called an aggregate.

Distribute paper plates to each child. Give each child 2 spoonsful of peanut butter. Ask the class what the peanut butter could represent. They might relate it to clay because of its thick, sticky texture. Distribute small amounts of the remaining ingredients. Have them be creative in thinking about what each additional particle could represent in the model of a soil aggregate. As they add ingredients to the plate, have the gardeners mix the ingredients thoroughly with their spoon "shovels."

Nutrients

We all need certain nutrients to keep our bodies healthy. We get nutrients from eating nutritious foods such as carrots, bananas, beans and cheese, and from vitamins. Just like people, plants need nutrients to stay healthy. Garden plants get nutrients from the soil and from nutrients we give them, called fertilizer.

There are no individual activities in the Nutrients section.

ACTIVITIES

✿ Nutrient Variable

Objective:	To use the scientific method to study the effects of fertilizer on plant growth.
Time:	25 minutes.
Observation:	6 weeks.
Materials:	Four planting containers (that can hold 1 pint of soil), teaspoon, potting soil, water soluble fertilizer, 15 bean or corn seeds, Nutrient Variable Lab Sheet (in the Appendix).

Ask the gardeners if any of them take vitamins. Ask them what they think is the purpose of vitamins. Tell them that people get nutrients from the food they eat and that some nutrients are vitamins that their bodies need. People can get vitamins from food, and extra vitamins from vitamin pills. Relate that plants, just like people, need nutrients to grow healthy and strong. Show them a container of fertilizer. Explain that fertilizer contains plant nutrients.

Ask the gardeners if they think it is important to read the directions on a bottle of vitamins. Discuss the need for safety when handling chemicals, and the importance of reading directions carefully. Have them tell you why it is important and what might happen if they took too many vitamins or not enough. Explain that they are going to conduct an experiment to see how plants grow with different amounts of fertilizer.

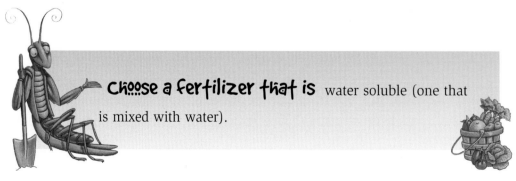

Choose a fertilizer that is water soluble (one that is mixed with water).

Have the gardeners make sure all containers are the same size and have the same number and size of drainage holes. Have them measure and pour soil into the five containers. They should push their finger or a pencil ½ inch into the soil and plant three seeds in each pot. Water the first container with water only—no fertilizer. Have the children water the second container with water containing the amount of fertilizer recommended on the label. Water the third and fourth containers with three and four times the recommended rate, respectively.

Each time the plants are watered, continue these fertilizer treatment variables.

The gardeners should chart the growth of the tallest plant of each container by measuring plant height once a week and including the heights on a graph (have older gardeners graph the average of the three plants).

In the Classroom
Have the gardeners repeat the activity using different brands of fertilizer or different nutrient ratios.

The Numbers on the Bag

Objective: To understand how nutrients in fertilizers help plants.
Time: 15 minutes.
Materials: Rhythm sheet (in the Appendix and JMG Handbook).

Sing the song, "The Numbers on the Bag," to the children so they can learn its rhythm. You can make up your own tune. As you sing it, you might have a bag of fertilizer as a prop to show them the numbers you are referring to. Have the gardeners use their rhythm sheets and sing the song as a group.

The Numbers on the Bag
It's time to fertilize,
you've got to realize
that plants need nutrients, too.
You want plants so strong,
it won't be long
before they'll be needing you.

Add nutrients to the soil,
like manure or fertilizer.
You'll learn plants grow better in the rich soil,
now you're a little bit wiser.

Chapter 2

When you use fertilizer
you'll have to figure out
what those three numbers printed on the bag
are all about....

Those three numbers side by side
tell you what's in the bag.
Each number means a certain amount
of nutrients to be had.

Nitrogen is the first number,
a nutrient that plants need.
It helps leaves grow strong
and grass grow long and makes plants stay green.

Phosphorus is for all of us,
the second number on the sack.
It helps plants bloom flowers
and make fruit for us to snack.

Potassium gives the plant some
nutrients so roots can grow.
It's the last number on the bag,
something everyone should know.

Plants need these three nutrients,
different plants need different amounts.
The plants won't just stay alive—they will thrive
and when you're gardening, that's what counts!

Bumps Below

Objective:	To become familiar with plants that produce their own nitrogen.
Time:	15 minutes.
Materials:	Mature bean plants.

For this activity, you need a few mature bean or peanut plants. You may plant a few bean seeds about 4 weeks before this activity. Pull up mature plants from your garden, buy a mature plant or just start this activity for the future.

Have the gardeners tell you what plant nutrients are called (fertilizer). Remind them that plants and people both need nutrients. Tell them that one of the main nutrients plants need is nitrogen; it helps plants stay green. Explain that although most plants we grow need fertilizer that has nitrogen, a special group of plants has figured out a way to get their own nitrogen.

This group of plants is called legumes.

Bluebonnets, Texas' state flower, belong to this group.

Explain that special bacteria in the soil make nitrogen; these special plants have developed so that their roots make a home for those bacteria. Tell them it is kind of like someone paying rent to live in an apartment—the bacteria get a place to live in the plant's roots, but the bacteria "pays" for living there by giving the plant nitrogen it needs.

Ask the gardeners if they want to see the bacteria houses. Tell them that they are called nodules and they look like little round bumps on the roots. Have the children pull up a mature bean plant and carefully wash away the soil. Have them try to find the bumps on the roots. Allow several minutes for each gardener to make a high-quality sketch of the entire bean plant. Have the children label all the plant parts they can think of—including the root nodules.

Soil Improvement

Even though leaves fall from trees year after year, they don't just pile up under the trees. Instead, after they die, they start to fall apart, or decompose. When leaves decompose, they are not leaves anymore; they become the part of the soil called organic matter. Organic matter is made up of bits and pieces of plants or animals that used to be alive. Organic matter is good for the soil because it helps loosen it so the roots can grow more easily. It also makes the soil better able to hold water.

ACTIVITIES

❧ Building Bins and Compost Sandwiches

Objective:	To build a composting bin for creating organic matter to amend soil.
Time:	30 minutes.
Materials:	Three wooden pallets, nails or 5-foot stakes, chicken wire or cinder blocks, plant wastes, soil, water, shovel.

Ask the gardeners to define recycling and explain why they think it is important. Tell them that composting is a way to recycle grass clippings, leaves and even vegetable food wastes. Explain that this material, which many people discard, can be composted into organic matter to make the soil better for growing plants.

For this activity, the gardeners will build a compost bin. If they are already using a compost bin, have them try another type of compost bin and compare the effects on the composting process.

Composting bins can be built in many ways. Wooden pallets can be nailed or wired together to make a three-sided bin; or, organic materials such as grass clippings and leaves can just be piled up. Here are photos of several ways to compost.

Composting can also be done on a smaller scale by drilling a couple dozen air holes into a trash can, filling it with the layers mentioned in the next activity, closing the lid, laying it on its side and rolling it every couple of days.

Have the group decide what method they want to use to build a bin.

After the bin project is completed, ask the gardeners to tell about their favorite sandwich. Have them describe what is on it. Make a rough sketch of a group sandwich with several layers of different items the gardeners named. Explain that when composting, you must make a "sandwich" of layers. When the wastes are put into the bin, layer them with alternating types of organic material listed below.

Green Stuff

Any plant material that is still green adds nitrogen to the composting material. This speeds the composting process by heating up the tiny animals, bugs and microorganisms in it.

Brown Stuff

This plant material, which has been dead long enough to become brown, adds carbon to the composting material.

Water

Water is essential to the composting process. Moisture allows the fungi, bacteria and other creatures, such as pill bugs and earthworms, to break down the material.

Soil

Soils naturally contain living organisms that eat the organic material to make the composting process take place. Add a thin layer of soil occasionally throughout the composting process to distribute these organisms within the organic matter.

Assign a child to be on the lookout for compostable materials. To begin, you might use lawn clippings or dead plants from clearing the initial gardening space, or the gardeners could bring vegetable wastes or lawn clippings from home.

Once the bin contains several layers, have the gardeners turn the composting material with a shovel to break up clumps of material and allow oxygen to permeate through it. Mix the ingredients in the bin every couple of weeks to break down the organic material faster. The organic matter will compost even if the "sandwich" layer technique is not used. The layering just helps the organic matter decompose more quickly.

As the organic material breaks down to a rich, brown, crumbly compost, it can be added to the soil to improve plant growth.

✿ Composting Critter Page

Objective: To identify organisms that are a part of the composting process.
Time: 30 minutes.
Materials: Markers or crayons, Composting Critter Page (in the Appendix).

Ask your gardeners if they think compost bins are alive. Tell them that any compost bin or, for that matter, anywhere along a forest floor is teeming with animals and microorganisms that can be seen only with a microscope. They may know that earthworms eat their way through organic matter to change it into compost, but have they ever heard of springtails, ground beetles or mold mites? All these creatures and many more play a role in eating the leaf litter and grass clippings, breaking them down. Explain that because these creatures are in organic matter munching away, they also attract other creatures that eat them.

Distribute copies of the Composting Critter Page. Have the gardeners look in the compost bin for any little creatures in their compost. They can use the Composting Critter Page to draw examples of some of the creatures they find. Also, allow them to visit the JMG web site at *www.jmgkids.org* under Leaders Links for more information and photographs of these creatures; or they can use encyclopedias or other reference materials from a library.

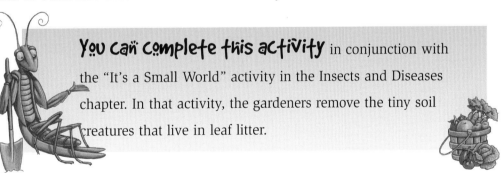

You can complete this activity in conjunction with the "It's a Small World" activity in the Insects and Diseases chapter. In that activity, the gardeners remove the tiny soil creatures that live in leaf litter.

✿ Compost Sandwich Composition

Objective: To write a paragraph to support the claim that it is important to compost.
Time: 45 minutes.
Materials: Markers, poster board, pencils, notebook paper.

Tell the gardeners they will write a sandwich paragraph. Their sandwich will be a slice of bread for the top and bottom, with three ingredients in between. Their job is to write a paragraph about why composting is important.

For this assignment, the gardeners will write a paragraph with at least five sentences. Just as the slices of bread that make up the top and bottom of a sandwich are basically the same thing, the first and last sentences of the paragraph will be the same—to say that it is important to compost wastes. And, just as the ingredients between the slices of bread in a sandwich make it better than just the bread alone, the sentences in the middle of the paragraph improve it by supporting the paragraph. The gardeners should write at least three sentences that tell why it is important to compost.

Below is a sample paragraph a child might write:

Composting your wastes from your yard in a compost bin is very important and everyone should do it. When you put your wastes in a compost bin, you recycle it just as nature does. Landfills are getting big because they are full of trash that people throw away, and composting helps get rid of some of your trash. The brown compost you get from your compost bin is very good for your soil. When you add it to your soil, it helps the plants grow. It is very important to compost your yard wastes.

Water Cycle and You

The water you used to brush your teeth with this morning may have been some of the same water that rained on your great-great-grandparents' heads or that dinosaurs drank millions of years ago. The Earth is sometimes called the "water planet" because most of it is covered with water. That's good for us, because all living things need water to live. All the water on the Earth is the same water we have used over and over again. We have not used up all of the water yet because of the water cycle.

Liquid water flows and sloshes in oceans, lakes and rivers. Solid water (that's ice!) is in the coldest parts of the world in ice caps and icebergs. Invisible gas water, called water vapor, floats around in the air. This makes the air humid.

Water rains down on the earth. Some of it soaks deep into the ground and may become a part of an underground river. This water can be pumped back up for people to use. Some of it flows into other bodies of water. Part of the water that rains down floats back into the air as water vapor. The water vapor changes to water droplets that make clouds. Those clouds produce rain that falls back down to earth. This is called the water cycle.

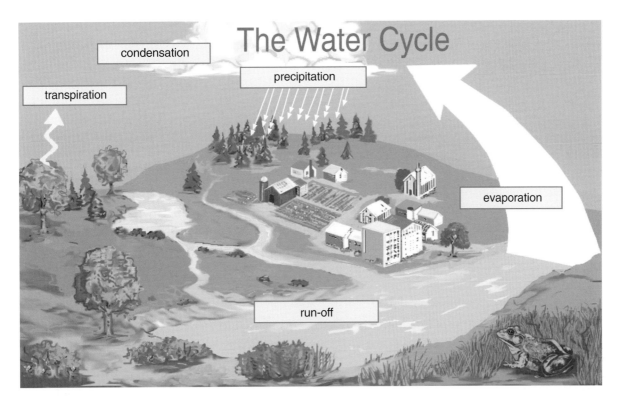

ACTIVITIES

❀ Earth Apple

Objective: To become familiar with plant needs.
Time: 20 minutes.
Materials: Apple, knife.

Tell the gardeners that the Earth is sometimes called the "Water Planet" because so much of it is covered by water. Show them an apple and tell them to pretend that the apple represents the Earth. Tell them that you will cut the apple into four equal sections, which will represent all land and water on the planet. Cut the apple and have them guess how many sections would represent the water on the Earth and how many would represent the land. Explain that about ¾ of the Earth is covered with water. Put one of the apple quarters away and tell them that today we will talk only about the water on the planet, because water is so important to life on Earth—without water, nothing could live.

Show them the remaining three quarters and ask them if they think we are lucky to have so much fresh water to drink. Explain that of those three slices of water left, most of it is saltwater that is undrinkable. Cut off ⅛ of one of the slices and explain that of all the water, only this amount is fresh.

Next cut the freshwater piece into three equal sections and explain that two of those are unavailable to drink because they represent the freshwater frozen in glaciers and polar ice caps. Explain that of all of the water on the Water Planet, only one of the remaining sections is freshwater available to us. So it is very important to conserve it.

In the Classroom

This is a good activity in which to introduce percentages. Distribute the Earth Apple Grid page (in the Appendix). Explain that the percent sign means "out of 100." Explain that if you were to take 100 people from their school, and 55 of them were boys, then boys would comprise 55 percent of the people in the school. Tell the gardeners that you want them to imagine that you took all of the water in the world and poured it into those 100 squares.

Ask: What percentage of the Earth's water is saltwater or ocean?

Answer: 97 percent. Have the gardeners color 97 squares and color-code the legend at the bottom of the page to match the saltwater color.

Ask: What percentage of the Earth's water is frozen?

Answer: 2 percent. Have them color two squares and color-code the legend at the bottom of the page to match the frozen water color.

Ask: What percentage of the grid is left uncolored?

Answer: 1 percent. Tell the children that only 1 percent of the earth's total water is available for us to use as freshwater.

Cloud Maker

Objective: To use a model to demonstrate the condensation process.
Time: 40 minutes.
Materials: Baking pan, ice, bowl.

Tell the gardeners they will make a cloud. Have one child pile several ice cubes on a baking sheet. Allow the sheet to rest over a bowl for a few minutes. Explain that water vapor is a gas in the air that we cannot see or feel. Tell them that when this water vapor rises into the cooler atmosphere high in the sky, it begins to cool. When water vapor is cooled, it condenses into liquid water droplets to make clouds and rain. The water vapor in the air in the bowl condenses into water droplets when it is cooled by the ice on the baking sheet. Have the gardeners hold the pan above the bowl to watch it "rain."

❧ The Cycle Song

Objective: To gain understanding of the water cycle through music.
Time: 15 minutes.
Materials: Rhythm sheet (in the Appendix and JMG Handbook).

Read the verse to the gardeners so they can learn its rhythm. Have them use their rhythm sheets and sing the "Cycle Song" as a group. Encourage them to create movements to go with the lyrics.

The cycle Song

The plants in the world just continue to grow,
because of the rain that falls and the water that flows.

The rain from the sky, it never runs out,
the water cycle keeps flowing just like a water spout.

The cycle keeps us wet, all around the nation,
when the rain falls down, it's precipitation.

The rain flows on the soil and ground,
some runs off and some soaks down.

The rain going down is drunk by the roots.
It's carried up to the leaves, the flowers and the fruit.

Once it gets to the leaves, the water starts to fly,
transpiration takes the water from the leaves to the sky.

The water that runs to rivers, oceans and the lakes
doesn't rest for long—there it cannot stay.

It doesn't stop long and take a vacation,
it travels up to the sky—evaporation.

From a liquid to gas and it travels up so high,
then it condenses to a cloud you can see floating by.

Some clouds get so big, they grow gray and tall,
they get so full of water that the rain has to fall.

The rain hits the earth as the water cycle starts again,
life on earth continues as the water cycle spins.

Chapter 2

✿ Apple Rings and Banana Chips

Objective: To measure the amount of water in fruit.
Time: 15 minutes.
Materials: Apples, bananas, lemon juice, knife, weight scale, cookie sheet, nonstick spray.

For this activity, you will need a scale to measure weight in grams or ounces. A postal scale, digital scale or a balance scale will work. If none of these is available, you can still use this activity to show the children how to make a healthful dried fruit snack that will be edible for several weeks.

Have the gardeners wash three to four apples. Remove the cores and cut the apples into rings about ¼ inch thick. Have the gardeners coat the rings with lemon juice. Next, have them weigh the rings and record the weight. Then they should spray a cookie sheet with nonstick spray and arrange the apple slices on it so that they do not touch each other.

Place the tray in the oven and set the oven to the lowest temperature setting. Allow the rings to warm for about 2 hours. The drying can be done between meetings so that the children can complete the activity the next time they meet. Remind the children about the water cycle and evaporation. Explain that evaporation occurs more quickly when air is warm and dry. Have them predict what the rings will look like and how much they will weigh after most of the water has evaporated. After 2 hours, check the rings. Completely dried apple rings have a leathery texture.

The gardeners should weigh the dried fruit and calculate the difference between the fresh and dried weights. Have them peel, slice and weigh three to four bananas and predict their dried weight. Repeat the drying process for the banana chips and calculate the difference in the fresh and dried weights.

The gardeners could also experiment with drying other fruits to see which types hold the most water and which taste best dried. Dried fruit is best kept in a sealed plastic bag.

In the Classroom
Have the children dry, measure and record the fresh weight of several different fruits, herbs or vegetables, predict the dried weight, dry them, and measure and record the dried weights. Have the gardeners calculate the differences between fresh and dried weights, then arrange the items in order of their water content.

Water Movement

When rain falls, some of it runs off the top of the ground and some soaks into the soil. When rain runs off the top and carries soil particles, it is called erosion. When water soaks into the soil, it is called infiltration. When water goes deeper into the soil, it is called percolation.

Plant roots absorb water that soaks into the soil. Good soil is loose because it has small spaces of air that allow water to infiltrate and percolate. If water does not seep into the soil, it cannot reach a plant's roots.

ACTIVITIES

✿ Out of the Spout

Objective:	To understand how water moves through different soil textures.
Time:	40 minutes.
Materials:	Three 2-liter bottles, three jars, three soil types (clay soil, sandy soil, potting soil), measuring cup, water, ruler.

Cut spouts from each 2-liter bottle. Have the gardeners invert the spouts over the jars to serve as funnels. Take the group outside to find differing soil types (a well-draining soil and a poorly draining soil are needed). Fill each spout with a different soil type. Have the gardeners slowly pour 1 cup of water into each funnel, record how long it takes to start and finish draining, and measure the amount of water that has drained into the jar.

Explain that water movement through the soil is important to plants' health. Soil that prevents water from traveling through it and soil that allows water to travel too quickly are unhealthy for most plants. Have the children evaluate which of the three soils they think is best. Remind them that organic matter helps water move faster through a poorly drained soil and helps it move more slowly in soil that drains too fast.

✿ Where Did It Go?

Objective:	To demonstrate that water can be held in air spaces in the soil.
Time:	30 minutes.
Materials:	Dry sand or gravel, water, two clear measuring cups (each must be big enough to measure at least 2 cups), a 1-cup measuring cup.

Ask the gardeners to pour sand into a measuring cup exactly to the 1-cup level. Ask them how much they would have if they added 1 cup of sand to that 1 cup of sand. Add 1 more cup of sand and measure it. Have them fill a measuring cup with water exactly to the 1-cup level. Ask them how much water they would have if they added 1 cup of water to 1 cup of water. Add another cup of water and measure it.

Ask the gardeners how much sand and water they would have if they added 1 cup of water to 1 cup of sand. Have the gardeners pour 1 cup of dry sand into the large measuring cup. Next, have them slowly add 1 cup of water to it. Point out that they can see the water as it seeps into the sand. Ask the gardeners if the sand and water reached the 2-cup mark. Have them try to explain why the mixture was less than 2 cups.

Remind them that sandy soil holds water very poorly because water drains right through it. Explain that sand does not absorb water; instead, water just fills in the air spaces surrounding the sand particles. The second cup of water does not sit on top of the sand to reach the 2-cup mark; it soaks down into the sand.

❧ Water Flows, Soil Goes

Objective:	To demonstrate the effects of water erosion on bare soil.
Time:	20 minutes.
Materials:	Water source (hose or 2-liter bottles filled with water), bare soil, soil with vegetation.

For this activity, prepare an area outside. Find an area of loose, bare soil. If none is available, you may need to scrape and break up an area with a hoe (about 2 feet by 3 feet). This works particularly well if the area slopes.

Tell the children that plants help protect the soil. Ask them how they think plants do that. Tell them that water is very powerful—one drop by itself has little power, but billions of drops falling from the sky or moving over the ground have a lot of power. Explain that water can cause problems for the soil because water can wash soil away—this is called water erosion.

Have a gardener write the word "erosion" in the soil and then pour water over the area for 1 minute. If you are using bottles of water, make sure the water keeps flowing. Next, find a grassy area. You might use a hand trowel to carve a letter E or some simple shape into the grass. Allow the water to flow over the grass the same way as the bare patch.

Have the gardeners point out erosion they see in both areas and look for differences between the bare and covered soils. Point out the differences they see in the erosion of the word "erosion" in the bare soil and in the design on the grassy soil.

LEADERSHIP/SERVICE LEARNING PROJECTS

Below are projects to complete with your JMG group. The group should choose at least one to complete.

❊ **Help Make Their Bed**

Have your group find a flower bed or garden in your community. It could be at school, a retirement home, city library or any place your group can think of. Obtain permission to take a soil sample from the bed. Send the soil sample to the county Extension service. When the results of the soil test come back, take it to the bed's owners and tell them how they can improve their soil.

❊ **Landfill Visit**

Arrange for your group to visit a landfill. Many facilities offer tours to show how trash is disposed of. Let the facility managers know that the group is studying composting. Have the group create visuals and share the information they learned at that facility with another group of children.

❊ **Wastewater Visit**

Visit a wastewater treatment facility. Many facilities offer tours to show how water is cleaned. Let the facility managers know that the group is learning about water. Have the group create visuals and share the information they learned at that facility with another group of children.

❊ **Make a Difference**

The JMG'ers can design posters that tell people in the neighborhood about the importance of composting. They should create at least 12 large colorful posters that try to convince people to compost. Posters could be hung on telephone poles, placed in windows of stores or on walls at school.

❊ **Super Soil Business**

Start a JMG business to raise money for the JMG group's needs. The gardeners can fill a few dozen large, sealable, plastic bags with compost from your compost bin. The compost can then be sold as a "super soil" to add to house or garden plants. The group can sell the soil for $1 a bag at an open house at a school, at a nearby business, or to neighbors. Have the JMG'ers post signs or create other advertisements before the sale to tell what the money is being raised for. You should also let the group practice handling money before the sale by conducting pretend sales with each other.

❊ **Create Your Own**

Your JMG group can have fun creating its own unique leadership/service learning project.

For a child to be certified as a Junior Master Gardener, one individual and one group activity should be completed for each section/teaching concept in this chapter. Your JMG group should also select one leadership/service learning project for this chapter to complete.

Balance and Interactions in Nature

GROUP ACTIVITIES

INDIVIDUAL ACTIVITIES

Your Own World
Wild Weeds
A Bee's Eye View
Water Balance
Become a Spider
JMG Web

Habitats

GROUP ACTIVITIES

INDIVIDUAL ACTIVITIES

Home Sweet Home
Toad Abode
Feathered Friend Feeder
Boarding House
Journal
JMG Web

Hand-in-Hand with Nature

GROUP ACTIVITIES

INDIVIDUAL ACTIVITIES

More Isn't Better
Organic JMG
Water, Water, Everywhere
Meter Reader
JMG Web

Recycling

GROUP ACTIVITIES

INDIVIDUAL ACTIVITIES

Grow Cards
Use it...Don't lose it!
Critter Condo
Composting Homework
Recycle Inventory
JMG Web

Eco-Art

GROUP ACTIVITIES

INDIVIDUAL ACTIVITIES

Seed Jewelry
Nature Garland
Mystery Boxes
Seeds Magnet
Recycle Sculpture
Garden Folks
JMG Web

Leadership/Service Learning Projects

Ecology and Environmental Horticulture

Balance and Interactions in Nature

Your JMG'ers have probably noticed that what they say or do affects other people. For example, if someone throws away a soda can, it may end up on the side of the road for someone else to pick up or go to the landfill instead of being recycled.

In nature, there is a balance between all living things. We are all interdependent, and every living thing has a purpose. Although many people think bees just cause trouble, many plants could not live without bees and other pollinators. Insects and animals that carry pollen from one flower to another are called pollinators. When a bee crawls into flowers to get nectar for its hive, it pollinates them so they can make fruits and seeds. Both the bee and the plants get what they need. Disturbing a natural balance such as this can cause problems.

Sometimes people do not know that their actions affect the delicate balance between people and other living things. Junior Master Gardeners need to realize that they have a responsibility to take care of the environment and this wonderful planet that is our home.

ACTIVITIES

✿ Nature Class Web

Objective:	To create a web to understand the interrelatedness of life on earth.
Time:	20 minutes.
Materials:	String.

Have the JMG group sit in a circle. Ask the gardeners to imagine that they are somewhere in their neighborhood. Ask the group about the interactions that occur in the area among animals, people and the environment.

As the children answer the questions, unroll the string and have them loop it around their fingers. As you ask more questions, connect more of the gardeners together in a "web" created by the string. Try to call on a different student each time until each has answered a question and been connected to the web. You might call on several students to give different answers to the same question. Below are questions you might ask to show the connections in nature around their neighborhood.

1. What is a plant that grows around here? (grass, oak tree, tomato plant)
2. What does that plant need to grow? (sun, rain, etc.)
3. What other living things in our area need rain to live? (crickets, birds)

4. Name something that might eat a part of a plant. (caterpillar, squirrel, people)
5. What happens to that plant during the winter? (It dies, loses its leaves.)
6. What happens to the plant when it falls to the ground? (It turns into part of the soil.)
7. How does a plant become part of the soil? (Insects and other creatures eat it.)
8. What is one creature that eats dead leaves? (earthworms, pill bugs)
   (Make sure to ask Question 8—it will be used later in the activity.)
9. Name an animal that eats one of these creatures. (robin, mouse)
10. What might eat one of these animals? (snake)
11. Name a plant that might grow in the new soil. (weeds, garden plants)
12. What would happen to the plants if the rain didn't fall for a whole month? (They might die.)
13. If the plants died, what would happen to the creatures that eat plants? (They might die.)
14. Name some plants that we eat. (corn, potatoes, carrots)
15. Where do these plants come from? (our gardens, stores, farmers)
16. What do all of these plants grow in? (the soil)
17. What are some things these plants need to grow? (sun, rain, etc.)

After each gardener has answered a question and is connected to the others by the string, ask them what the string resembles. Explain that the connection among all living things is like a web. Each strand of the web is connected to all the other parts of the web. A problem with one part of the web causes problems in other parts. Tell them that every living thing in nature plays a special role. Ask them what would happen if one part of the web was missing.

Have them describe what would happen if the world had no animals to eat dead leaves. Clip the strings of the gardeners who answered the question about what animal eats dead leaves. Have them notice how the web is not as strong even if one part is changed.

In the classroom

Ask the students what they think pollution is. Have the group decide whether pollution can kill some of the living things in the food web. Tell the students that there are different kinds of pollution—it can be in the air, in water, in the ground and sometimes just in a pile. Ask them what would happen if you added pollution to the water in the web. Have the student who earlier answered "water" or "rain" raise his or her hand. Take that student's string and tug on it sharply. Ask the group who felt the tugging. Explain that all things in this web and in the whole world are connected and that a problem with one part of the web causes problems with other parts of the web.

Read the book, "Brother Eagle, Sister Sky," to the students. Have them discuss what the author may have been feeling as he wrote those words.

✿ The Food Chain Gang

Objective: To play a game that represents the interrelatedness within the food chain between animals and the environment.

Time: 25 minutes.

Materials: Chalk or markers, chalkboard or poster board, a few dozen slips of green paper.

Write the following words on a poster or chalkboard:

dead leaves ◇ worm ◇ beetle ◇ mouse ◇ rattlesnake ◇ hawk

Tell the gardeners you will play a game in which all the players will pretend to be animals that you have listed. Have each child choose an animal to be. After all have chosen, have each write the name of his or her animal on a sheet of paper and hold it up. Group the gardeners based on the animals they chose.

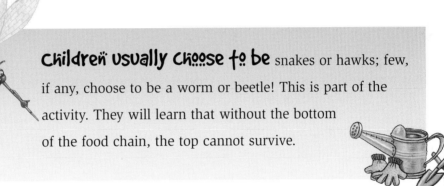

Children usually choose to be snakes or hawks; few, if any, choose to be a worm or beetle! This is part of the activity. They will learn that without the bottom of the food chain, the top cannot survive.

This activity works best with a group of about 20 or more.

Tell the gardeners that they will play the food chain game. Ask them what the animals listed above have in common. Explain that these animals all must eat one of the other animals listed to be able to survive and that this is an example of a food chain. Draw circles to link the animals.

Sprinkle a few dozen slips of green paper over the floor to represent fallen leaves. Tell the players to slowly start moving about the room just as if they were animals moving about the forest floor. Call out FOOD CHAIN! Then have all the players stop and tell the group that the worms are hungry. Have the worms raise their hands.

Instruct the worms to each find four leaves to munch. Ask if there is enough food for them to survive. (If no worms are in the group, explain that if there are no worms, the beetles die. Ask them what would happen if all the beetles were gone. Then ask what if all of the mice are gone and so on.) Have them start moving again, and again call out FOOD CHAIN! Have the group stop, and tell the beetles to raise their hands. Tell the group that the beetles are hungry and need four worms to survive. Have the beetles take their worms and set them to the side. If there are no worms, all the beetles die; if there are not enough worms, the beetles that didn't eat enough worms die.

Have the group start moving again. Continue playing. Each time you stop, tell the players what the next animal on the food chain needs. As animals at the top of the food chain die because there is not enough food for them, the gardeners will understand that many more members are at the bottom of the food chain than at the top. Below is a breakdown of what each animal must consume:

Each worm eats four leaves (12 children are worms).
Each beetle eats three worms (four children are beetles).
Each mouse eats two beetles (four children are mice).
Each snake eats two mice (one child is a snake).
Each hawk eats one snake (one child is a hawk).

Play the game again, letting the gardeners pick which animal to play again. On the final game, assign the children roles to play from the breakdown above.

In the Classroom

Ask the group what would happen if they didn't study for a very important test. As they say they probably wouldn't do very well, ask them why.

Explain that the CAUSE of the problem was they didn't study for the test. The EFFECT of not studying was they didn't do very well. Give the gardeners a few more examples like the ones listed below and have them think of an effect of that happening:

Their shoes aren't tied when they have a race.
They forget to take an umbrella on a very cloudy day.
Their lunch money is lost on the way to school.
They don't feed a pet goldfish for 3 days.

Mark half the leaves with a dark X, which represents a tree that has absorbed pollution dumped on the soil.

Play the food chain game one last time, assigning roles to the gardeners from the breakdown above. Have the worms hold the leaves they pick up. Once the game is finished, explain that the leaves with Xs are leaves that were polluted. Have all worms that ate at least one polluted leaf raise their hands. Tell the group that those worms were poisoned. Ask them what caused this problem. What was the effect of the pollution?

Have all the beetles that ate at least one poisoned worm raise their hands. Tell the group that those beetles were poisoned. Ask them what caused this problem. What was another effect of the pollution?

Have all the mice that ate at least one poisoned beetle raise their hands. Tell the group that those mice were poisoned. Ask them what caused this problem. What was another effect of the pollution? Have the snake that ate a poisoned mouse raise his or her hand. Tell the group that the snake was poisoned. Ask them what caused this problem. What was another effect of the pollution?

Have the hawk that ate a poisoned snake raise his or her hand. Tell the group that the hawk was poisoned. Explain that pollution has become so concentrated in the snake's and hawk's bodies that the hawk dies. Ask them what caused this problem. What was another effect of the pollution?

Show your group that sometimes a single cause can have many effects by having them complete, then illustrate, the following statement:

The pollution was dumped on the ground and that caused the leaves to absorb the pollution and that caused....

Have them include in that statement each animal that become poisoned and in turn caused another animal to be poisoned.

❧ Polluting Your Planet

Objective: To observe the effects of pollution on a model of the Earth.
Time: Initial activity, 40 minutes.
Materials: Four 2-liter bottles, soil, small plants, decomposer creatures (such as pill bugs or earthworms), a handful of organic material (such as dead leaves or grass clippings).

Ask the gardeners what the name of our planet is. Tell them that today they will make their own little Planet Earth. Their tiny earth will contain a life cycle and a water cycle. Have the gardeners cut off the spouts from four 2-liter plastic bottles. They should fill each bottle with a few inches of soil, a small plant, several small decomposer creatures and a handful of organic material. These ingredients will help maintain the life cycle. Have them sprinkle enough water into the bottle to dampen the soil. The top can be sealed later with plastic wrap and taped to help create an environment for a water cycle.

Explain that these worlds were created to be real models of the Earth, so the group can see what happens when pollution is added to an environment. Ask the group where pollution comes from in our world. Of the four bottles, three will be polluted in different ways; one will remain pollution-free to show the different effects.

The first bottle should be polluted with a tablespoon of salt to represent too much fertilizer being applied or allowed to run off and contaminating surrounding areas. Explain that because of its more widespread use, incorrect fertilizer application (such as using too much, applying incorrectly) causes more problems for the environment than even pesticides. Spray the second bottle several times with a solution of half vinegar and half water to represent acid rain. Explain that acid rain is caused by air pollutants from burning fossil fuels (such as oil or coal). These fossil fuels combine chemically with rainwater to create sulfuric acid and nitric acid. The third bottle should contain an oil spill. Have one of the gardeners pour 3 tablespoons of motor oil on top of the soil. Leave the fourth bottle clean.

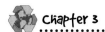

Ask the group where pollution ends up on our planet. Does it eventually escape out to space or just disappear? Explain that because the Earth's atmosphere seals in pollution, they, too, will seal the pollution in their little earths. Seal the bottles with the plastic wrap and tape.

Instruct the group to place all four bottles in a location that receives light but not direct light. Have them observe any changes every other day. It would also be a good idea to have them record in a journal their observations of each bottle.

After a few weeks, have the gardeners discuss their observations. Ask them to share their ideas about why the pollutants caused changes in the bottles.

Exploding Cactus

Objective: To demonstrate how cacti store water.
Time: 10 minutes.
Materials: None needed.

Have a volunteer stand before the group and pretend to be a strong, healthy plant. Have the child act as if the plant is getting just the right amount of sun and rain. Then tell the child to act as if the plant is becoming very hot and dry and wilting.

Ask the group what kinds of plants grow where it is very dry—those that grow spines instead of leaves. Tell the group that cacti are special plants because they have adapted to grow in harsh conditions and can last a long time between rains. Cacti have spines that don't lose water as leaves do; their waxy covering helps keep them from losing water; and they can store water for a long time after a rain. Ask the group where a cactus stores a lot of water.

Take the gardeners out to an open area and hold hands to form a circle. Tell them to imagine that they are part of a cactus—the outer edge. Walk the group through the passage of time.

1. The cactus is growing nicely and is well watered. After a period of no rain, the cactus draws in as it loses water. Have group take a small step in.
2. Now, weeks have gone by and the cactus shrinks even more.
3. A brief, heavy rain falls, and the cactus soaks up as much water as it can. The group takes a step back as the cactus stretches to hold the water it has soaked up.
4. More time passes and no rain has fallen; the cactus again draws in as water is lost. Have the group take a small step in.
5. More than 2 weeks have passed, and the cactus shrinks dramatically. Have the gardeners take two big steps in.
6. At the end of the year, a heavy rain falls and the cactus soaks up a lot of water—so much that it has expanded. The outer edge forms a tight circle. The children should be as far apart as possible while still holding hands.
7. Another rain falls; the cactus begins to soak up more water. Have the group take a large step back to see what happens to the cactus.

❧ Garden Weather Station

Objective: To create weather instruments and monitor weather conditions.
Time: Initial activity, 45 minutes.
Materials: 2-liter bottle, ruler, permanent marker, broomstick, duct tape, plastic sheeting, thumbtack, outdoor thermometer.

Explain to the group that weather is vital to a garden's success. Your gardeners can create a weather station to monitor weather conditions in your area. They can choose to add one or all of the following items to the station.

Rain gauge

The group can make a rain gauge for your garden by recycling a 2-liter bottle. Cut off the spout and invert it into the bottle opening. The JMG'ers can use a ruler and a permanent marker to place notches marking the inches along the length of the bottle. The gauge needs to be in an area that is not protected from rainfall, but that does not catch run-off from a nearby roof. Attach the gauge to a stake or weight it with a rock to prevent it from blowing over on windy days.

Wind Direction

Have the JMG'ers pound a stake or broomstick into the ground so that the top is 4 or more feet from the surface. Then they should cut a strip of white or light-colored plastic from a trash bag or plastic sheeting. Have them use a permanent marker to draw large arrows on both sides pointing to one end of the plastic strip. Use duct tape to reinforce the end that the arrows are pointing to, and tack the strip to the stake so that the arrow points toward the stake. Have the children observe that when the wind blows, the arrows point to the direction the wind is coming from.

Thermometer

To monitor the temperature in your area, you will need an outdoor thermometer. Place it out of direct sunlight.

In the Classroom

Have the class record and chart the temperature and rainfall every day. After a few weeks, help them draw conclusions on the relationship between days of rainfall and changes in temperature. (Another way your class could measure the temperature is to listen. Crickets are nature's music makers. They chirp not only to make noise, but also to attract a mate. The rate at which they chirp varies with the temperature. The children can sharpen their math skills while determining the temperature in Fahrenheit. Have them count the number of cricket chirps they hear in 1 minute, subtract 40 from that number, divide the difference by 4, and then add 50. That number is the temperature in Fahrenheit.)

Habitats

When your gardeners visit someone else's house, their host may offer them something to eat and drink. If the JMG'ers want to invite wildlife such as birds, squirrels, butterflies or other creatures to visit their yards or gardens, then they should offer the animal visitors something to eat and drink. All living creatures need water and food, especially during the winter.

If they want wildlife to live near their homes, the gardeners must also be sure that the area provides shelter, or a safe place to stay. This could be a nest, birdhouse, plants or trees that the creatures like to live in or around. If your gardeners don't know what type of home creatures might like, have them look out in nature. They can attract wildlife to their landscape just by copying what they see around them.

ACTIVITIES
✤ The Tree Community

Objective: To observe the variety of life supported by a single tree.
Time: Initial activity, 30 minutes.
Materials: Paper, pencils, colored pencils, magnifying glass, binoculars.

Ask the gardeners what living things need to be able to live. Although they might list more than the basics, the three main needs are food, shelter and water. Take the group outside to an area that has a mature tree. Explain that trees can provide shelter for people, and that some trees even produce food for people. Have the group choose a tree to adopt for the rest of the year. Ask the gardeners if their tree provides shelter for living things. How about food?

Allow them to bring materials with them to make a drawing of the tree, including as many details as they can. If possible, let them use magnifying glasses to study the lower trunk bark and leaves and include in their drawing the details they see. Also, binoculars can be an excellent discovery tool to help gardeners notice the details and observe life in the upper branches. Tell them that you especially want them to include the signs of life they see in the tree.

Have the gardeners label all the signs of life they find, and date the picture. Then each can tell the rest of the group about the discoveries. Tell the JMG'ers to pay special attention to the tree any time they pass by it and look for signs of life they haven't already noticed.

Plan to have the group come back to the tree after several weeks to make another drawing and recording of the tree and the life it supports.

❧ Gourd Bird House

Objective:	To grow and build habitats for birds using gourds.
Time:	Variable.
Materials:	Gourd seeds, garden space, bleach, water, scrub brush, drill, wire, acrylic paint, paintbrushes.

For this activity, your gardeners will need gourds.

They can be grown in the group's garden or bought from a market. Bottle, Bushel and Calabash gourds work especially well for this activity. Initially, this activity must begin with gourds being planted, harvested and set aside to dry for several months. After the gourds have dried, the gardeners can make birdhouses while planting seeds or harvesting for the next JMG group.

This activity requires time and preparation by adults. It would be a good activity in which to use Master Gardeners or other volunteers. Although children can plant, harvest, decorate and enjoy the bird houses, adult volunteers might be needed to clean, store and drill the gourds.

Ask the JMG'ers if they have ever seen a house grow. Tell them that you know of houses that can grow on vines! Gourds are a fun crop to grow, because once harvested they can be used for natural, long-lasting homes for birds. Have them help plant a new crop of gourds as they are working to prepare their dried gourds into bird houses.

Once the gourds are mature, leave them on the vine until the stems have dried. Then harvest them and lay them, without allowing them to touch each other, in an open area to dry. Gourds harvested in the fall should be dried and ready for use by late spring/early summer. Turn them every week to prevent soft spots. Gourds that have dried completely feel hollow, and the seeds can rattle around. At that time, the gourd has "cured" and is ready to be drilled. Drill an appropriately sized hole using a ½-inch wood drill bit. Drill the hole about two-thirds of the way down the gourd. Also, drill two small holes near the top so the gourd can be hung with wire.

Have the children thread wire through the holes at the tops of the gourds to serve as hangers. If possible, give them acrylic paint and brushes to use to paint designs on the gourds. Take them for a walk to scout for a place to hang their birdhouses. The gardeners will enjoy watching and waiting for a bird to make its home in the new gourd birdhouse.

❧ Our Pocket Park

Objective: To beautify an outdoor area.
Time: Variable.
Materials: Variable.

Have your group find a small, unkempt or neglected area in your neighborhood or school grounds to beautify. It could be at the corner of a building, in an alleyway, or any other area needing improvement. Take the gardeners to the location and have them brainstorm ideas for beautifying it.

In the classroom
If needed, have the class write letters to various local businesses asking for donations of specific items to use in the park. Have the children be very specific about what they need and why. Be sure to have the gardeners write thank-you notes to each business that contributes.

Explain that their job is to create their own "pocket park."

Ask those who have been to a park to describe what they liked about it—what did the park have that made it an inviting place? Tell the gardeners that for this project, the area must be cleared of litter and weeds, and it must contain the following items to attract local wildlife: a water supply (such as a birdbath or pond), shelter (such as a birdhouse or toad abode), food source (such as a bird feeder or hummingbird feeder) and some type of flowering plant (to attract pollinators).

It is also important for the group to make the area easy to maintain. Feeders and water containers that need to be filled should be easy to reach and big enough to hold large amounts. This will help the park last longer.

❧ Backyard Buddy

Objective: To reward environmentally friendly people in your community.
Time: 20 minutes.
Materials: Backyard Buddy Checklist (in the Appendix), Backyard Buddy Award (in the Appendix), pencils.

Ask the gardeners if they like for people to tell them they have done a good job. Ask them if they would like to receive an award for doing a job well.

Tell your gardeners that they will have the special task of rewarding people who are doing a good job. Show them the Backyard Buddy Award. Explain that this award is given to those who take special care of the environment in their backyard or neighborhood.

Distribute copies of the Backyard Buddy Checklist. Have each gardener make a list of people who might be eligible for such an award. Explain that anyone they know who earns more than 90 points can receive the award. Their job is to talk to people they think might be eligible for this award and ask them questions from the checklist.

Go through the list to make sure the gardeners understand each question and why it is being asked. Instruct them to find at least two people who score more than 90 points. Have the children sign and award certificates to those individuals. The certificates are found in the Appendix. Make a list at your JMG meeting place of all the Backyard Buddies recognized by your group. Have the JMG'ers leave a copy of the Backyard Buddy checklist for those people who scored less than 90 points, which will give gardeners a chance to recommend ways those people can be more earth friendly.

🌿 Visit with a Vet

Objective:	To understand needs and habitats of animals in your community.
Time:	30 minutes.
Materials:	None.

Invite a veterinarian or naturalist (from the state or county parks and wildlife department) to visit with your JMG group. An animal expert can provide interesting insight about habitats of animals living in a garden and in your community. Encourage the expert to bring anything that could serve as a visual aid for the visit. Give him or her a list of questions to be prepared to address, such as:

1. What does a veterinarian do?
2. What are some common animals in this area that might be found in a garden?
3. What types of homes do those animals live in?
4. How can we encourage more wildlife to visit our garden?
5. Are there some animals we don't want to invite? Why?
6. How can we attract those we want in our garden, while discouraging those we don't?
7. What can we do to help animals survive during the winter?
8. If someone found an injured animal (nondomesticated), what should that person do?
9. Where can injured animals (nondomesticated) be treated?

After your guest finishes speaking, invite the gardeners to ask questions of their own.

Hand-in-Hand With Nature

Everyone enjoys visiting a beautiful yard, schoolyard or park. We can keep these green spaces looking great by removing things that stress the plants and animals living there. Many factors can stress plants: insect pests, diseases, lack of water or even too much water. Your group can work hand-in-hand with nature in your neighborhood.

Nature often can take care of itself without our help. For example, if a pest insect is feeding on a plant, often a good insect will come and eat the pest. Your gardeners will learn that to work "hand-in-hand" with nature, they must first find out if a problem exists, decide if they need to help, and be sure that if they do help they don't disrupt the balance of nature.

ACTIVITIES
✿ On the Move

Objective: To understand that pollution can create many indirect negative effects.
Time: 30 minutes.
Observation: 3 hours.
Materials: Aquarium or clear plastic bin, sand, water, red food coloring, small plant (even a weed from the garden will do).

For this activity you need to prepare a model of the Earth. Fill an aquarium about half full of sand. Dampen the sand and push most of it to one side of the aquarium to create a slope, like on a beach. Gently pour water in the "ocean" part until the water is a few inches high. Put a small plant somewhere along the highest part of the sand.

Mix a spoonful of soil in a glass of water. Set it in front of a gardener and ask, "Are you thirsty?" Invite the child to take a drink. When the drink is refused, ask why. Ask the gardeners what the word "pollution" means. Have them list as many types of pollution as they can. Write down the answers as they call them out. Ask them which types of pollution are the most serious. Explain that all types of pollution can be dangerous and that they will conduct an experiment to see how the pollution moves in a miniature replica of their world.

Show them the aquarium. Have them imagine that the aquarium is like their world—it has both land and water. They can imagine fish swimming in the ocean and people and animals roaming on the land.

Tell them that some types of pollution occur when people dump wastes or chemicals on the ground. Ask them what problems could be caused by dumping just a little pollution on one small part of the land in that miniature world. Have them think about how pollution would hurt the animals living in that small area.

Drop 10 drops of red food coloring about 1 inch from the edge of the water. Explain that the color represents some kind of pollution being dumped onto the ground. Tell them to watch the red color

closely to see if pollution remains where it was dumped or if it spreads. As the red spreads some, tell the group that it might be important to check during the day to see how much it spreads.

After a few hours, the red coloring should seep farther into the sand and water. Here are questions to initiate a discussion:

1. Did the pollution stay in the same spot?
2. Why is it such a problem that pollution doesn't stay in the same place?
3. What could happen when pollution seeps to the ocean?
4. If pollution poisons the animals in the ocean, what happens to the other animals that eat them?

Explain that much of the water that people get is pumped to the surface from groundwater. Show them the visible layer of water through the sand. Tell them that is called an aquifer. What would happen to us if we drank water contaminated by pollution?

Explain that one small spot of pollution in their area of the world can touch many other parts of the world.

✿ Both Sides of the Fence

Objective: To voice opinions in a debate format.
Time: 30 minutes.
Materials: None.

> **This is a good opportunity for your gardeners** to develop their communication skills. Although debates can be lively, it is good for the gardeners to make decisions on certain issues, to feel strongly about something and to make a case for it.

Tell your gardeners a story about two neighbors who have a problem. After you read the following background to the group, have them each decide which neighbor is right.

The Farmer

A farmer lives in a very small town. He has about 10 acres of land where he raises corn, a few other crops and some cattle. He uses part of the corn to feed his own livestock, but sells most of it at a market. He has a wife and three small children. He uses the money he makes from selling the crops to pay for his family's house, food, clothes and everything else they need. The farmer must grow as much corn as he can on his land to have enough money to provide for his family. He increases the amount of corn he produces by using:

Pesticides to kill harmful insects that can destroy his crops;
Fertilizers to make the crops more productive; and
Herbicides to get rid of weeds in his fields.

The farmer is always very careful to follow the directions on the chemicals and use them correctly.

The father

The farmer's neighbor downhill on the other side of the fence is furious. He is very concerned about all the chemicals the farmer uses, because much of it is washed down from the farmer's land into his yard. He is especially worried because his 3-year-old twin girls spend a lot of time playing in their yard. Their favorite game is to make little roads in the dirt and to build pretend towns to play in with their toys. The father worries that the farmers' chemicals could end up in his soil and harm his daughters and the rest of his family. He has heard about many children becoming very ill because of chemical exposure.

The problem

The farmer is using the chemicals. The neighbor doesn't like it. Should the farmer continue to use the chemicals?

Use string to divide the room into two sections and have the gardeners get on the side of the "fence" they agree with—the farmer or the father. Tell each group to think about the problem and come up with reasons why its position is right. Ask for a volunteer from one of the sides to start a debate by stating one of the reasons why that side is correct. The other side then can respond. Allow the responses to continue until the points are exhausted.

After one point has been debated fully, allow the gardeners on the other side to start again with a statement of their own.

Once both sides have been heard from several times and have made all their points, ask the groups a few questions: Does the farmer have a right to use those chemicals? Would you be upset if you were the father? Is the farmer doing anything illegal? Would you want to live next door to the farmer? Who is right?

Explain that there is no right side to this problem and both have good arguments. Tell them that problems often have no easy answer; they must decide for themselves what is right and what should be done.

In the classroom

Have the students write a short paragraph on one of the following points:

1. Describe the problem between the farmer and the father.
2. Pick a side and give some reasons why you think that side is correct.
3. If you were deciding a solution to this problem, what would you do and why would it be fair?

❀ Weighing Wastes

Objectives: To measure the amount of food wastes produced at a meal and to work to reduce waste for the future.

Time: 45 minutes.

Materials: Container for food wastes, spring or bathroom scale.

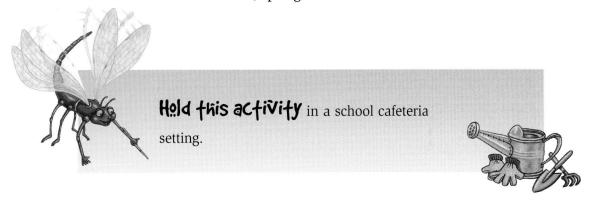

Hold this activity in a school cafeteria setting.

Ask the gardeners if they usually clean their plates or if they usually have food left over that is thrown away. For those who usually have food left over, ask them why: Is too much food on their plate, or do they dislike the food? Have the group predict how many pounds of food waste their class produces at just one meal.

Set aside a special container for the students to drop their food wastes into when they finish lunch. Instruct them to drop in just the leftover food, not the plastic ware or paper products. After lunch, weigh the bag of wastes. If you don't have a spring scale, just weigh a student on a bathroom scale and then weigh him or her again holding the bag. The difference between the two weights is the amount of food waste.

Ask the students if they are surprised by how much food was thrown away. Find out the total number of classes that ate lunch today. Have them estimate the total weight of food thrown away by the whole school by multiplying the weight of that class's waste by the number of classes at the school that eat lunch. Have them think about all the waste being produced, and ask if they think that much waste is a problem.

Tell the group that they will devise a plan to reduce the amount of waste being produced. Have them brainstorm ways that can happen. Ask if it can be reused or recycled somehow (some food wastes can be recycled using vermi-composting, in which earthworms eat waste and recycle it). One way to reduce waste is to lower the amount they throw away. This can be done by having the cafeteria serve more foods that the children will eat and not throw away.

Have your group come up with questions to ask in a poll of other classes to find out which foods are thrown away and which they would like to see served more often. A list of questions that could be used are below.

1. Who buys lunch? Who brings a lunch?
2. What is your favorite food the cafeteria serves?
3. What food does the cafeteria serve that you usually don't eat?
4. What is your favorite side dish from the cafeteria?

5. What cafeteria side dish do you usually not eat?
6. What food not now served in the cafeteria would you like to see offered?

Have the group visit several classes and record their responses. The information can then be compiled into a graph.

Invite a manager from the school cafeteria or the district nutrition service to come speak about how menus are chosen when planning meals for students. Have your students then share with the visitors the information they gathered from other classrooms and the graphs they created. Have the children ask if menus can be adjusted to reflect what is more likely to be eaten while still meeting nutritional guidelines.

Let's Try Organic

Objective: To implement organic gardening practices in a garden.
Time: Variable.
Materials: Variable.

Organic gardening is a way of raising plants that is safer for the environment. In organic gardening, a gardener uses organic, nonchemical methods to control pests and weeds, to improve the soil and to fertilize.

Explain to the children that organic gardening is a way to have a beautiful garden and yard in a natural way. Tell them that they will maintain an area in their garden using some organic gardening practices.

Ask them how chemicals are used in gardens. List on the chalkboard or a poster the ideas they call out. They might include several items such as bug spray or plant food. As you write their ideas, group them into the categories of Weed Control, Pest Control, and Soil Improvement. Have the gardeners circle the names of chemicals that have been used in their JMG garden or a garden at home.

Explain each of the following organic gardening concepts to the children and discuss how to use these ideas in your group's garden.

Weed Control

Weeds can challenge any gardener. Some weeds, such as crabgrass and bermudagrass, can take over a garden space and choke out other plants. There are organic ways to keep weeds from stealing sunlight, moisture and growing space from other plants. One organic method is to simply pull them out of the soil. Some weeds can be pulled by hand; others come out more easily if the soil is loosened with a trowel or hoe.

Mulch also reduces the problem of weeds in your garden while helping keep the moisture in the soil from evaporating. It also helps keep the soil from becoming compacted. Mulch is a layer of nonliving material that covers the soil surface. Mulch can be made up of organic material such as wood chips, compost or grass clippings, or it can consist of inorganic material such as rock. Although some weeds can grow through any layer of mulch, a layer about 4 inches thick will reduce weed populations.

Pest Control

Instead of spraying plants with an insecticide at the first sign of insect damage, first be sure that the insects are harming the plants. If they are harmful, decide if they are large and visible enough to be picked off and squashed. If that won't work, you can control and even eliminate many insects by knocking them off the plant with water. Pay special attention to the undersides of leaves, especially for controlling spider mites and aphids.

Organic gardeners also sometimes use a kind of soapy water called insecticidal soap that is an environmentally friendly way to control many pests. Beneficial insects can also help control your pests. Ladybugs and praying mantid egg cases can often be bought at nurseries.

Other methods also can prevent and control specific pests. For example, a collar of paper can be wrapped around the base of the stem of tomato plants so the collar dips slightly below the surface of the soil. This prevents cutworms from damaging those stems. A board can also be laid on the soil. This attracts slugs. The board can regularly be stomped on to squash the slugs.

Many gardeners believe that planting certain crops can trap or repel certain harmful pests. Growing garlic around other plants is thought to repel some insects. Other types of companion plants are believed to reduce populations of certain pests.

Soil Improvement

One of the most common ways to improve soil is to amend it with compost or some other type of organic material. These soil improvements can give your plants needed nutrients. Compost can also be top dressed around existing plants. This means the compost is spread over the ground around the base of the plants. Good sources of material include organic matter from a compost bin and earthworm castings from a vermi-composting bin.

Have your gardeners decide which organic gardening ideas to implement in their garden. For more information, see the JMG web site at *www.jmgkids.org*.

❀ Xeriscape

Objective: To build a garden site using water conservation concepts.
Time: Initial activity, 45 minutes.
Materials: Chalkboard or poster, chalk or markers, plants, hoses, mulch.

Have your gardeners imagine that they have just finished a very long walk in the hot sun. Ask them what they would like to have to drink. Tell them that water is the best thirst quenching drink in the world. Write the word DRINK on the chalkboard or poster. Have them call out other ways people use water and add them to the list (washing clothes, flushing, brushing teeth, etc.).

Tell them that in urban areas one particular way people use water requires about half of all the water people use. Have them guess what this use is. Tell the group that the biggest use of water is watering plants in gardens and landscapes.

Ask them how we can save water in our gardens and in our yards—can we just stop watering? What would happen if we did? Write the word Xeriscape (pronounced ZEER-escape) on the

chalkboard or poster. Show your group how this combines the word landscape with the Greek word "xeri," which means dry.

Tell them that Xeriscape is a way to have a beautiful garden and yard without using so much water. Tell them they will create a Xeriscape area outside.

Explain each of the following concepts and discuss how to use them in a garden and landscape.

Plant Choice

Many plants and even different kinds of grasses can live very well in your area with little irrigation. These plants are more "in tune" with the local environment. The local nursery sells all sorts of plants, but they may require a lot of extra water. For a list of plants that are native or are well adapted to your area, contact the county Extension agent, or see the JMG Web site at *www.jmgkids.org.*

Irrigation

An irrigation system gives your plants water. Your group should irrigate to give the plants only the water they need without wasting water. Most lawns receive twice as much water as they need to be healthy. Your gardeners' Xeriscape should not receive regular irrigation, as it is likely to overwater the specially adapted plants or grasses.

There are many different types of irrigation systems. One of the easiest and most inexpensive ways to irrigate efficiently is to use a soaker hose system. A soaker hose bought from a nursery can be attached to a water hose and laid on the ground around the base of your plants. Areas can also be watered using a dripper system, a less efficient hose-end sprinkler or an underground sprinkler system.

Mulching

Mulch is a layer of nonliving material that covers the soil surface. Mulch helps keep moisture in the soil from evaporating, reduces weeds in a flower bed, and helps keep the soil from becoming compacted. Mulches can be made up of organic material such as wood chips, compost or grass clippings, or can consist of inorganic material such as rock.

Have your group find a small area that can be developed into a Xeriscape. The gardeners can write the county Extension office for information or go on-line to select plants for the Xeriscape. They should decide on a way to irrigate and a type of mulch that can be spread around their plants. Once the area is established, your group might be surprised at how easy the Xeriscape is to maintain!

Recycling

When you recycle you are actually turning trash into treasure. We can all make the Earth a better place when we take the time to recycle. Did you know that plastic, glass, newspapers and even tires can be recycled?

Nature has also been recycling for thousands of years. In the forest, leaves, twigs and dead plants and animals are recycled to make rich new soil. How does this happen? Small microorganisms, fungi and even worms help break down these things to turn nature's trash into treasure.

These activities will help your group learn more about recycling.

ACTIVITIES

❧ Vermi-composting

Objective: To recycle food wastes with vermi-composting.

Time: 30 minutes, ongoing.

Materials: Plastic bin with lid, newspaper, water, soil, food wastes, 1 pound of red wiggler earthworms (There are many mail order sources. Contact your county Extension office or search on-line for sources of earthworms.).

Your group can create an earthworm bin to keep indoors for composting food wastes into earthworm castings. The castings that earthworms produce are ideal nutrients for indoor and garden plants. Many different types of containers can be used to house your group's earthworms. Plastic bins about 1 foot wide and 2 feet long work especially well.

1. Drill small holes (about the width of a toothpick) around the base of the container about 1 inch from the bottom. Space the holes about one per inch. These holes allow air flow to and from the soil.

2. Next, add bedding to the bottom of the bin. Bedding can be made by shredding newspaper into inch-wide strips. Wet the strips by dipping them into water. Fill about 6 inches of the bottom of the bin with wet newspaper bedding.

3. Sprinkle a 1-inch layer of soil over the bedding and sprinkle it with water to make the soil damp.

4. Then bury food scraps under the soil.

5. Now add your earthworms, and they will go to work!

Earthworm bins do poorly with food scraps that are fatty or contain meats, but work well with newspaper, coffee grounds and even eggshells.

Ask gardeners what the word RECYCLING means. Have them call out items they have recycled before. Make a list of those items. Ask the gardeners if the food can be recycled. Tell them to imagine they are in the cafeteria at their school. Have them try to think of ways they can use the leftover food being thrown away to make something else. (This question will probably elicit interesting responses.)

Ask the group what happens to leaves in the forest during the winter. (They fall to the ground.) Ask them why the leaves that fall from the trees every year don't just pile up higher and higher each year. (They break down/decompose and become part of the soil.) Explain that food can be recycled the same way plants are recycled in the environment. Tell them that they will recycle their leftovers into a special soil that will help give plants the nutrients they need. The secret is earthworms.

Explain that earthworms live in soil all over the world. They help change bits of dead plants and animals back into nutrients that plants can use. Show them the earthworms in the bin and allow them to find a worm and look at it closely. Tell the group that these red wiggler earthworms are especially suited for composting food scraps inside an indoor bin.

Assign one or two JMG'ers a week to give food scraps to the worms. Explain that although earthworms eat a lot, they need only a couple of small handfuls of food a week. As the worm population grows, they should be able to eat more food. Have them make sure the scraps are buried, which should prevent food odors.

After a few months, the compost can be harvested. Open the bin and shine a bright light onto the soil. The earthworms will migrate to a deeper level, and the top layer of soil can be scraped away. Continue this process until you get close to the bottom of the bin and mostly earthworms remain. Then add fresh bedding and soil to the bin to give the worms a new home again.

The compost that is scraped away makes a wonderful soil amendment for garden and indoor plants.

For more information and helpful links on vermi-composting, go to the JMG web site at *www.jmgkids.org.*

In the Classroom
Have your group experiment with measuring the effect of the vermi-compost on plant growth. They could use such variables as growing seeds with differing amounts of compost added or adding differing amounts of compost to plants growing in the garden. Have them predict which amounts of compost will produce the best results. The gardeners can then use tape measures to record growth and observe the changes in the plants.

❦ Supermowing Machine

Objective: To be creative in inventing a new mowing machine.
Time: 25 minutes.
Materials: Paper, pencils, colors.

Tell the children that they just landed a new job as an inventor. They will work for a lawn mower factory; their first job is to invent an all-new, improved lawn mower. It will be called the Super Mowing Machine. To begin the activity, have the group call out the parts to a lawn mower as you make a rough sketch for the group on a chalkboard or poster. Try to include the following parts in the group sketch: motor, blade, pull string, wheels, handle and gas cap.

Label each part and ask the gardeners to describe what each of the parts does for the lawn mower. Have those with mowing experience explain how to mow. Ask them what is hard about mowing. Have the group think about and call out ideas to make mowing easier, cleaner, more comfortable or more efficient, or to make the mower do more things. Encourage them to be creative.

Allow the children to spend several minutes working on a rough sketch of the Super Mowing Machine. Have them share their sketches and ideas with each other. If they like, allow them to partner with other gardeners to continue working. Spend the remaining time with them working on a final drawing in color with all the parts labeled telling what each part does.

❦ Grow Cards

Objective: To recycle newspaper to create plantable greeting cards.
Time: 30 minutes.
Materials: Newspaper, window screen, bin, water, cookie cutters, blender, flower seed (any seed will do, but larger seeds make the final product more attractive), brown paper bags, raffia, glue.

For this activity, you need to use a window screen or make a screen frame.

Ask the gardeners if they have ever received a card for their birthday, holiday or other special occasion. Then ask if they have ever planted one of those cards in a garden. Tell them that today they will make a greeting card for someone they know that can be planted in the garden and will grow a plant.

Your group will need to gather scraps of paper and tear them into small pieces about the size of postage stamps. Have them fill a blender half full with scraps and ¾ full with water. Blend the water and paper mixture on high speed until the mixture has an oatmeal-like consistency. The

gardeners can choose a cookie cutter shape they like and place the cutter onto the screen. Next, they should pour the blended paper mixture into the cutter, so a thin layer of the mixture fills in the shape. The gardeners can then sprinkle on a few seeds and push the seeds into the mixture with their fingers.

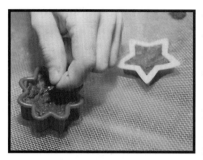

They should then place the screen with the wet paper shape onto a towel and carefully remove the cutter. Then have them lay another towel over the paper shape and firmly press it to remove most of the remaining water. The paper shape will still be damp, but will be strong enough to keep its form. The card should dry and be ready for giving in a day or two. Because the cards have seeds embedded in them, they can be planted. The seeds will germinate and the paper pulp will break down in the soil.

If they attach ribbon or raffia to the grow card, it can be given as a hanging ornament. The group can also cut rectangles (about 8 by 6 inches) from a brown paper bag, fold the paper in half and then attach the grow card to the front. Special messages can be written inside. Have the group experiment using a combination of different types and colors of papers when blending the mixture for the grow cards.

In the Classroom
Have the gardeners write a short paragraph explaining what a grow card is and how to plant it. This can be copied neatly on the back of the brown paper part of the card so the recipient will know what to do with it.

🌿 Know & Show Recycling Sombrero

Objective: To create wearable works of art that display recyclable materials.
Time: 1 hour.
Materials: 2-inch clear tape, newspaper, miscellaneous art supplies (markers, yarn, glitter, pipe cleaners, tissue, etc.).

The gardeners will create pieces of wearable art—newspaper hats decorated with items that can be recycled. Assist the gardeners or have them partner up to make a hat for each member of the JMG group.

To make a hat, take two large, square sheets of newspaper and place the middle of both sheets on top of a gardener's head. Lay the rest of the paper flat against the gardener's head. Tape around the newspaper, starting right over the gardener's ear and continue wrapping until the tape goes all the way around the head.

Curl up the edges of the newspaper to form the brim of the hat. Have the gardeners decorate the newspaper hats using art supplies to depict materials that people can recycle instead of throwing away. Encourage them to have fun and be creative.

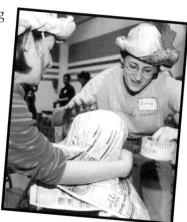

When all are finished, have them show what they have created and discuss what each decoration means. You may want to have hooks for the gardeners to hang their hats on for storage when they are finished. This is a good activity to help the JMG'ers look for items that can be recycled.

Eco-Art

Your JMG group can use items found in nature to make unique and special art projects and gifts. Many years ago, people used materials from nature to make dyes, paints, musical instruments and even jewelry.

In this section, your gardeners will have fun making Eco-Art.

ACTIVITIES
❀ Plant Pounding

Objective: To transfer the likeness of plant parts to fabric.
Time: 45 minutes.
Materials: Fresh leaves and petals, cutting board, plastic wrap, hammer, old sheet.

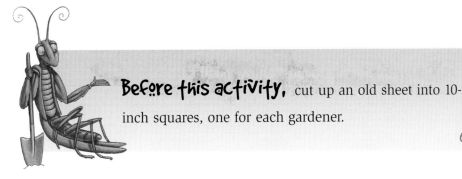

Before this activity, cut up an old sheet into 10-inch squares, one for each gardener.

There are wonderful patterns and designs in nature. Lines and shapes of flowers and leaves can be captured onto fabric, and they last a long time. Ask the gardeners if they have ever hit a flower or pounded a leaf.

Explain that they may have rubbed leaves or other plant parts to get an impression of the shape and design, but with pounding, they can copy the shape, design and color of the plant. Take the gardeners out for a walk in the morning. Have them choose leaves, grasses or flowers they have permission to pick and would like to try pounding. Encourage them to be selective and pick only an item or two to try. Because these first selections will be for practice, have the group try a variety of plants to see which ones leave the best likenesses of the plant used.

Have each child lay the fabric on a cutting board, flatten a flower or leaf face down on the fabric, and then lay a sheet of plastic wrap over the plant parts. A hammer can then be used to pound over the plant parts until an impression is left. After several strikes, the children can gently peel back the leaf or petal to see if the part needs more pounding or not. Although fresh plant parts work best, your group might also try using flowers from a florist. (Florists often will donate wilted blooms.) The gardeners will discover that some plants leave beautiful impressions that capture colors, while other plants don't seem to do anything!

Once the gardeners are successful in making plant impressions on their practice squares, plan another pounding day when they can each bring a T-shirt and create botanical shirts for themselves or for gifts. Clothing decorated with plant poundings should be hand-washed in cold water with a mild detergent.

Let's Dye It

Objective: To color eggs or fabrics using dyes created from natural materials.
Time: 1 hour.
Materials: Hard-boiled eggs, various plant materials, water, vinegar.

As spring arrives, many gardeners may be interested in dyeing eggs. Your group can color eggs using dyes made from plant parts and other natural materials. The chart below shows several possibilities for creating homemade, natural dyes.

Material	Color
Yellow onion skins	orange
Beets or cranberries	red
Spinach leaves	green
Red cabbage or blueberries	blue
Orange or lemon peels	yellow
Coffee or tea	brown

Have the gardeners clean the eggs by wiping them with vinegar. They can then cut or tear plant parts into small pieces, mixing 4 cups of the plant material with 2 quarts of water in a pot. Bring the water to a boil and have them add 2 tablespoons of vinegar. The gardeners can then place the eggs in the colored water and allow them to soak for 30 minutes.

Have the group experiment with different dyeing methods. Ideas might include soaking eggs with the plant materials removed versus allowing them to soak with the materials, wrapping eggs with string or rubber bands before soaking, or dipping eggs in different colors. Your group might even try dyeing fabric with your homemade dyes.

Nature Windows

Objective: To create art using natural materials.
Time: 30 minutes.
Materials: Scissors, clear contact paper, natural materials, brown construction paper cut in ½-inch strips.

Have the gardeners go outside and collect natural materials. They should collect flat, easily dried materials such as leaves and flower petals. Have them dry the materials in a plant press or book.

Next, have each gardener cut two 8-inch squares of contact paper. Have the children remove the paper backing from one of the sheets and lay it on a flat surface with the sticky side up. They can then apply the materials in any design they like. The remaining sheet of contact paper should be laid over the arrangement to seal it into the paper. The gardeners can then glue brown strips around the edges and in a plus sign down the middle to create a window pane. Hang the nature window in an open area so light can shine through the design.

🌿 Garden Folk

Objective: To build a scarecrow.
Time: 20 minutes.
Materials: Plastic jug, broomstick, coat hanger, old clothes, safety pins, permanent marker.

Scarecrows have been used to scare bird pests from gardens for a long time. Your gardeners can make their own versions of scarecrows, called garden folks, to protect the plants and make your garden a more friendly place.

Have the gardeners hammer a stake or broomstick into the ground and top it with the plastic jug by putting the spout over the end of the stick, as seen in the picture. Then they should push the hook of the hanger into the spout to create shoulders. Next, dress the character with the old clothes, holding them in place with safety pins. The last step is to use a permanent marker to add a face. Your gardeners will enjoy seeing the scarecrow standing in the garden and keeping watch over their plants.

🌿 Nature Masks

Objective: To create wearable art using natural materials.
Time: 30 minutes.
Materials: Tagboard, Nature Masks (in the Appendix), poster board, twigs, hot glue gun/sticks, glue, natural materials.

For this activity, your group should gather twigs and other natural materials for decoration, such as leaves, seeds, petals and seed pods.

Copy the mask forms onto tagboard. Have the group cut out the forms. Your gardeners can use these forms as stencils to trace the patterns onto poster board and cut them out. Assist them by hot-gluing a small twig to the side of each mask. This will serve as a holder.

They can then use natural materials to cover the surface. Use glue to attach the items to the mask. Encourage them to be creative in decorating their masks. Once masks are completed, your group might decide to have a JMG masquerade party.

Mother Nature's Children

Objective: To create art using natural materials.
Time: 20 minutes.
Materials: Paper, glue, various natural materials.

Before this activity, gather many different types of natural materials, such as seeds, flowers, acorns and leaves of various shapes and sizes.

Ask the gardeners if they have ever heard of Mother Nature—and if they have ever seen her. Have them describe what their imagination tells them Mother Nature might look like. Next, ask them to imagine what Mother Nature's children might look like. Tell them that these are imaginary characters; their job is to create on paper how some of her children might appear. Have them use glue, paper and an assortment of natural materials to craft their creatures. Encourage the gardeners to be creative—the creature might resemble people or animals, or might have some completely original form.

LEADERSHIP/SERVICE LEARNING PROJECTS

Below are projects to complete with your JMG group. The group should choose at least one to complete.

❧ Winter Wildlife Tree
In the cold months of winter, many animals cannot find as much food as during the rest of the year. Your JMG group can create edible decorations, such as pine cone bird feeders, fruit or bread, for an outdoor tree that is beautiful and provides food for birds and other creatures.

❧ Backyard Habitat Garden
If the gardeners like butterflies, birds, squirrels and other creatures in their garden, they can invite even more of them by building a Backyard Habitat Garden. Certain creatures are attracted to certain plants. When the group plants them, these special creatures will stop in to visit and build their homes in the group's own backyard, school or neighborhood.

❧ Recycled Art Show
Your JMG'ers can create art sculptures using only recyclable materials. These works can then be displayed in a JMG art show. The group could hold the art show at a school, grocery store, bank or any other place in your area to bring attention to all of the common items that can be recycled. People might come by to vote on which recycled sculptures should be awarded prizes for the "Most Creative," "Most Beautiful" or even "The Trashiest."

❧ Create Your Own
Your JMG group can be creative and decide on a special project to complete for the Leadership/Service Learning requirement.

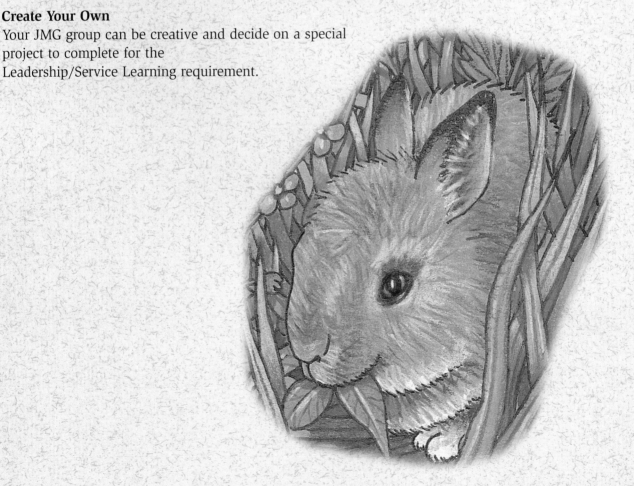

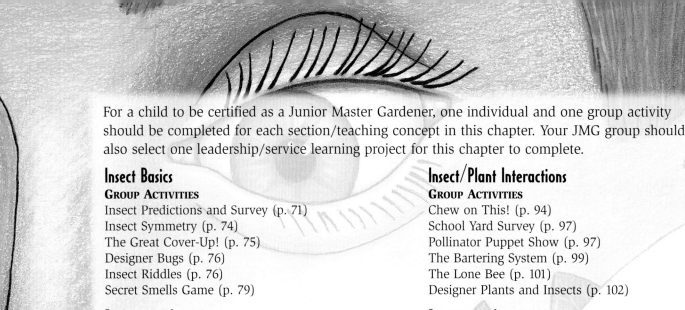

For a child to be certified as a Junior Master Gardener, one individual and one group activity should be completed for each section/teaching concept in this chapter. Your JMG group should also select one leadership/service learning project for this chapter to complete.

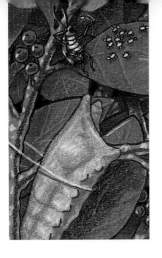

Insects and Diseases

Insect Basics

If all the insects on earth were piled together, they would weigh more than all the people. Insects are everywhere, and they play a very important role in garden life. In this section, you will guide your JMG'ers in exploring the world of insects by finding and studying insects, learning about their unique characteristics, making insects and even eating them!

ACTIVITIES

✽ Insect Predictions and Survey

Objectives: To predict insect characteristics and learn what all insects have in common.
Time: Variable.
Materials: Chalkboard or flip chart and easel, clear plastic bags and/or clear jars for collecting insects, enough tweezers and/or gloves to have one for every four to five students, Insect Drawing and Insect Predictions Chart (in the Appendix), book about insects.

Ask the gardeners what an insect is. Write down their descriptions, and draw an insect using their suggestions. As the JMG'ers respond, question them further to elicit more specific responses. (For example, if someone suggests that insects have wings, ask "How many? Where are they located?") Although most children have a fairly good image of what an insect is, they may be confused about some specifics, such as whether all insects have wings (they don't) or whether some creatures typically thought of as creepy crawlers, such as spiders and centipedes, are insects or not (they aren't).

You may also have the gardeners work independently to draw their own "typical insect" including all the features they think insects have.

After you have created a representative picture of the gardeners' predicted insect features, stand back and look at the picture. It may look pretty wild. Ask students if they have ever seen an insect that looks like the picture. Let students know that they will participate in an insect survey and conduct research to determine which of their predictions are accurate.

Discuss with the students what a prediction is. The insect you draw represents the gardeners' predictions of what an insect looks like, based on what they already know.

Insect Walk

Before this activity, review the safety principles with the gardeners. They should not try to pick up or catch insects that are unfamiliar or known to be harmful. Demonstrate how to use tweezers and gloves, or how to place a bottle over an insect without touching it.

Organize the group into smaller work groups with four to five students each. Take them outside and ask each group to look for insects in a different area. The intent is not to catch every insect in the area, but to gather a sample of common insects against which to test their predictions. If more adult volunteers are available, it is helpful to have one adult with each group. This should take about 20 minutes.

After the Survey

After the insect survey, ask the gardeners to observe the captured organisms using clear plastic jars as temporary observation chambers. Have them use the Insect Prediction Chart and record on the left side of the page the names of each organism and the number of each characteristic listed across the top. In the last column they should indicate whether or not the organism is an insect. If they do not know the name of an organism, they can make up a descriptive name. Ask each group to chart the features of two or three organisms; some groups may be able to do more.

As they study their insect catches, they can check off each specimen's features. For example, under the column named "Body parts," they can write in the number of body parts of each specimen. Do the same for other features they observe, such as antennae, wings and legs.

Name _____ Date _____

INSECT PREDICTIONS CHART

Name of organism	Number of body parts	Number of legs	Number of wings	Antennae present?	Is it an insect?

When all the groups have created charts, ask them to compare what they found with the other groups and with their original predictions. Which features were the same? Which varied? Cue the gardeners to observe what this tells them about insect features. (Some features are common to all insects; some can vary or are difficult to see.)

Draw a new insect, based on their new observations. Their new predictions will probably differ from those made earlier. Discuss with them that they are updating their predictions based on new information. Scientists continually update their predictions as they discover new information. They usually cannot answer all their questions; some may remain unanswered, and more questions may arise. Discuss with the gardeners which features changed, and why. What questions still exist? Are there any new ones to be added? If so, how would the gardeners go about answering them? The gardeners may disagree on some features. However, after having examined a variety of insects, they will have a better idea of which features are shared by all insects, and which creatures may not be insects at all.

Conclude the activity by reading aloud from a book about insects. Ask the gardeners to listen carefully for information pertaining to insect characteristics, and to change the insect drawing as needed. When it is finished, compare the different stages of insect drawings and predictions, and discuss how they have changed. You may also want to have children label the insect drawing in the Appendix.

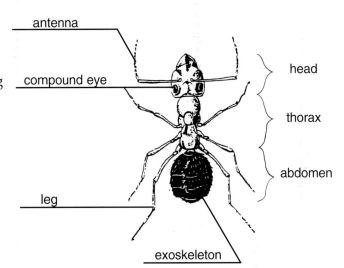

Chapter 4

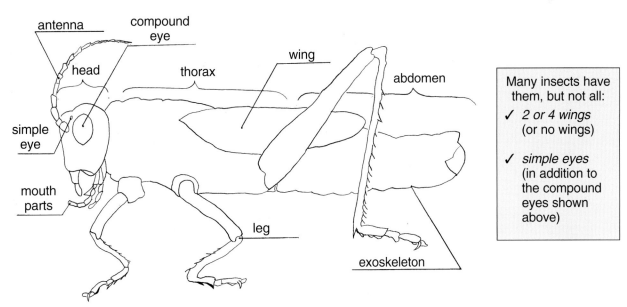

All insects are covered by a hard exoskeleton, or skeleton covering the outside of their bodies like armor.

❀ Insect Symmetry

Objective: To learn and understand the concept of symmetry.
Time: 45 minutes.
Materials: Masking tape, construction paper, poster paints, paintbrushes.

Attach tape to yourself so that your body is split horizontally into two halves. Have the gardeners do the same to themselves. Are you symmetrical? Prompt the gardeners with questions such as, "Is there an arm at the same place on both sides of the tape?" until they understand that you (and they) are not symmetrical horizontally. Divide yourself (and the gardeners) in half with tape again, but this time apply the tape vertically, so that you are split in half lengthwise. Ask gardeners the same questions: "Is there an arm (or eye, or leg, etc) at the same place on both sides of the tape?" This time the answer is yes. You have divided yourself in half symmetrically, so that each side is a mirror image of the other. Discuss the term "symmetry" with the gardeners.

Give each student a sheet of construction paper. Demonstrate how to fold the paper in half and draw the outline of half a butterfly on the fold. Cut out your example and unfold it to show the gardeners that it creates a perfectly symmetrical butterfly. (Most children will have done this part of the activity using heart cutouts for Valentine's Day.) Have the gardeners make and paint their butterflies in any pattern they wish, but on one side only. When they have finished, they should fold the butterfly in half, and press the two halves together.

For the paint to transfer, it must still be

wet when the butterfly is folded back together. The gardeners must work quickly to paint the first half. When they reopen their butterflies, the pattern will have transferred to the unpainted half. Set the butterflies aside to dry.

In the classroom
Use mirror tiles to reinforce the concept of symmetry. Show the students how to place an item such as their painted butterflies flat on a table. When a mirror is placed on its edge in the center of the butterfly, the mirror image is reflected in its surface, creating a complete and symmetrical butterfly.

❧ The Great Cover-Up!

Objective: To learn and understand the concept of camouflage.
Time: 30 minutes.
Materials: Insect Templates (in the Appendix), several colors of paper that will blend in to your meeting room.

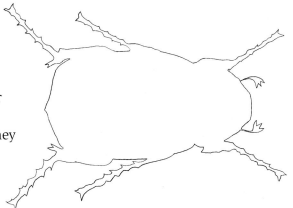

Before the activity, use the insect templates and cut three to six insect shapes from a variety of types of paper, using colors and/or patterns present in the meeting room. For example, use paper similar to the color of a chalkboard, another paper with a wood-grain look like a desk top or coat rack, another the color of a countertop, etc. Before the gardeners arrive, tape the insects to the various surfaces that they match, creating a camouflage environment.

To introduce the following discussion, you might want to wear army fatigue-type clothes, such as camouflage pants or T-shirt, if available, to stimulate the gardeners' interest.

Lead the JMG'ers in discussing the concept of camouflage. Ask them, "What is camouflage?" They may have heard the term before in reference to camouflage clothing worn by members of the military. Ask the gardeners what camouflage clothing looks like. What is its purpose? Through discussion, make sure that the gardeners know that the purpose of camouflage clothing is to conceal the person wearing it. Camouflage is a type of disguise that hides people (or animals) by helping them blend in with their surroundings. In addition to people in the military, many animals and plants use camouflage to allow them to either sneak up on their prey or hide from a predator.

Inform the gardeners that, before they came in, you placed some insect shapes around the room. Tell them how many there are. Ask them to pretend they are hungry predators, looking for a juicy insect snack. Keep track of the time it takes for them to find all the insects. Afterward, discuss camouflage again. Were the insects hidden well? How long did it take to find all the shapes? If the insects had been real and the gardeners real predators, which insect would have been caught and eaten first? What advantage is there in being camouflaged well?

> **JMG Trivia** Some insects use reverse-camouflage. That is, they are brightly colored to stand out rather than hide. Usually, these insects taste bad or are toxic, and the bright colors serve as a "DO NOT EAT!" warning to other animals. Some other insects use bright colors to disguise themselves as toxic or bad-tasting insects, even though they aren't. This technique of imitation is called mimicry.

☙ Designer Bugs

Objective: To reinforce concepts learned thus far: insect characteristics; the concepts of symmetry and camouflage.

Time: 1 hour.

Materials: Paint, paintbrushes, construction paper, miscellaneous craft items such as paper towel cylinders, pipe cleaners, pompons, etc.

Discuss with the gardeners the parts of an insect. You may want to use the insect anatomy work sheet from the Insect Predictions activity in the Appendix, and have the JMG'ers color in the various body parts and structures as you discuss them.

Ask the gardeners to create three-dimensional insect models from available craft materials. They should make them as accurate as possible, including the basic insect characteristics—correct number of body parts, legs, etc. The models should be symmetrical, and may be camouflaged to fit into a certain environment. (For example, insects living in the grass would probably be green; those living on a tree would be brown.) Their creations may be patterned after real insects (for example, a dragonfly or a walking stick), or they may be "fantasy insects" (for example, a rainbow beetle that has rainbow-colored stripes to blend in with rainbows, etc.).

Ask the gardeners to write descriptions to display with their insects, including the names of the insects, what they look like and where they live.

This activity does not present new concepts;

rather, it combines previously learned skills and concepts. You can use it to evaluate whether the JMG'ers understand the concepts and to reinforce these concepts with a fun art activity.

optional Extension

Have the gardeners display their creations or present them orally to another group. Organize a contest with a secret ballot box. Vote on the best insect for various categories, such as the Most Creative, Most Realistic, Brightest, etc.

☙ Insect Riddles

Objectives: To reinforce basic concepts learned about insects so far and to experiment with creative writing concepts by writing riddles.

Time: 1 hour.

Materials: Pens or pencils, paper.

Have the gardeners compose riddles about insects or other garden creatures that are not insects, using the information they have learned about insect characteristics. Read the riddles below as examples. When each JMG'er has composed one or two riddles, have them all present their riddles to the others or another group. Have the other children try to guess the identity of the mystery creatures. Examples are included of both rhyming and nonrhyming riddles—use whichever is appropriate for the children's skill level.

You may want to revisit this activity later in this unit. As the gardeners learn more about insects and other garden creatures, they will be able to add more detail to their riddles. Creating riddles or simple rhymes will help you assess how well they understand the concepts you are teaching.

Nonrhyming riddles

(Dragonfly)
I am an insect.
I have four long, narrow wings that make a whirring sound
    when I swoop over ponds and lakes searching for mosquito larvae.
I scoop them up with my basket-shaped front legs for a snack on the run.
I have two large compound eyes
    so I can see what's sneaking up behind me,
    and a long, narrow body that may be brightly colored, blue or green.
I like to rest on reeds or cattails by the water and bask in the sun
    while I am looking for my next meal.
What am I?

(Spider)
I am not an insect.
I have two body parts instead of three, as insects have,
    and I have eight legs instead of six.
I am a very helpful friend to have in the garden,
    because I eat many pest insects that would eat your plants.
I catch my prey using silk threads.
What am I?

Chapter 4

Rhyming riddle

(Caterpillar)

I cannot fly, spin a web, chew through wood, or even hop!
But when it comes to eating plants, I'm pretty much nonstop.

My chewing mouthparts munch on leaves morning, evening and at noon
In preparation for the BIG DAY when I change in my cocoon!

In the Classroom

1. Discuss the terms onomatopoeia (the name given to its corresponding sound, such as buzz, hiss, drip-drop) and/or alliteration (a sentence or phrase in which many words begin with the same letter, such as "blue buzzing bees") with the gardeners. Ask them to include examples of onomatopoeia in their riddles, and/or alliteration where appropriate. This is also a good activity for practicing the use of descriptive words such as adjectives or adverbs.

Example (Dragonfly)
Whirring wildly, I whip above the water, winging on the wind as I watch for wigglers (mosquito larvae) in the water. Who am I?

2. Use descriptive terms about insects to reinforce the students' knowledge of the parts of a sentence, using the follow-up activity below

Ask the students to call out names of insects. List these words on the chalkboard. Explain that the name of a person, place or thing, such as an insect, is a noun. Next ask the students for words that describe how insects look, and list these on the board as well. Explain that words describing a person, place or thing are called adjectives.

Next, ask the children to call out words that tell what insects do. Make another list of these, and explain that these words—which show action—are called verbs. Finally, ask them for words that describe how insects do each of the action words listed. (For example, for the action word "fly," how do insects do it? Swiftly? Silently?) Explain that words describing verbs or adjectives are called adverbs.

Tell the students that they will create special poetry riddles about an insect of their choice. Show them the Poetry Riddle template. Ask them to think of an insect and fill in the blanks of their Poetry Riddle with words describing this insect. Once they have finished, have them share their Poetry Riddles with the rest of the class to see if other JMG'ers can guess the insects.

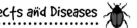

Poetry Riddle Template:		Example Poetry Riddle:
_____ (adjective),		small
_____ (adjective),		brown
_____ (adjective),		quiet
_____ (adverb)	_____ (verb)	quickly hop
_____ (adjective)	_____ (noun)	old logs
_____ (verb sound)		chirp

❧ Secret Smells Game

Objective: To discover how insects use pheromones to communicate.

Time: 30 to 45 minutes.

Materials: Black plastic film canisters (one per student), or other opaque jars, cotton balls, a variety of scents (possibilities listed below).

Obviously, insects cannot talk. However, like other species, they have developed specialized forms of communication. Many use special scents and hormones called pheromones. Many insects identify another as a potential mate (or a potential enemy) by scent recognition.

People are so accustomed to talking that it may be difficult for your gardeners to imagine using scents instead of language to identify and recognize each other. One fun way to illustrate the concept is by playing the Secret Smells Game. Ahead of time, prepare the film canisters by placing in each one a cotton ball that has been dipped into a scent of some sort. Make two film canisters using each scent, and then mix them up.

Tell the gardeners they are going to be insects. Their mission is to search out their partner insect using only their sense of smell. They absolutely positively cannot talk! Ask each student to take one film canister, and lift the lid just long enough to smell the scent. Then ask them to go from person to person, sniffing containers, to try to identify the student who has the scent that matches their own. See how long it takes all the gardeners to locate their Secret Smell Partners.

Some possible scents to use:

✓ Peanut Butter
✓ Orange Juice
✓ Scented soap or lotion
✓ Chocolate

✓ Mint-flavored mouthwash
✓ Perfume
✓ Vanilla, peppermint or
   other types of extract or flavorings

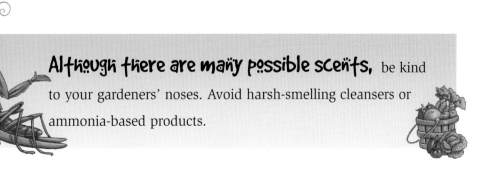

Although there are many possible scents, be kind to your gardeners' noses. Avoid harsh-smelling cleansers or ammonia-based products.

Insect Life Cycles and Classification

Insects are divided into different groups, called orders, according to their characteristics and the type of life cycle, or metamorphosis, they undergo. Imagine being able to totally change your appearance. Instead of hands and feet, you might have suction cups for walking up walls. Or, you might grow wings and fly instead of walking. Imagine having different eyes that could see the world in dazzling colors invisible to humans! In this section, your JMG gardeners will learn about insect groups and some of the many incredible ways that insects transform themselves into new creatures as they go through their life cycles.

✿ All in the Family: Insect Flash Cards

Objectives: To learn that insects are organized into groups based on their characteristics; to learn the characteristics common to all insects as well as those specific to a few insect groups, called orders.

Time: 1 hour.

Materials: Note cards, a hole punch, clear contact paper, something that will connect the cards such as a metal shower curtain ring or twist tie.

Look at the Insect Orders chart on page 82. Insects, like all other plants and animals, are grouped into different categories called orders. All insects share some characteristics—three body parts, six legs, two antennae, a hardened exoskeleton and compound eyes. They may or may not also have simple eyes and two or four wings.

All insects grouped together in an order also share other characteristics and are more closely related than those from different orders. For example, all insects in the order Lepidoptera have scale-covered wings—the butterflies, moths and skippers. All insects in the order Diptera have two wings, instead of the more common four, and are specialized for fast flying. This order includes flies and mosquitoes.

Ask the gardeners to use the Insect Orders chart on page 82 to list the specialized characteristics of each order. (There are many more orders of insects than are shown here; we have just highlighted a few of the common ones.) Have the gardeners draw sketches of insects from each order they learn on one side of a note card, and write the characteristics common to that order on the reverse side to create a set of Insect Flash Cards. The basic characteristics common to all insects can also be included on a separate card.

To make the insect flash cards more durable, you can have the gardeners cover them with clear contact paper, which is sold in the wallpaper section at hardware stores.

Next, have the gardeners punch a hole in the upper left corner of each card and connect the cards with a shower curtain ring or twist tie. This will be a set of flash cards they can carry with them to help them classify some of the insects they see.

In the Classroom

The section on insect characteristics and grouping is a good one to use to introduce Venn diagrams. Make a Venn diagram with two insect orders. (See the illustration below as an example.) In the overlapping space, write in the characteristics that the two orders share. In the spaces of each circle that do not overlap, write in the characteristics of each individual order. Ask the gardeners why each characteristic is in that space, to make sure they understand the purpose of each space in the diagram. Have them make another Venn diagram on their own using different insect orders.

Lepidoptera (Butterflies)

4 large, showy wings covered with colorful scales; siphoning (straw-like) mouthparts

Insects

3 body parts
6 legs
2 antennae
compound eyes
hardened exoskeleton

Diptera (Flies and mosquitoes)

2 wings, which are small and not showy, but are specialized for fast flying; sponging or piercing/sucking mouthparts

Ordering Insects

Objectives: To learn to sort insects by similarities and differences, and to make a basic insect key.

Time: 1 hour.

Materials: Poster board and markers, jars of insects and leaf and grass debris gathered on a previous insect hunt and placed in the freezer overnight.

Insects are grouped into orders based on their characteristics. Those with similar characteristics, such as the scaly wings of butterflies and moths, are placed in one order. The order for butterflies and moths is called Lepidoptera. Insects without scaly wings but with enlarged hind legs for jumping, such as crickets and grasshoppers, belong to another order called Orthoptera.

Show the gardeners how to draw an organizational chart illustrating hierarchical levels. This kind of chart is used for family trees or for personnel in organizations. It shows not only the different units, but also how they relate to each other. Each level on the chart has all the characteristics of the level above it; the levels below it are divided further. Refer to the chart on the next page as an example.

Ordering Insects

Class Insecta

Order Coleoptera
- **Beetles**
- Two pairs of wings
- Chewing mouthparts
- Complete metamorphosis
- Bodies usually stout
- Hardened outer wings form straight line down back when folded

Order Orthoptera
- **Cockroaches, grasshoppers, crickets**
- Two pairs of wings—may not have during juvenile stages
- Mouthparts typically chewing
- Gradual metamorphosis
- Enlarged hind legs for jumping

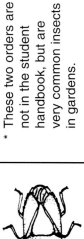

Order Hemiptera*
- **True bugs**
- Two pairs of wings
- Mouthparts typically piercing/sucking
- Gradual metamorphosis
- Have a triangular plate formed by wings that overlap
- Body usually broad and flattened

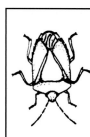

Order Lepidoptera
- **Moths, butterflies**
- Two pairs of membranous wings covered with scales, may be brilliantly colored
- Mouthparts are sucking
- Complete metamorphosis
- Larvae known as caterpillars with chewing mouthparts

Order Hymenoptera
- **Ants, wasps, bees**
- Winged, usually two pairs
- Mouthparts chewing or chewing and sucking
- Complete metamorphosis
- Abdomen connected to thorax by thin constriction ("wasp-waisted")

Order Diptera
- **Flies, mosquitoes, gnats**
- One pair of wings
- Mouthparts are piercing/sucking, lapping or sponging
- Complete metamorphosis

Order Homoptera*
- **Aphids, scale insects, leafhoppers, cicadas**
- When present, two pairs of wings; many wingless forms; wings come to a point above body on adults, giving tent-like shape
- Mouthparts are piercing/sucking
- Gradual metamorphosis
- Excretion of honeydew common to many members

These drawings are examples to show the main characteristics of each order. To identify a specific insect, see the JMG web site or another insect guide.

* These two orders are not in the student handbook, but are very common insects in gardens.

Divide the JMG'ers into smaller work groups, with three to four gardeners in each group. Give each group a jar containing insects and leaf and grass debris. Ask the groups to first sort out all the insects they can from the grass and leaves. Then have them examine their insects and sort them into groups based on the insects' similarities and differences. (They can use any characteristics they wish for their chart—size, shape, color, etc. The grouping criteria they use do not matter; this is an exercise to practice sorting and grouping according to whatever organizational criteria they choose.)

Ask the gardeners to make an organizational chart for their insects showing the different types of insects they have and how they relate to each other. Each division should have all the characteristics of the level above it, but some that distinguish it from other groups at the same level. When they are finished, ask the groups to present their charts to the group.

The chart the gardeners created will be the same kind scientists use to classify insects and all other organisms. These charts are called keys, because they are the key to identifying insects and other organisms. The process of using a key to identify an insect is called keying out the organism. There are so many different organisms that scientists make separate keys for insects, plants or other organisms from a certain area. These are often referred to as the flora or fauna of a certain area. Keys have been developed specifically for the insects of Texas, of the tropics, and of New England. Some counties have their own keys for the insects found there.

Use the basic insect key from the Appendix to make a classroom-sized insect key on poster board. Hang it up to give the gardeners an ongoing reference to "key out" insects they find at home or in the group garden. Discuss with the group the similarities and differences in the keys they created.

In the Classroom
Create a collection of the insects found in and around the group garden. Show the different insect orders and examples of insects from each order found. You can use pictures or specimens that have been dried and mounted. This is a great ongoing activity, as the children will continually find new and different insects in their garden.

✿ Metamorphosis Bracelets and Belts

Objective: To learn the stages of metamorphosis.
Time: 1 hour.
Materials: String or cording, cardboard, markers, beads.

Insects go through different life stages as they grow. This process is called metamorphosis, which means "change of form." Some insects, such as butterflies, change form completely as they go through the different stages. Their larval forms, caterpillars, look very different and even have

different types of mouthparts than their adult forms, butterflies. Other types of insects may look similar to their adult forms throughout their life.

There are two different types of metamorphosis: complete and incomplete. The insects grouped together in an order all undergo the same type of metamorphosis. The stages of each type of metamorphosis are pictured below. (Note: Level I of the JMG Junior Master Gardener program focuses mainly on complete metamorphosis.)

Complete Metamorphosis: egg, larva, pupa, adult

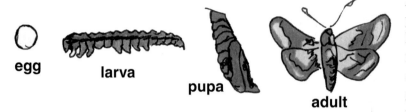

egg **larva** **pupa** **adult**

An adult insect lays its eggs in a protected place where the hatching larvae can easily find food. When the larvae hatch, they are eating machines! As a larva grows, it sheds its skin several times because its skeleton is on the outside of its body and cannot expand and grow with it. When it has reached full size as a larva, it is ready for the next stage, called the pupa (plural: pupae). The larva may form a cocoon, or chrysalis. Inside the cocoon, the insect's body changes form and is transformed into the adult form. Then the adult insect breaks out of the cocoon and mates. The cycle starts over again.

Incomplete Metamorphosis: egg, nymph, adult

There are several types of incomplete metamorphosis. Insects that undergo incomplete metamorphosis may change features somewhat as they grow, may change very little except for the addition of such features as wings or sex organs, or may not change at all. Some insects with this type of metamorphosis may live part of their lives underwater as aquatic insects.

 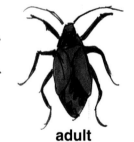

egg **nymph** **adult**

An insect that undergoes incomplete metamorphosis sheds it skin during its growth stages; however, it doesn't completely change form (such as from caterpillar to butterfly), as insects do in complete metamorphosis.

Discuss metamorphosis with the gardeners using the cycle illustrations above as a guide. Discuss the different insects that undergo complete metamorphosis—butterflies, beetles, ants and wasps are a few examples.

Ask the gardeners to draw and cut out small pictures of each stage of the life cycle in complete metamorphosis (egg, larva, pupa, and adult). Each picture should be no larger than a 3- to 4-inch oval. Have them use a hole punch to make holes at both ends of the ovals, and tie a piece of cord or string through the holes. Tie all four pictures together to make a metamorphosis bracelet or belt. If they wish, they may add colorful beads or other decorations between the four segments. When they are finished, discuss again the four stages of metamorphosis, emphasizing the ongoing cyclical aspect of life cycles.

In the classroom
Compare and contrast the life cycles of different organisms such as dogs, cats, plants, people and insects.

Morpho Puppets

Objectives:	To learn the stages of complete metamorphosis, and to teach them to a younger group.
Time:	Variable.
Materials:	One sock per student, miscellaneous craft materials to decorate with (markers, sequins, glue, pipe cleaners or chenille stems, pompons).

For this activity, refer to the complete metamorphosis life cycle from the activity above. Have the gardeners make puppets illustrating the life cycle of a butterfly or another insect that goes through complete metamorphosis.

Socks work especially well for this activity. Give each student a sock, or ask each to bring in one from home. (Here's an opportunity to use those pesky, unmatched socks everyone has lying around in their sock drawers!) The gardeners can use miscellaneous craft materials to create a caterpillar on the outside of the sock and a butterfly on the inside. They can decorate them as they choose, as long as the sock can be turned inside out. ("Crumply" wings made of felt or tissue paper, or netting with thin wire for reinforcement, work well.)

To show the different stages of complete metamorphosis, begin with the sock turned to the caterpillar side. As the caterpillar eats, it grows and grows, and the sock can be stretched longer and longer. To show that the caterpillar is ready to pupate, roll the sock into a ball by pulling the toe end up into the cuff. Then, when the butterfly emerges, pull the toe all the way through the sock, turning it inside out, revealing the butterfly on the other side. Younger children will be amazed at this "magic trick." Using the same item to illustrate all stages also helps convey the idea of transformation better than if separate items are used for each stage.

Work with the gardeners to create a "Metamorphosis Play" to perform for a younger group of children or for a senior citizens center.

JMG Web Activity: Journey North*

Objective:	To become familiar with the Internet as a research tool.
Time:	Variable.
Materials:	Computer workstation with Internet access, map of the United States.

* The Journey North web site is used as a JMG activity with permission.

The Journey North web site can be accessed through the JMG Website at *www.jmgkids.org*. Preview it to explore its features before logging on with your group. The gardeners can choose a species from a list of animals and plants on the web site to monitor in their area, or they may track the occurrences of the first "signs of spring," such as the date that tulips first sprout and bloom. The site provides a work sheet to record observations; the accumulated data from classrooms all over the nation are then plotted on a map. This allows the gardeners to see the north/south journey of animals and the gradual growth and development of emerging plants in spring.

You can track the arrival/emergence of species in your area without using this site. However, when your gardeners compare their dates with those of others, they can better understand gradual climatic change. They also learn that seasons change at different times in different locations—the farther north you live, the later spring arrives.

The program is free, but to enter updates and sightings on the web you must register your group. The Journey North web site also offers many other activities and lesson plans that you may wish to pursue with your gardeners.

Explore this site with your gardeners, and select a species to monitor. You may want to divide the group into smaller work groups and have each select a species or perhaps a plant and an animal to watch. Ask them to plot on a map the locations and dates in the spring that their chosen organism appears from north to south, and discuss the climatic transition from warmer southern locations to cooler northern ones.

In the Classroom
The USDA Hardiness Zone Map in the Chapter 6 Appendix divides the United States into 10 climatic zones according to each area's first and last average frost dates. Have your students find out which climatic zone they are in and the dates of the average first and last frosts. Ask the students to write a report including this information, as well as how their climatic zone affects the type of plants and animals living in the area. (Plants are specialized to grow in different climatic regions, such as deserts, plains, or cold winter areas.)

You can also use this activity as part of a latitude/longitude lesson.

Insect Collecting

You may have at some time caught an insect, or watched one closely to see what it did next. Where you were at the time (the environment) and what you used to catch it (the method) influenced the type of insect you observed and/or caught. There are many places to look for insects, and a variety of specialized techniques have been developed for collecting them. Most methods take advantage of insect instincts in one way or another. In this section, you can teach your group a variety of enjoyable ways to collect insects to study. Your JMG'ers can set a trap for insects, make an insect night-light, sweep up insects, or create their own insect farm.

❧ Suck-A-Bug!

Objectives: To make a simple aspirator and use it to collect and observe small insects.

Time: 30 minutes to make the aspirator, plus 30 minutes to 1 hour to collect and observe insects.

Materials: Small plastic containers—clear if possible (film canisters are the perfect size, although usually opaque; you also can use small plastic herb bottles, small butter dishes or plastic test tubes), plastic drinking straws or flexible plastic tubing (tubing works better, but is a little more expensive), modeling clay, netting or gauze, tape, awl, ice pick or drill (for adult use).

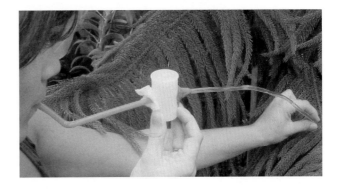

There are many insects to see, and many ways to catch them so you can observe them. Nets work well for large insects, but tiny ones often go unnoticed. One way to catch these small ones is with a Bug Sucker, also called a pooter or an aspirator. Bug suckers are easy to make, but you will probably need to practice making and using one ahead of time before doing it with your gardeners.

Clean a small (preferably clear) plastic container and remove the label if it has one. Clear containers are handier because they allow the gardeners to observe the insect inside without opening the container. However, film canisters are the perfect size. (You can create a "window" in one by cutting out a section and replacing it with clear plastic, such as a piece from an overhead transparency. If you do this, make sure to seal the edges of the window with glue to keep air from entering. You will need good suction to be able to suck up a bug.)

Tape a piece of netting or gauze over one end of the drinking straw or tubing.

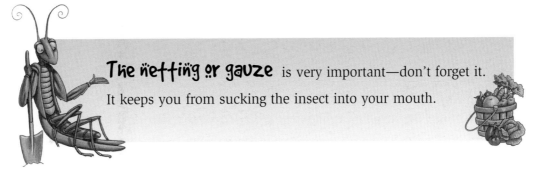

The netting or gauze is very important—don't forget it.
It keeps you from sucking the insect into your mouth.

Use the awl or ice pick to make two holes in the top of the container. (If possible, use a drill to make holes in the lids ahead of time.) Insert the straw or tubing through one of the holes so that the gauze end is down in the container and the uncovered end is sticking out of the top. Insert the other straw or tubing through the other hole. Finally, seal both holes with a bit of modeling clay, but be careful not to pinch off the tubing.

When you suck on the straw with the gauze on the end of it, you create a vacuum. Use this suction to capture small insects. Gently place the end of the straw without the gauze next to a small ant or other creature, and suck on the other straw. The suction will pull the insect into the container, where you can safely hold and observe it. It takes a little practice to be able to keep the straw next to the insect while sucking on the other end. This is why the flexible tubing is better: It can be longer and is more flexible. However, straws are inexpensive and easy to obtain. Children love practicing their bug-sucking technique, and usually spend quite a while working on it.

Do not use the bug sucker for large insects such as bees and butterflies. They can't fit up the tube, and the suction may damage their wings. (You don't want an angry bee that wouldn't fit up the tube flying around you!) Also, avoid using the bug sucker with "true bugs" (Order Hemiptera), such as stinkbugs; when sucked up a tube, they can spray irritating odors that leave a bad taste in your mouth.

❀ It's a Small World

Objectives: To make a Berlese (burr-lay-z) funnel and use it to collect and observe insects living in the ground and soil.

Time: 30 minutes plus additional time later that day and the next for observing.

Materials: 2-liter soda bottle (1 per child or group), coarse screening or hardware cloth (different materials may be used, but they should have holes at least ¼ inch wide to allow insects to crawl through it), light with extension cord, place to hang light, bowl, soapy water.

Many insects live in the soil or the leaf litter just above the soil. Although we usually do not see many of these insects because they hide below ground, they can easily be collected using a Berlese funnel.

Show the gardeners how to make a funnel out of a 2-liter soda bottle by cutting the bottle in half. Turn the top part over to make a funnel. If you cut the bottom from the remaining portion of the bottle, you can use the resulting cylinder as a holder for the funnel to keep it from falling over. Have the gardeners place a piece of coarse screening or hardware cloth around the outside of the

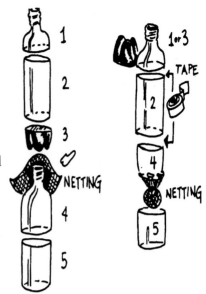

funnel. Hold the screening in place by inserting the funnel into the bottom portion of the bottle. The screening allows insects to crawl through, but retains the soil. Place some leaf litter or soil inside the funnel. Then have the gardeners place the entire funnel/holder apparatus in a bowl containing a few inches of soapy water. Do not let the bottom of the net touch the water.

Suspend a light source a few inches above the funnel. The heat and light will drive the insects deeper into the soil, and they will fall into the soapy water below.

See which insects collect in the water immediately, after 2 hours, after 4 hours, and the next day. Have the gardeners make a chart showing the number of insects, and the number of different types of insects. You can also ask them to write a journal entry telling why they think the bugs traveled downward. (The insects are ground-dwellers; most live on or under the soil's surface where it is cool and damp. They instinctively travel away from light and heat. A Berlese funnel takes advantage of these instincts to collect these insects.) You will be amazed at how many insects can be collected in a small patch of soil. Yes, it is a small world—especially if you are a tiny little soil mite who may never travel more than a yard away from home!

In the Classroom
Try sampling soil and leaf litter from different habitats to see what types of insects and other arthropods (centipedes, spiders, pill bugs, etc.) the children find. For example, have one group collect leaf litter from under a shady tree, another from a sunny meadow, and another from a damp spot. Some might get soil from the JMG garden or from the compost pile. Ask the students to chart what is found in each habitat area, and discuss the different types and number of insects they find.

❧ Insect Nets

Objectives: To make an insect net and use it to collect samples of insects by sweeping.

Time: 2 hours to make, plus time to practice sweeping and to collect insects.

Materials: Broom handle cut in half or ½-inch dowel rod, hose clamp (from hardware store) or duct tape, heavy gauge (⅛-inch) wire, muslin (about 1 yard per net), netting or curtain sheer, sewing machine, drill or X-Acto® knife, large plastic jars, Insect Nets pages (in the Appendix).

One common way to catch insects is with a net. You can buy many different specialty nets from science supply catalogs or pet supply stores and hobby shops, but you can make them much more inexpensively.

If you use this method, for only a few dollars you can make a net that looks just like those sold in stores for $15 to $20. The pattern for the fabric portion of the net should be made by an adult/parent volunteer and sewn with a machine, unless the children are old enough to sew the seams by hand. Once the fabric portion is done, the JMG'ers should be able to assemble the nets themselves. (Instructions for making a simpler version with a pillowcase and a coat hanger are in the JMG handbook. Both versions will work well.)

Making the net (fabric) portion

Use the pattern from the Appendix.

Preparing the frame of the net

1. Using the drill or X-Acto® knife, make two 4-inch grooves on both sides of one end of a dowel rod. (The wire ends will be fitted into these grooves to hold them more securely.)

2. Bend the $1/8$-inch wire to form a circle. Leave several inches extending straight on each end, and bend these ends down to form a 90-degree angle. The circle will serve as the frame, and the two ends will be attached to the dowel rod. (The ends of the wire extending past the circle should be as long as possible, up to 4 or 5 inches. This makes the net more sturdy. If the wire is shorter, the net will be flimsier and may come apart.)

Sewing the net

3. Cut a piece of muslin to 22 by 36 inches. Fold the piece of muslin in half so that it now measures 22 by 18 inches.

4. Measure 4 inches from the top of the muslin and mark the point A. At the bottom, measure 11 inches from the center fold and mark this point B. Make a diagonal cut from point A to point B. The top 4 inches of the muslin material should now be 18 inches wide and the bottom portion, 11 inches wide (see diagram in the Appendix).

5. Fold a 14- by 22-inch piece of netting in half to make it 14 by 11 inches.

6. Measure an 11-inch width from the center fold and mark this point C. Next, measure 12 inches in length and mark this point D. At the top, cut the material lengthwise from point C to D. The material should measure 11 inches at the top and 8 inches at the bottom. Now, make a rounded bottom by cutting the netting to form a semicircle (see diagram). You should now have two pieces, a muslin piece and a netting piece.

7. Sew the bottom of the muslin piece (11-inch end) to the top of the netting piece (11-inch end).

8. Sew the open side together to form a net. Be sure to leave the straight unsewn edge of the muslin piece open to serve as an opening for the wire.

9. Fold down the open muslin edge 2 inches. Fold it down 2 more inches to form a casing. Sew along the edge of the casing, leaving enough room to insert the wire.

10. Insert the wire through the casing. Fit the ends of the wire into the grooves in the dowel rod. Place the hose clamp around the wire and tighten it, or wrap it tightly with duct tape.

11. Hand-sew the opening for the wire closed.

12. Have the gardeners use permanent markers to write their names on their nets. They may also add an artistic element by decorating the nets using insect stencils and/or stamps.

You can make the entire net of muslin if you wish. But if the end piece is made of netting, you can more easily see what has been caught and where it is in the net. You can also make a net entirely of netting or curtain sheer, but it will be less durable. (It would be best used for aerial collecting, not for grassy or brushy meadows where sticks and brambles would tear it.) For land or water collecting, muslin or lightweight canvas is the most durable.

Safety Rules

Be sure to review the safety rules with your group, including no running with the nets, and always be aware of others around you so you don't hit someone with the net as you swing it back and forth.

Collecting with nets

Nets are used to collect insects in grassy areas by a process called sweeping. Sweeping with a net is very much like sweeping with a broom. Make an arc back and forth in front of you as you walk, making sure to keep the top of the net even with the top of the vegetation so that the entire net is scooping through the grass. (Sweeping works best in meadows with tall grass. You will get some insects in a mown lawn, but there just aren't as many there to catch.) As you sweep back and forth, turn the net at each end of the arc before sweeping it back down, so that the open end is always coming down. As you (and your gardeners) become more proficient, you will be able to sweep and walk at the same time more easily.

You can also use the net to catch flying insects. Sneak up on an insect, carefully hold the net above it, and then drop the net on it. This method is much more effective than chasing them—they can usually out-fly you!

Getting your catch into a jar

When you catch an insect using the sneak-and-drop method, keep one hand on the handle against the ground, and use the other to lift up the tip of the net. The insect will instinctively try to escape by flying or crawling upward, where it can be easily trapped in the small tip portion and transferred to a collection jar.

After sweeping, turn the net over so that it closes off the opening. Use the same technique as above, encouraging all the insects inside to travel up into the tip of the net. Then you can insert an open jar under the net and release the tip of the net containing the insects and plant material into it for observation.

Practice makes perfect!

After you have practiced your netting techniques, demonstrate them for your JMG group. Allow the group to practice in a mown yard first, then go on a collection expedition in a grassy field or meadow. Ask each student to sweep an area, and then dump the contents of the entire net, grass and all, into a jar. Then take the jars back to your classroom or meeting place to observe how many and what kinds of insects they caught. Depending on the time of year, they should be able to see many different insects, large and small. If they look closely, they may even find large insects such as a 3-inch walking stick or praying mantid camouflaged as a piece of grass. It's truly amazing what you can find! Ask your JMG'ers to write down what they found and where they caught the most insects—in the mown yard or the grassy meadow.

Children love making and using insect nets. The nets your group makes will come in handy on many other JMG insect expeditions.

🐝 By Land or Sea

Objective: To compare the types of insects living in different habitats.
Time: Variable.
Materials: Variable, By Land or Sea chart (in the Appendix).

Divide the gardeners into groups and have them use one or two of the three types of collection methods from the activities above to collect samples of insects from several different habitats. For example, ask one group of gardeners to collect in a sunny meadow, another under the shady canopy of a group of trees, and another along the banks of a stream (or in it, if possible). Or you might choose to sample a series of sites that range from highly maintained (for example, the lawn around a school) and moderately maintained (outlying soccer fields) to not maintained at all (a field, woods, or park near a school).

When the gardeners are reassembled, ask each group to list the types and numbers of insects collected. You can use the sample chart in the Appendix as a guide. Ask each group to read its list aloud, and compare them with other groups. Discuss the groups' findings. Did the types or numbers of insects vary from those collected in different habitats? Ask the gardeners to write a short comment on this below their chart, stating if there was variation and, if so, why they think it was so.

✿ Ant Lion Farm

Objectives: To make a living collection of one type of insect and to observe it closely as it builds a home.

Time: 30 minutes.

Materials: Pie plate and/or small paper cups, hand lenses.

Ant lions, sometimes called doodle bugs, are little insects that create perfect funnel-shaped burrows in sandy areas. You may have seen groups of these "upside-down cones" under bridges, carports, or in other sandy areas out of the hot, direct sun. These are the traps built by immature ant lions; they use them to catch small insects such as ants, as might be guessed from their name.

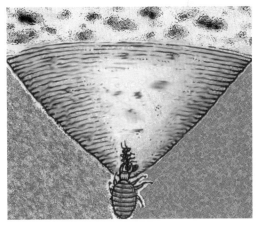

When an ant falls into an ant lion trap, the sandy funnel's slippery slope prevents the ant from escaping. Its scrambling alerts the ant lion waiting at the base of the trap. The ant lion feels the vibrations and runs out to catch the ant in its pincer-like mandibles, or jaws, which are perfectly suited for catching and eating ants. (They are not aggressive toward people, and will run away rather than bite; however, if trapped, they might pinch a child's finger. Instruct your JMG Group to handle them with the same care as for any other insect that might bite or sting.) After catching its prey, the ant lion repairs any damage to the funnel, then retreats back to the base of its trap to await the next unwary insect. You can sometimes trick them into coming out by tapping very, very gently on the sides of their trap with a blade of grass.

A quick, easy activity for your gardeners is to scoop up a pan full of ant lion traps. Use a pie pan or other shallow container and scoop about the top 2 inches of soil from an area where you can see their telltale funnels. You are sure to get at least a few. Afterward, just wait. After a few hours or perhaps overnight, the ant lions will make new funnel traps, right in your meeting room.

Ant lions are harmless and great fun to watch. Show the gardeners how to gently scoop out one ant lion and separate it from the sand. If you place it on a small dish or in the bottom of a small cup, it will scoot around backwards. If you place a small amount of sand in the cup with it, it will busily begin flicking sand around in an effort to hide itself. If you shine a light on part of the cup, the ant lion will move away from it into the shadows.

If there are enough ant lions, give each gardener a paper cup and allow him or her to scoop out an ant lion to observe. If you have only a few ant lions, have the gardeners work in groups. Ask them

to try some of the mini-experiments described above, and to observe the ant lions' behavior. Ask the gardeners to think of other simple tests, such as with sound or color, to see if the ant lions show distinct behavior patterns.

Remind the gardeners to be kind to their live experimental subjects, and not to use the same insect for long. Give the insects a chance to rest between observations, and allow them to burrow back into the soil where they are less exposed.

Remember, the ant lions making all those perfect little funnels are just larvae. After undergoing complete metamorphosis, adult ant lions are winged insects.

In the classroom

Ask the gardeners to write a description of their ant lions and the behaviors they observe, and to draw a picture of one and its trap. For each experiment conducted, ask them to write down the question the experiment will answer, what they predict will happen (hypothesis), and what actually happens (the results).

Insect/Plant Interactions

Insects prefer certain foods and colors, just as people do. Many of the plants in your JMG garden have flowers of a certain color or fragrance just to attract a particular kind of insect. What do the plants want insects for? Pollination—so they can be fertilized and produce seeds for the next generation of plants. Many plants and animals depend on each other in bizarre ways. Many of these relationships involve some kind of exchange, or trade, of food or shelter for services. Your JMG'ers will enjoy learning about these relationships as they discover how plants and animals interact. They can become plant detectives as they search plants for signs of insect damage, create a puppet show to illustrate pollination, or design their own plants and insects that are uniquely suited for each other.

❧ Chew on This!

Objective:	To learn the four types of insect mouthparts and how they are specialized.
Time:	30 minutes to 1 hour.
Materials:	Pair of pliers, M&M's®, Fruit Roll-Ups®, red gelatin (slightly liquefied, or use water with red food coloring) in a clear cup with the top covered tightly with plastic wrap, a turkey baster, a sponge, some sugar on a saucer, juice boxes with straws.

Most organisms have mouthparts specialized to catch and eat certain types of food. For example, dogs and wolves have long, sharp teeth specialized for tearing meat. Birds have beaks specialized for scooping water and fish (pelicans), pecking through wood to catch insects (woodpeckers), cracking seeds (cardinals and many others) or drinking nectar from long, tubular flowers (hummingbirds).

Insects have specialized mouthparts, too. There are four types of insect mouthparts, depending on what type of food the insects eat. Below are descriptions of those mouthparts, along with fun ways to teach them.

Chewing Mouthparts

Insects with chewing mouthparts use jaw-like mandibles to grasp food and bring it close. Ask the gardeners if they've ever watched a grasshopper or cricket close up. They may have watched the mouthparts working from side to side.

Grasshoppers, crickets, bees, ants, beetles and caterpillars all have chewing mouthparts. Most of these eat plants, except for some beetles such as ladybugs, which eat other insects. Other insects with chewing mouthparts include most of the predatory insects—praying mantids, dragonflies and ladybugs.

A plant damaged by an insect with chewing mouthparts usually looks as if someone took an insect-sized bite out of the edge of a leaf—like a bite from the side of a sandwich. (Explain to the gardeners that they don't usually see a sandwich with a bite out of the middle, because people have to work their way in from an edge of the sandwich. Likewise, chewing insects must work their way in from the edge of a leaf.)

Activity: Use pliers to pick up an M&M® from a bowl and bring it to your mouth. Or, show the gardeners how to use their fingers as a pair of pincers on both sides of their face: Make a fist on both sides of your face, and extend the first finger of each hand to form "mandibles." Have them use their mandibles to pinch off a small piece of a Fruit Roll-Up® or other food item and bring it to their mouths.

Piercing/Sucking Mouthparts

An insect with piercing/sucking mouthparts has a long, thin proboscis that it inserts into a juicy leaf (or a juicy arm, in the case of mosquitoes). Then it sucks up the nutritious plant sap from the leaf (or blood from an arm). Many plant pests have piercing/sucking mouthparts. Instead of holes along the edge of the leaf, like from chewing insects, plants damaged by piercing/sucking insects have small spots or speckles across entire leaf surfaces. Often these spots turn brown or yellow because the plant cells in the surrounding area die when the sap is extracted. Leaves with piercing/sucking damage often appear dull and sandpapery. Mosquitoes, aphids, stinkbugs, harlequin bugs and many others have piercing/sucking mouthparts.

Activity: Use a clear plastic cup containing liquid red or green gelatin or water colored with red or green food coloring. Place clear plastic wrap tightly over the mouth of the cup. Then, with the tip of the turkey baster, pierce the plastic wrap surface and suck some of the liquid into the stem of the baster. The gardeners can pretend they are mosquitoes biting on someone's arm (with red gelatin) or a bright green stinkbug piercing the surface of a leaf to suck out the juicy sap inside. (If you do not have a turkey baster, you can give each child a straw and let him or her pierce the plastic wrap and suck up some nectar.)

Siphoning Mouthparts

A siphoning mouthpart is a type of piercing/sucking mouthpart specialized for sucking nectar from flowers or rotting fruit. Insects with siphoning mouthparts are some of the most familiar to us, including butterflies and moths. They have a long, tubular proboscis, like insects with piercing/sucking mouthparts. However, instead of piercing through the surface of a leaf, they use these long tubes as straws to suck up nectar from flowers such as zinnias and honeysuckle. When not using the straw-like siphoning proboscis to drink a meal, they coil it up to keep it out of the way. When they find a sweet flower, they roll it out and suck up some nectar.

Activity: This type of mouthpart is very easy to simulate using juice boxes with straws. The gardeners will enjoy pretending to be butterflies drinking nectar from a flower. You can also simulate the coiled-up proboscis using a party blower that unrolls when you blow in it. Give each student a party blower to blow and watch the paper roll out and in. Siphoning mouthparts will be a favorite.

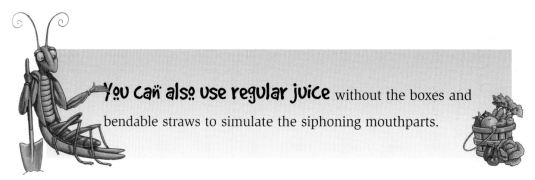

You can also use regular juice without the boxes and bendable straws to simulate the siphoning mouthparts.

Sponging Mouthparts

Sponging mouthparts are perhaps the least known of the types of mouthparts, but your gardeners will find them fascinating. An insect we see most often, the fly, has sponging mouthparts. If you've ever watched a fly crawling on a cabinet, you may have noticed that it continually presses its proboscis against the counter, sponging up food. The end of the proboscis is blunt and rough looking, as opposed to the tubular-shaped proboscis of a mosquito or butterfly.

However, there is another component to the story—one that will disgust and fascinate your group. A sponge can't pick up crumbs and sticky messes unless it is wet. The fly's mouthparts work the same way. If a fly lands on a bowl of sugar, it can't sponge up dry sugar. To wet the food, the fly spits fluid on it to moisten and soften it. The liquid dissolves some of the food, and the fly can then sponge it up.

Disgusting, right? This is part of the reason flies are considered such pests and germ spreaders in homes. They also can carry disease organisms on their feet as they crawl from dirty to clean surfaces. Tell the gardeners not to think too badly of flies, though. In spite of their poor table manners, they are vital as pollinators—second only to bees.

Activity: Show the gardeners how to take a dry sponge or paintbrush and touch it to the surface of some sugar. Very little sugar will stick to it. Then wet the sponge or paintbrush and touch it to the sugar again. The sugar will instantly begin to dissolve and can then be absorbed and picked up by the sponge. (We don't advise that you simulate the spitting part!)

❧ School Yard Survey

Objectives: To survey the school yard for signs of insect damage and to determine the types of insects that caused the damage.
Time: 30 minutes.
Materials: Hand lens, bag for collecting.

Using the guide to insect mouthparts above, divide your JMG'ers into small work groups and ask each group to survey part of the school yard for signs of insect damage. The gardeners will be looking mainly for signs of chewing or piercing/sucking damage, since siphoning and sponging mouthparts do not damage plant tissues directly. Remind them of the types of damage that insects with these mouthparts cause:

Chewing: Holes, or "bites" from the edges of leaves.
Piercing/sucking: Small brown dots scattered over the surface of the leaf. Leaves may look dull or "sandpapery" from loss of sap.

Although not essential, a hand lens can help the children look closely at leaf surfaces. It's also an important tool for scientists, and may help remind the gardeners that they are conducting a scientific survey. After the survey, ask each group to present its findings to the others. Make a group chart on the types of insect damage they found, what types of mouthparts would have caused the damage, and any guesses as to the type of insect that caused it.

❧ Pollinator Puppet Show

Objective: To learn the basic process of insect pollination.
Time: 1 hour.
Materials: Materials to make into a puppet (brown paper lunch bag, sock, etc.) for each student, markers, miscellaneous craft materials, small Styrofoam balls, pieces of Velcro or crumpled-up balls of masking tape.

For this activity, paint some small Styrofoam balls (or newspaper balls) yellow or orange, and glue small pieces of Velcro onto them. These will be the pollen grains in the activity, with the Velcro enabling them to stick to gardeners' clothes. (You can also use circles made of construction paper with pieces of tape to attach them. The material just needs to be able to stick to the gardeners' clothes when they are being "pollinated.")

Many gardeners have trouble understanding why plants produce flowers. Plants must use much of their energy to create their showy, colorful or fragrant flowers. This is hard work in a harsh environment, and plants don't do it just to look pretty or smell good or for the enjoyment of others. Rather, they make flowers with bright colors or sweet-smelling nectar to attract pollinators.

A pollinator—such as a bee, fly or moth—collects nectar and pollen to eat, and while collecting it from flower to flower, transfers some of the pollen onto nearby flowers. The pollen then travels down the pistil and fertilizes the egg in the ovary of the pistil, which develops into a seed. The fruit matures (usually with the seeds inside), the seeds are then dispersed, and the cycle begins again.

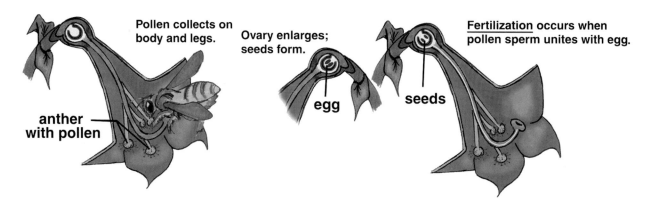

Review the process of pollination with your JMG Group using the Pollination Reference page in the student handbook. Have the gardeners act out the process, with several playing flowers and others playing pollinators. "Flower" gardeners can hold the Styrofoam balls that have been painted yellow or orange. As the "pollinators" travel among them, some of the pollen grain balls can be stuck to their clothing and transferred to other flowers. This active demonstration may help your group better understand the process.

If possible, have the group observe pollinators at work in the garden. They can readily see pollen sacs on bees, and often can see pollen smeared on other insects' legs and bodies.

The children should be very still and quiet during the observation in order to see the pollination process. If possible, have several adult volunteers help with this activity so you can divide the group into several small groups and rotate them between playing the pollination game and observing in the garden.

After discussing pollination and playing the pollination game, ask your group to create a skit or puppet show demonstrating the pollination process for a younger group. They can make puppets from socks or brown paper bags, or they may prefer to make simple costumes and act out the skit as a play rather than as a puppet show. They can make simple costumes using headbands with antennae attached; felt or net wings with a wire edge that have elastic straps attached for arm holes; and small decorated paper bags with elastic straps glued to them to pull over pants as "pollen pockets." Arrange to have them perform their show or skit for a younger group.

🌿 The Bartering System

Objectives: To learn how plants and insects trade services, and to become familiar with the concept of an energy exchange.

Time: 30 to 45 minutes.

Materials: Energy Credit Pieces (in the Appendix), paper, string, markers or colors to create signs, small paper bags (brown lunch bags will work well) to collect pollen with, masking tape to use as pollen grains.

Creating flowers requires a large input of energy (i.e., hard work!) on the part of plants. This energy is expended for a reason. In nature, living things survive by maintaining or acquiring as much energy as possible, while expending as little as possible. For plants, this means generating as many leaves and getting as much sunlight as possible while attracting pollinators to the flowers for pollination services.

Some plants take a completely different pollination path: Instead of developing flowers for attracting pollinators, they produce long catkins, which scatter pollen when the wind blows. This process, called wind pollination, is used by many plants such as grasses and oak trees. Still other plants are pollinated by splashing water that carries pollen away. These methods are less efficient, because pollen is scattered widely and may or may not reach its target. However, less energy is expended than to produce the flower. It's a trade-off. Like with most activities, the more energy and effort put into something, the better chance it will be a success.

Activity: Photocopy the Energy Credit pieces and have gardeners cut them out.

Divide the JMG'ers into two groups, with 25 percent pretending to be pollinators and 75 percent pretending to be plants. Distribute 10 energy credits to each child who is a plant. Each gardener playing a plant should choose to be either a showy, animal-pollinated plant (such as a sunflower or petunia) or a nonshowy, wind-pollinated plant (such as grass or trees). Each gardener playing a pollinator should choose to be a bat, bee, fly, moth, beetle, butterfly, hummingbird or other pollinator.

The game will proceed by stages: Insects will make one pass around the room to barter pollination services for energy, which will make up one "rotation." After each rotation, the plants will use sunlight to produce 10 new energy credits, which the leader provides. (Explain that plants transform energy from the sun into food through a process called photosynthesis.) The game consists of two to three rotations, or more if you wish, until the group understands the concept of energy exchange.

Wind-Pollinated Plants

Space apart the wind-pollinated plants. Either you or an assigned student can play the wind and carry (or "blow") pollen around the plants. Remember: The wind doesn't know which plants need which pollen—it is only a matter of chance that some of the many pollen grains produced hit their targets.

You can simulate the mass production of wind-disseminated pollen by using small balls of tape that stick onto gardeners' clothes, or you can use confetti. The confetti will better convey the concept of mass production. The gardeners will be able to see that most of the pollen ends up on the floor or on other plants, while only a few grains end up on the other wind-pollinated plants. This is why wind-pollinated plants produce so much pollen. Many wind-pollinated plants trigger people's allergies because of the huge amounts of pollen they produce.

Chapter 4

Animal-Pollinated Plants

Space the animal-pollinated plants evenly around the room for the most part, although you might want to consider creating one or two "clusters" of animal-pollinated plants so that their pollinators can work more efficiently. (Insect pollinators often are more attracted to groups of plants). Have them stick pollen grains (balls of sticky tape) to their shirts and arms, so that insect pollinators can come by and collect them. They also will need a bag (a brown paper bag will do) to use for the pollen grains they receive. After collecting pollen from one flower, an insect will drop it off at another flower. The recipient should place the pollen in his or her pollen bag, so that it is not collected again inadvertently. Their goals are to send their pollen away and to gather new pollen. They will use this pollen to fertilize their eggs and produce seeds, which is the overall goal of all plants—to reproduce.

Animal Pollinators

The animals' goal in this game is to collect pollen and nectar (represented by energy credits) for a meal. There should be only a few animal pollinators, mostly insects. This is most representative of nature, which has many more low-energy organisms (plants) than higher-energy organisms (animals). As you go up the food chain, the organisms become more complex and use more energy, and there are fewer of them.

The pollinators should travel around the plants, gathering pollen from some in exchange for an energy credit and dropping it into the pollen bags of others in exchange for another energy credit. The energy credit is the price plants pay, and the reward pollinators receive, for being pollinated or for pollinating.

The pollinators will begin the game with one energy credit each, and will need to use the plants to obtain the additional energy credits they need to survive. The animals can "barter" with the plants to get nectar to eat in exchange for transferring pollen to other flowers, or they can be animal raiders that decimate a plant's leaves (such as a grasshopper). The animal raiders do not pollinate. They just take an energy credit from each plant on demand. Each of the pollinators gets an energy credit from a plant for each flower they pollinate (the one that it cost the plant to produce the flower) and for each leaf they eat, which takes away from the plants' energy reserve. The pollinators use their energy in moving about the room—one energy credit for one rotation around the room—and must have five energy credits left at the end to produce eggs. The plants must have pollen in their bags to produce seed.

Managing the Game

Begin the activity by assigning roles to the children. Ask the students to create signs to hang around their necks identifying their roles, and to draw pictures of the organisms they are portraying. About 75 percent of the gardeners will be plants that remain stationary in designated spots around the room. The other 25 percent can be animal pollinators, with only one or two being plant-eaters such as grasshoppers. (You may need to set limits on the amount of plant material a grasshopper can eat, to maintain a balanced ecosystem within your group.)

Allow the pollinators to circle the room one time in exchange for one energy credit, which they must give back to you. During their rotation they must barter with some of the plants for energy credits. Most do this by providing pollinating services, while one or two may feed on plants to obtain their energy.

After each rotation, pause to discuss what is happening with your group. Who has gained energy? Who has lost energy? What would happen in nature if this occurred? Some plants may accumulate pollen and produce seeds, while others may not. Likewise, some insects will have enough energy credits remaining at the end of two or three cycles to produce eggs for the next generation of insects, while others may not. What are the advantages of being a plant? What are the advantages of being a pollinator?

The rules are flexible and can be adjusted to fit your group's needs. You may need to use more plants and fewer animals to balance the available energy, or you may add some varying climatic conditions, such as drought versus adequate rain. It is important that your group experiment with and understand some of the complexities of energy exchanges between plants and animals, and to think about how delicate a balance it is.

The Lone Bee

Objectives:	To learn about solitary bees and to create a bee home for them.
Time:	30 minutes.
Materials:	Coffee can or other metal container for each student, paper straws, nontoxic glue.

Most of us think of bees as "social insects" like ants and termites. They live in hives, have workers, guards and a queen, and work together cooperatively. However, this is true of only one category of bees, called social bees. Many other bees do not form social colonies—instead, they live alone. These types of bees, called solitary bees, are often overlooked. But solitary bees include some important pollinators—carpenter bees, leaf cutter bees and mason bees, to name a few. Each solitary bee creates its own nest, gathers and stores its own nectar and pollen, lays its own eggs, etc. A novel concept for most people, these solitary bees can be interesting to study.

Although solitary bees live alone and build individual nests, they do nest near each other and often take advantage of ready-made nest sites. In nature, these insects make their homes by tunneling into dead or soft wood. Your JMG group can make Lone Bee Houses, described below, and attract some of these unfamiliar bees to pollinate the flowers in your JMG garden.

To make a Lone Bee House, first coat the inside of a coffee can with nontoxic glue. Then pack the can tightly with paper straws. The glue helps the straws adhere to the edges and prevents them from slipping out. The gardeners may decorate the outside of the can if they want and tie a string around the outside for hanging. The can should hang horizontally to prevent water from collecting inside; it may need two pieces of string to hang level. Hang it near the garden out of direct sunlight, and keep an eye out for solitary bees entering and leaving individual chambers.

If you can't find paper straws, an alternative to making the coffee can home is to drill a series of $\frac{5}{16}$-inch holes into the face of a block of wood. Attach a second piece of wood to serve as a protective overhanging roof, and hang it up. The holes will attract solitary bees to use them as nest sites.

❀ Designer Plants and Insects

Objective: To combine previously learned concepts in creating insects and plants that are designed to work together.

Time: Several sessions—one for planning, and two or three for creating plants and insects.

Materials: Papier-mâché materials (newspaper, flour or glue, water), paint, miscellaneous craft supplies.

Ask the gardeners to use their imaginations to create a plant and insect pair uniquely suited to work together. They might create a unique pollinating/nectar exchange relationship such as:

✓ A keyhole bug that has a keyhole-shaped proboscis, and a plant whose flower is shaped like a keyhole, so that only a keyhole bug can pollinate it;

✓ A plant with a unique new color of flower that only one certain type of insect can see—the flower would be invisible to other insects.

The gardeners can create a real or imaginary service that their plants and insects provide for each other. Whether or not the organisms are real is unimportant. This activity, which unites several concepts learned in previous activities, allows you to assess whether the gardeners have mastered the concepts of energy exchange, plant/animal partnership and pollination.

Encourage the gardeners to be creative. They may use papier-mâché or some other material to create their plant/animal partners. They may want to paint and decorate their creations. Ask the gardeners to write essays describing the plants and animals they have created, and explaining their partnerships. If possible, arrange to have the creations displayed in a school or local library.

Insect Management

Before you squash that bug. . .WAIT! You might be squashing one of your garden's best friends. There are many more good insects than bad insects. Of every 100 insects, only about two or three are bad or harmful. In this section, you and your JMG group will learn how to distinguish insect friends from insect enemies, how to attract helpful insects to your garden, and how to manage those pesky bad guys.

❀ Garden Friends and Foes

Objectives: To learn the difference between beneficial and pest insects, and to learn examples of each type.

Time: Variable; ongoing.

Materials: Poster board, camera, markers.

Many people assume that all bugs are bad, but that's just not true. Your JMG garden, if kept healthy, will be full of life from all the insects it attracts. Most actually benefit the garden in some way. These insects, called beneficials, should not be stomped on or sprayed.

Insects can be grouped into two large categories: pests and beneficials. A pest is something that bothers you. In the garden, pest insects feed on plants and disrupt their growth cycle or cause stress to the plants, which makes them less healthy. A beneficial is an organism that provides some service. The vast majority of insects are beneficials. There are four kinds of beneficial organisms:

predators, parasites, pollinators and poopers.

It is difficult to determine whether an organism is a beneficial or a pest. Use the pictures on this page or visit the JMG web site at *www.jmgkids.org* to help your JMG group identify the harmful and beneficial creatures in their garden. You and your group will be surprised at how many beneficials you find. Remember: These are just a few common ones. More complete guides of insects and other organisms in your area can be obtained at local bookstores or from your county Extension agent.

Have the gardeners create a poster of pests and beneficials to help others identify these creatures. If possible, display the poster at a local school or library so other people can learn the difference between the good guys and bad guys in their gardens.

Beneficials

Predators prey on other insects. Ladybugs, praying mantids, dragonflies and spiders are all examples of predators.

ladybug

praying mantid

lacewing

Braconid wasp eggs on back of tomato hornworm

Parasites destroy pest insects by laying their eggs on or inside them. Here, a tomato hornworm carries tiny white eggs of braconid wasps on its back. When the eggs hatch, the wasps will feed on the hornworm, eating it alive! Most parasitic insects are tiny and usually go unnoticed.

Pollinators provide important services to the garden by pollinating many plants so they can produce fruit.

butterfly

bee

wasp

Poopers, otherwise known as decomposers, provide nature's own recycling service in your garden. They eat, digest and excrete (poop) dead plant material. By doing this, the nutrients in the plant material are returned to the soil.

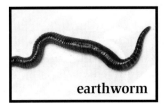
earthworm

pill bug

dung beetle

Pests

Here are ten garden pests that might be seen in the JMG garden.

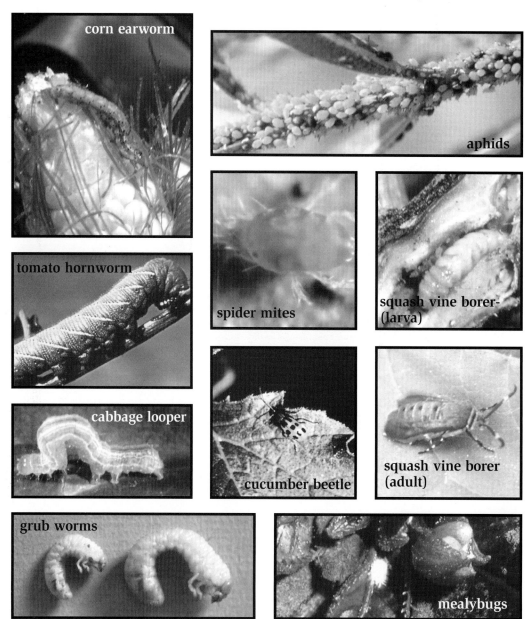

corn earworm

aphids

tomato hornworm

spider mites

squash vine borer-
(larva)

cabbage looper

cucumber beetle

squash vine borer
(adult)

grub worms

mealybugs

🐝 Don't Bug Me!

Objectives: To identify pest insects of various organisms and to discover the interrelatedness of all living organisms.

Time: 30 minutes.

Materials: Paper, pencils.

Discuss with the gardeners the concept of a pest. Some insects may be a pest to people (for example, gnats that buzz around your face in the garden); however, these same gnats may be an important food source to a bird or frog. Those animals would probably not consider a gnat to be a pest at all.

Ask the gardeners to make a list with the following categories: People, Dogs and Cats, Plants/Garden, and any other categories the gardeners or you suggest. For each category, ask the gardeners to think of pests and beneficials. (Hint: To come up with beneficials, try to think of something that would eat or otherwise get rid of the pests listed.) Some insects may appear on the pest list for one category, and on the beneficial list for another category.

Another aspect to consider is a pest's life stage. For example, butterflies help pollinate plants and are beautiful to look at, and would be considered a beneficial by most. However, some species can greatly damage agricultural crops during their larval stage as caterpillars. Discuss this with the gardeners and try to find other examples of insects that might change categories as they go through different stages of their life cycle.

✿ Who Goes There?

Objectives: To learn the basics of Integrated Pest Management (IPM) and to create a classroom IPM charting system.

Time: 1 hour, plus 15 minutes for pest checks twice a week.

Materials: Paper, pencils.

It is vital that your gardeners manage pests in their garden because it makes a big difference in how well the garden grows. Gardeners and professional horticulturists use a method of managing pests called IPM, which stands for Integrated Pest Management. IPM discourages pests in a way that is environmentally friendly. The steps involved in IPM are discussed in the "What is IPM?" section on the next page.

Your JMG'ers can follow a simplified version of IPM by using the chart below. Help them follow the steps of the flow chart to manage pest outbreaks in your garden.

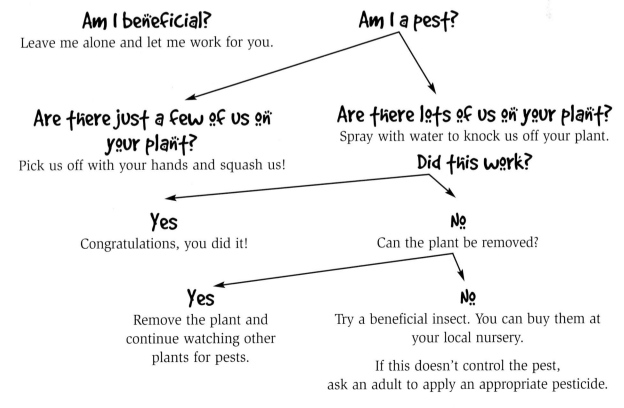

Am I beneficial?
Leave me alone and let me work for you.

Am I a pest?

Are there just a few of us on your plant?
Pick us off with your hands and squash us!

Are there lots of us on your plant?
Spray with water to knock us off your plant.

Did this work?

Yes
Congratulations, you did it!

No
Can the plant be removed?

Yes
Remove the plant and continue watching other plants for pests.

No
Try a beneficial insect. You can buy them at your local nursery.

If this doesn't control the pest, ask an adult to apply an appropriate pesticide.

Chapter 4

Ask the gardeners to scout the garden each week to see what types of insects or signs of insect damage they see. For each insect, go through the flow chart process above to determine what action should be taken. Then make an ongoing list of Organism Observations to keep track of what insects are seen in the garden, what plants they were on, whether they were pests or beneficials, what type of damage they caused, and what action was taken, if any. (Members also could record this individually as journal entries.) This can be done as an activity for several weeks, but is best used on an ongoing basis as a regular garden maintenance duty.

What is IPM?

Integrated Pest Management, or IPM, is an effective way to address pest problems. Rather than applying chemical pesticides on a routine schedule, people who practice IPM use pesticides only when and where they find unacceptable numbers of pests. They choose and time the treatments to control pests while trying not to disrupt natural controls, such as beneficial organisms. An IPM program aims not to eliminate pests totally, but rather to keep the number of pests below levels at which they cause too much damage.

Treatments are made only after a series of steps have been followed:

1. Gather and study information about the site, plants, potential pests and problems.

2. Monitoring is the next step. Observe the site and plants regularly to spot pests or problems early.

3. As soon as a problem arises, establish an injury threshold. If and when you see that the damage reaches that threshold, take corrective action, trying the least toxic treatment first.

4. It is critical to keep good records, so you can base your future decisions and treatments on previous experience.

5. Evaluate each treatment on its effectiveness, and record any side effects.

The various ways that gardeners treat a pest problem are the "integrated" part of IPM, which has six basic strategies:

1. Choose plant materials that resist pests, support natural controls or promote ecosystem diversity. Make sure the plants and the design are appropriate for the climate, soil conditions, available resources and available maintenance levels.

2. Modify the habitat to discourage pests from harboring or feeding there and/or to encourage natural predators, parasites, diseases or competitors of those pests.

3. Some people will need to change their practices and attitudes. They must change their cultural practices—such as mowing, fertilizing, watering, etc.—to eliminate problems. They also can change their attitudes by learning more about the need for "perfect" fruits and vegetables, manicured landscapes and total elimination of pests.

4. Use biological controls against pests. This may include creating an environment that helps existing natural enemies, as well as adding to the natural population by periodically releasing natural predators.

5. Physically control small populations of some insect, disease and weed pests through handpicking, barriers, traps, water sprays and dry conditions.

6. If you use chemical controls, emphasize those of an organic origin. There are scents that lure, repel and confuse pests; hormones that either stop pests from developing or act as contraceptives; fumigants; and poisons that kill either on contact or after eaten. You also can use any combination of these controls.

✤ Critter Creations

Objective: To learn four types of beneficial insects and the reasons they are considered beneficial.

Time: Two to three 1-hour sessions or more, as time allows (extended art project).

Materials: Papier-mâché supplies (newspaper, glue or flour, water, container), art supplies for decorating (paint, pipe cleaners, wire, netting, miscellaneous craft supplies).

Discuss with the gardeners the four types of beneficials, referring to the categories listed in Friends and Foes, Activity 1 of this section. You can discuss them all at once, or spread the discussion over several sessions, focusing on one type of beneficial in each. Ask the gardeners to list the insects they know that belong in each category, highlighting ones they have seen in their gardens.

Ask the gardeners to select a category of beneficials that interests them most, and make a papier-mâché model of an insect in that category. The models should have the correct insect anatomy (see Insect Basics). The gardeners will need one to two sessions to create the models, which will then need to dry for a day or two. After they are dry, they can be painted and decorated. Ask the gardeners to write a description to accompany their Critter Creation, including the insect's name, what it does, what it eats and what category of beneficial it is.

You can specify that the insects be real or allow the gardeners to make up imaginary insects. If they create their own insects, they should also create an imaginary plant or animal for which the insect is a beneficial. This can lead to some interesting and imaginative creations.

Work with school administrators to display the Critter Creations in a school or community library. If you wish, cover the student names and have visitors vote on the best Critter Creations for each category, as well as Most Colorful, Largest, Smallest, etc. Host an awards ceremony for the Bennies. ("Bennies" is short for Beneficials. The movie industry has the Oscars; TV has the Emmys, and JMG has the Bennies.)

Plant Diseases

Pest insects are not the only threat to a garden. Plants can also contract diseases, just as people can. Fungi, bacteria and viruses are in the air all around us, and can make people as well as plants sick. Preventing most diseases in plants is like keeping diseases away from ourselves. We keep ourselves healthy by eating right, taking vitamins, exercising and keeping ourselves and our homes clean and free of germs.

There are similar things we can do to keep our garden plants healthy. In this section, your JMG group will learn how to water correctly so that their plants are not exposed to diseases, choose plants that will succeed in their garden, plant at the right time, and give each plant its own space. Keeping harmful insect populations at a minimum helps, too. All these factors help minimize plant stress, which, just as for people, helps them resist diseases and stay healthy. Most important, having healthy, disease-resistant plants in your JMG garden means that you minimize the need to control diseases and insects by spraying.

Prevention really is the best medicine. Use these activities to help your JMG group find out which fungi are used to make food products as well as those that cause us grief in the garden.

ACTIVITIES

❧ Exploratory Fungi

Objective: To observe the variety of fungal spores present in the air.

Time: One 30-minute session for the activity, plus several additional 10-minute periods for observation.

Materials: Paper plates, samples of different foods (such as bread, apple, banana, etc.), Fungi Finds chart (in the Appendix).

Many people think a fungus is a strange type of plant, but in fact, fungi are neither plants nor animals. They are a completely separate kingdom of organisms. Fungi grow from spores rather than seeds. Different groups of fungi have a wide range of forms and uses—mushrooms are the most commonly recognized, but there are also yeast fungi (molds used to make products such as cheese) and fungal medicines such as penicillin.

Most fungi are saprophytic, meaning that they feed on dead organic matter and by-products of other organisms. These are recyclers, which help out in the compost bin. Other fungi establish mutually beneficial (symbiotic) relationships with algae to form lichens. Still others are parasitic and feed off plants. These can be serious garden pests.

Thousands of fungus spores are floating in the air all the time. When a spore lands where conditions are favorable for it to germinate, it begins to grow. You and your gardeners can observe various types of fungi. Set out a variety of foods on paper plates. Set some inside, some outside, some in the sun, and some in a moist, cool place. Put one in the refrigerator to use as a control group. You will probably be able to observe several different colors and shapes of fungal splotches beginning to grow on some of the items after a few days. Ask the gardeners to check the plates daily to see what types of fungus they attract and record their findings on the Fungi Finds chart.

Use the questions and activities below to stimulate additional discussion and for writing exercises.

1. List each food and the number of types of fungi that grew on it. Describe their color, shape, size, appearance, etc.

2. Which types of food attracted the most fungal growth? Why do you think this is so?

3. Under what conditions (sun, shade, dry, moist, etc.) did the most fungi grow? Why?

4. Why is it important to put food in the refrigerator at home instead of leaving it out?

❧ Yeast Bread

Objectives: To learn how one fungus—yeast—is used in cooking and what purpose it serves; to learn about safety guidelines in the kitchen.

Time: 2½ to 3 hours (not continuous; dough must set and rise twice).

Materials: Ingredients listed on the next page, access to an oven.

Some fungi can be used to help people. A good example of these good fungi is yeast. Yeasts are simple, one-celled fungi that have been cultivated by scientists to use in many foods, such as bread, cheese, yogurt and alcoholic drinks.

By making yeast bread, your JMG group can observe what happens when yeast cells multiply. As yeast divides, it produces carbon dioxide, which causes the dough to rise and puff up. Then, when baked, the carbon dioxide expands and rises, giving bread its light fluffiness. Help the gardeners follow the recipe below. Discuss the yeast division process and its effects on the dough.

Before making the bread, open a packet of yeast and show your group what it looks like. Explain that people eat fungal organisms such as yeast every day—in bread, yogurt and many other food products. Ask the gardeners if they have eaten bread today, and tell them that they have eaten yeast. To illustrate the production of carbon dioxide (CO_2) as yeast multiplies, put a packet of yeast in a small bowl along with a cup of lukewarm water. Have one student stir the mixture for a minute, and then let the group observe as the mix begins to thicken and form bubbles of CO_2.

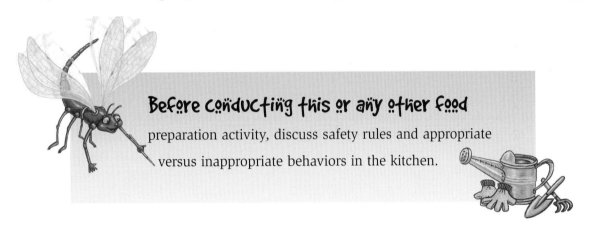

Before conducting this or any other food preparation activity, discuss safety rules and appropriate versus inappropriate behaviors in the kitchen.

Magic Cheese Bread

2$\frac{1}{2}$ cups flour
2 teaspoons sugar
1$\frac{1}{2}$ teaspoons salt
1 package active dry yeast

4 ounces (1 cup) shredded cheddar cheese
$\frac{3}{4}$ cup milk
$\frac{1}{2}$ cup margarine or butter
3 eggs

In a large bowl, combine 1$\frac{1}{2}$ cups flour, sugar, salt and yeast; blend well. Stir in the cheese. In a small saucepan, heat the milk and margarine until it is very warm (120 to 130 °F). Add the warm liquid and eggs to the flour mixture. Blend at low speed until moistened; beat 3 minutes at medium speed. By hand, stir in the remaining 1 cup of flour. Cover it loosely with plastic wrap and a cloth towel. Let it rise in a warm place (80 to 85 °F) until it is light and doubled in size, about 45 to 60 minutes.

Generously grease a 1$\frac{1}{2}$- or 2-quart casserole or a 9- by 5-inch loaf pan. Stir the dough to remove all the air bubbles. Turn it into a greased casserole dish. Cover and let it rise in a warm place until it is light and doubled in size—20 to 25 minutes.

Heat the oven to 350 degrees F. Uncover the dough. Bake it for 40 to 45 minutes or until it is deep golden brown. Immediately remove it from the casserole, and let it cool on a wire rack.

🌿 Lacy Leaves

Objective:	To observe organic matter (decaying leaves) being decomposed by fungi.
Time:	45 minutes.
Materials:	Construction paper (dark colors work best), white paint, glue, skeletonized leaves from around your meeting area or brought in from a wooded site.

Many fungi are saprophytic, which means that they eat dead organic matter such as dead grass, last year's leaves and other plant and animal remains. These fungi are extremely important—without them, the leaves that fall each year in autumn would not decay or be incorporated back into the soil.

As plants grow, they take up nutrients. These nutrients are held above ground in tree trunks, leaves, etc. When the plants die, decomposers feed on the organic matter. Then, when they excrete it, the nutrients from the organic matter are returned to the soil. This is called nutrient cycling. The death and decomposition part of the life cycle is seldom a focus of life cycle studies; however, without it, life could not begin anew because there would not be enough nutrients. Discussing decomposition through plant decay and nutrient cycling—building new soil and starting the life cycle anew—is a positive way to explore this important aspect of the life cycle.

Decomposition takes a season or more for most types of leaves. If you look under a deciduous tree in the fall you can see mounds of freshly fallen leaves. Dig under them, and you will find last year's leaves. This layer is much thinner because they have been decomposing for a year, and are probably tattered and partially decomposed. Leaves at the top of this layer may still be complete for the most part, but the leaves at the bottom have been exposed to more soil-dwelling decomposers.

You may be able to find leaves from which the tender, juicy leaf tissue has been eaten away, leaving only the tougher veins and stems behind. These are called skeletonized leaves, because the body of the leaf has been removed, exposing the stem and vein framework, or skeleton, of the leaf. They are very delicate and lacy; handle them carefully to keep from tearing them.

Under the layer of partially decayed leaves is a rich layer of completely decomposed organic matter, called humus. This is fresh soil and is a darker color, which indicates that it is high in nutrients. (See Shake, Rattle, & Roll activity, p.26.) Depending on the type of tree, leaves may take 1 to 3 years to decay completely. For example, oak leaves are tough and leathery, so may take several years. Maple leaves, on the other hand, are more tender and may be decomposed completely in a single year.

If a wooded area is nearby, such as a park or an unmaintained grove of trees where the leaves have not been raked, take your JMG group on a leaf skeleton hunt. Show them how to carefully push the fresh leaf layer aside to reach the partially decayed leaves beneath and find skeletonized leaves. Ask them to look under several trees to find a variety of leaf shapes. Collect several types of leaves at various stages of decomposition.

After you have collected the leaves, ask the gardeners to select several to make a picture of decomposition on a sheet of dark-colored construction paper. They might show a complete leaf at one end of the page, and progress to a skeletonized leaf at the other end. Or, they may compose an artistic arrangement of leaves. (The lacy appearance of skeletonized leaves could be used to represent the net-veined appearance of insect wings, for example.) Once they have arranged their leaves, they can paint over them very gently with a white or other light-colored paint and glue them to paper when dried. The light-colored paint on a dark sheet of construction paper makes the fine lines of the veins show up better.

Spray paint actually works best for this activity, because the fine spray coats the leaf veins without being too heavy. You may want to use spray paint if you have extra adults to help and access to a well-ventilated area. Or use poster paint and have the gardeners apply it with sponges.

The gardeners can create several additional effects using leaves as patterns. By sponging paint on or around a leaf, the gardeners can create a leaf or a leaf silhouette shape. The leaves can also be used as stamps. Brush a small amount of paint onto the leaf, and then press the leaf to the paper. The children can mix different techniques and leaves to create a layered look on the paper. Try these techniques before demonstrating them to your gardeners. You can create a very attractive picture if you glue a combination of skeletonized leaves over a background of more subtle sponged leaf shapes. This also encourages the gardeners to work with leaves at all stages of decomposition.

❧ Likin' those Lichens

Objective: To learn about lichens and mutually beneficial relationships.
Time: 30 minutes to 1 hour.
Materials: Likin' those Lichens puzzle art (in the Appendix).

You may have seen lichens growing on rocks or the branches of trees and shrubs, and wondered what they were. They look like hard, crusty moss or stiff seaweed. A lichen is unique because it is actually two organisms, an alga and a fungus that live together in a symbiotic relationship. A symbiotic relationship is one in which both organisms benefit in some way.

In the case of lichens, the alga and fungus interact so closely that scientists regard them as a single organism and give them a single scientific name. The two organisms work together in all aspects of their life cycle—the algal part makes food for both species through photosynthesis; the fungal part obtains water and minerals, forms the vegetative body of the organism and develops the reproductive structures. Many of the algae and fungi that form lichens can also live on their own as individual species. When they unite to form a lichen, they take on a completely different shape, form and texture. Lichens grow slowly, are very delicate and are found only in clean, undisturbed places. They are very sensitive to pollution, and should be handled as little as possible to avoid disrupting them. You and your JMG'ers have probably seen lichens growing on tree branches along a creek or in the woods. They often live on oak trees. Lichens also grow on rocks, where they make a variety of rough, circular patterns in different colors such as green, yellow, brown or pink. Lichens are an excellent example of teamwork, and can be used to focus on the benefits possible

through teamwork. Bring a lichen to a JMG gathering or, if possible, find a place where lichens grow and take your JMG group there to observe them. Have them feel the lichens—they are hard and rough, with an interesting variety of textures.

Discuss the concept of teamwork and pooled resources. In the case of lichens, each of the two organisms contributes certain defined resources, and each benefits from contributions of the other organism. Use the Teamwork game described below as a focus on working together.

Teamwork Game

Divide the group into teams of three gardeners each. Explain the following rules:
One person cannot talk.
One person cannot see (use a blindfold).
One person cannot use his or her hands (they must put them behind their backs).

All other abilities can be used, although you can add other conditions if you wish. Photocopy the puzzle from the Appendix, and cut out pieces so that each group has a complete puzzle to assemble. Ask the members of each team to work together to assemble their puzzle. Give them 10 minutes to complete the puzzle. To complete the puzzle, the gardeners must work together by pooling their resources and abilities.

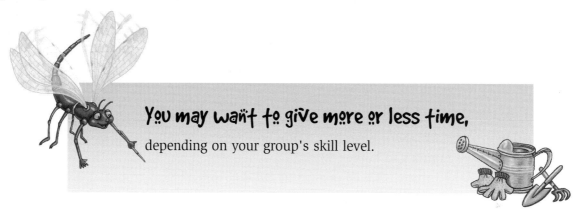

You may want to give more or less time, depending on your group's skill level.

After the activity, ask each group member to write a short paper that discusses the following points:
✓ How well did your group perform in the teamwork activity?
✓ How did you feel during the activity (Excited? Frustrated?)?
✓ Could your group have improved its performance? How?

At the end of the activity, discuss teamwork with the group. It's not always easy to make sure all members of a team are included in a group process. With a team, the group takes on characteristics that are unique and different from the individual team members, with results that are often better than any one person could achieve alone.

❦ Prescription for Prevention

Objective: To learn the components of the disease triangle and the concept of IPM.
Time: Variable.
Materials: None.

For a disease to successfully attack an organism, three things must be present. These components make up the Disease Triangle.

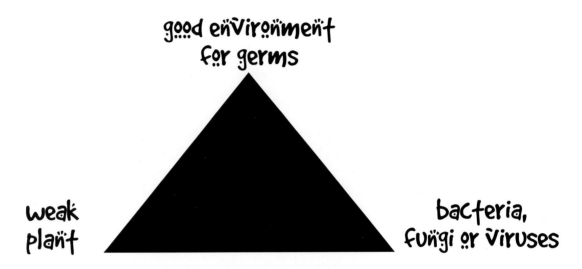

good environment for germs

weak plant

bacteria, fungi or viruses

If any one of these three parts is missing, a plant is less susceptible to disease. The best way to prevent disease is to keep the plant healthy. Read through the tips below, and discuss them with your group. Ask the gardeners how these components prevent plant disease. Include as many of these practices as possible in the JMG garden.

1. Make sure your plants are healthy when you buy them, and use plants well suited for your area. (Your local nursery can help you select good plants to use.)

2. Check the tags that come with your plants or seeds. Space your plants just as the directions say. Overcrowded plants become thin and weak.

3. Layer mulch around your plants to prevent mud, which can carry fungus spores, from splashing up on your plants when you water.

4. Fertilize your plants regularly to keep them strong and healthy.

5. Be careful when you water. Avoid splashing water on the leaves.

6. Keep the garden clean. Don't let dead plants and weeds pile up (except in the compost pile). They can be a home for many pests.

The group could make a mobile of the disease triangle. Each point (weak plant, good environment for germs, bacteria/fungi/virus) could have pictures or statements hanging from it that relate to it.

Chapter 4

❧ There's a Fungus Among Us!

Objective: To observe and identify fungi that act as pests in the garden.
Time: 30 minutes.
Materials: Photographs on this page, notebooks for making observations.

Fungi cause many plant diseases. The photographs on this page depict a few very common plant diseases, but there are many others. You may need to consult a general gardening reference to identify and find recommendations for treating these and other plant diseases.

black spot

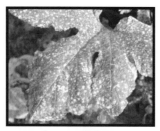

powdery mildew

sooty mold

Take your group on a neighborhood hike, and ask them to look for signs of plant diseases. Plant diseases are more prevalent during damp, rainy periods, as these conditions promote spore development and transfer. Ask your group to look for examples of these diseases. Have them record the plant diseases they see, their locations and the kinds of plants they were on.

LEADERSHIP/SERVICE LEARNING PROJECTS

Below are projects to complete with your JMG group. The group should choose at least one to complete.

❦ Collect and Share

Your group can take a younger group on an insect expedition and show them techniques for catching and collecting insects.

❦ Butterfly Garden

If the gardeners like butterflies fluttering around their garden, they can attract even more of them by building a butterfly garden. Certain butterflies are attracted to certain plants. The JMGers can contact your local county Extension office for a list of butterfly attracting plants in your area. Have them select some butterfly plants and plant your own butterfly garden in your neighborhood.

❦ Butterfly Release

Have you ever been to a ceremony and seen balloons being released? Why not try the same idea with butterflies? Your JMG group can raise your own butterflies to release at a school ceremony, garden dedication, or even at your JMG graduation! Check with your local nursery, county Extension agent, or the World Wide Web for resources.

❦ Create Your Own

Your JMG group can have fun creating its own unique leadership/service learning project.

For a child to be certified as a Junior Master Gardener, one individual and one group activity should be completed for each section/teaching concept in this chapter. Your JMG group should also select one leadership/service learning project for this chapter to complete.

Landscape Horticulture

Design Process

A landscape designer looks at an area outside and finds ways to make it more beautiful and useful. People who have a spot they want improved will first meet with a landscape designer to talk about it; the designer learns about the clients and their family, asking them what plants they like, how they use their yard and many other questions. The designer also visits the house to look at the yard. He or she learns such things as: Is it a front or backyard? Does it get mostly sun or shade? Do any plants in the yard need to be removed? The designer wants to learn much about the family and the area where they live, in order to make a plan just for them. This section will help your gardeners see what it would be like to be a landscape designer.

ACTIVITIES

❧ Rooms

Objectives: To define areas within a space and to show that they serve special purposes.
Time: 45 minutes.
Materials: Poster or chalkboard, markers or chalk.

Just as homes have private areas (such as a bedroom or office), public areas (such as a living room) and transitional areas (such as an entry or hallway), landscapes have spaces that serve similar functions. For this activity, choose a building site with a back, side and front area.

Ask the gardeners what rooms they have in their home. Have the group call out names of different rooms as you list them on a poster or chalkboard. Circle the word "bedroom" and ask the group what special items are in this room to give it that name. Have them do the same for the living room and hallway. Then ask the group if each of the rooms listed can be closed off from the rest of the house. If so, how?

Let them know that different parts of their homes are used in different ways. Explain that different rooms in a house can be considered public areas, private areas or transitional areas. Public spaces are usually open, so anyone who visits the home can see them. Explain that these areas usually have more formal decorations. Private areas are more personal and are usually closed off from other areas. Transitional spaces lead people from one part of the house to another.

Make three columns on a chalkboard, one for each of the three different types of spaces. Have the group think about each room listed and decide what type of space it is.

When you arrive at the word "bedroom," ask the group how they'd feel if the front doors of their homes opened into their bedrooms. Why would they feel this way? Explain that a bedroom is a private area and that visitors generally go into the back part of the house only if they are invited there. When a room has four walls and a door enclosing it from the rest of the house, it signals to guests that this is a private space. Because this room belongs to a family member, it contains his or her special things, such as posters, pictures, games, and special mementos and furniture.

ROOMS

When the gardeners discuss the living room, ask them how that room is used in their house. What about this room makes it a space for the whole family as well as guests? Explain that public rooms are generally in the front of the house, where the family and guests gather.

Tell the group that public, private and transitional spaces can be outside as well. These spaces are what make up landscaping. Take the group outside to an open area in the back of the building. Explain that a backyard is a private place where people gather to spend time and have fun. Take the gardeners to the side of the building and ask them if this space is public, private or transitional. End the walk with the front area. Explain that front yards are normally considered public spaces to be viewed by everyone. They are community areas that welcome people to the house. A front yard leads such people as the mail carrier, visitors, friends and the family members themselves to the front door. An attractive front yard says "welcome."

After the group defines this space as public, ask if an area in the front could be considered a private space. (People usually consider public spaces to be the areas in front of a building that are open for everyone to see.) Have the gardeners think of ways that a place at the front of a building could be a private space. Explain that even a 1-foot wall around a small space in the front could make that small space more secluded and private. Plants and low walls are designed to keep people from walking through certain spaces, and help create the sense of privacy. .

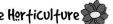

🌼 People and Places

Objective: To understand that different people use yard space differently.
Time: 45 minutes.
Materials: Different Strokes, Different Folks activity page (in the Appendix), scissors, hat or bowl.

For this activity, cut out the phrases from the Different Strokes, Different Folks page. Later, each learner will pull one slip out of the hat.

Have the gardeners look around at their neighbors and imagine that they are all adults. Ask them whether any of their neighbors is exactly like them. Explain that everyone is different. Because we are different, we all might use our yard space differently. Ask them to think of a sport they like to play, and explain that they might choose to have a space in their yard to practice that sport. For example, a golfer might have a putting green in the backyard.

Would someone who loves to garden need a putting green? What would people with small children most likely need in their backyard? Explain that a landscape designer meets with the clients at the site to discuss their needs. The designer learns such information as whether the clients have small children, what hobbies they have, whether they like to read outside, and whether they have friends over often. Explain that sometimes a client may have more needs than the space allows. When faced with this dilemma, the landscape designer must decide which needs are most important.

Divide the gardeners into groups of two or three. Ask each learner to take one or two slips of paper from the hat. The phrases represent a client's needs. Each group is to brainstorm and design a yard that meets all the client's needs. Later, have the members of each group tell the class about their design and explain how they met their client's needs.

🌼 Money Trees

Objective: To understand that trees help people save energy and money.
Time: 30 minutes.
Materials: None.

This activity involves visiting two different areas around a building on a sunny day. Choose a large area where a nearby tree shades the building, and a second site that receives sun all day.

Chapter 5

The south and west sides of a building are generally warmer, especially during the summer. Deciduous trees (those that lose their leaves in the fall) planted on the west and south sides of buildings help shade them during the hottest part of the year. This helps conserve energy and money. During the winter months, however, the trees allow the sun to warm the building, because the sun can shine through the bare branches. Evergreen trees provide shade year-round.

JMG Trivia Decidous trees planted on the south or west side of a house help lower the indoor air temperature in summer and help raise the indoor temperature in winter.

Begin this activity by taking the gardeners outside to stand under a large tree. Warm, sunny days offer a chance to experience the temperature difference between sunny and shady areas. Ask the group why they think people plant trees. Some might respond, "They're pretty," "Trees give us shade," or "It's a place where we can get out of the sun." Explain that trees have many functions, including offering shade, beauty, edible fruits, and food for wildlife. Ask for other benefits that trees provide. Tell the group that trees also help protect buildings from heat and cold. When trees protect buildings, people use less energy and money to heat or cool them. Ask the gardeners how they think trees could be used to provide this kind of protection.

Lead the gardeners to the side of a building with no trees. Have them notice the difference in temperature. Would this be a good spot to plant a tree to shade the building and save energy? On very warm, sunny days, building surfaces may be hot. Ask the gardeners what time of the year a building needs to be protected from the sun. Ask them when it would be good for a building to be warmed by the sun. Explain that during the winter, some trees lose their leaves and allow the sun to shine through the branches. Tell the group that these trees are called DECIDUOUS. Point out an EVERGREEN tree. Explain that the evergreen tree branches are full of leaves all year long. Have them decide which tree would better protect the building from the sun. For more information on distinguishing deciduous from evergreen trees, visit the JMG web site at *www.jmgkids.org*.

Have the group visit the sites at different times of the day or in different seasons to observe differences in temperature and energy savings the trees provide for the building.

Discussion Questions
1. What effect would a row of trees have on the north side of a building?
2. In what area around a building would you plant a tree or a row of trees? Why?

It would be wonderful to have a tree or trees donated for the gardeners to plant. This would provide a chance for them to apply the skills they learned, as well as give them the feeling that they've made a real contribution to the environment. Plant trees at least 10 feet from a building. Trees planted too close to a structure can cause problems with its foundation as they mature.

🌿 Site Map

Objective: To experience an initial step in the landscape design process.
Time: 45 minutes.
Materials: Site Map Survey (in the Appendix), Site Map Symbols pages (in the Appendix),
              graph paper, blank scrap paper, tape measure, glue, black marker.

for this activity, the JMG'ers will become landscape designers who conduct a site analysis of an area in your neighborhood. A site analysis plays an important role in the overall landscape design. After the initial client meeting, the landscape designer conducts a site survey. Once all the data is collected, the landscape designer returns to the office to produce a site analysis. The Site Map Symbols page contains some of the most common symbols used by landscape designers in an evaluation.

Tell the gardeners that they will be landscape designers for this activity. Explain that one of the tasks for a designer is to conduct a site analysis, which is like a map of an area to be worked on.

Distribute copies of the Site Map Survey and the Site Map Symbols pages to be used on their site analysis. Discuss each symbol so that everyone understands what the symbol represents.

Give each gardener a blank sheet of graph paper to make sketches and notes on during the site analysis. Take the gardeners outside to the designated area. Keep the site to a size that can be managed on graph paper. They will observe more if the space has plant materials, trees, low sites, high areas, slopes, dirt pathways or a building than if they were working with a bare, flat area. Have the gardeners fill in their Site Map Survey forms.

Choose at least five items and conditions for your group to include in the site analysis:
✓ Are any structures on this site?
✓ Which direction is north?
✓ Where are the trees and shrubs?
✓ Note the kinds of trees and/or shrubs.
✓ Are there any sunny areas? Where?
✓ Are there any shady areas? Where?
✓ From which direction is the wind blowing?
✓ From where do gentle breezes usually come?
✓ Are there low spots on the site?

✓ Does water stay in this spot for a long time, or does it drain quickly into the soil?
✓ Does the site have a slope or is it flat?
✓ Do any overhead telephone lines or other utility lines cross the space?
✓ In which directions are the good views?
✓ Are any unsightly obstacles around or on the site that should be hidden?

Have the group think of other symbols they can use to represent other objects and characteristics of the site.

In the Classroom

To plot objects in the area more accurately for the site analysis, your group can measure the area being mapped. They can transfer the measurements to the graph paper by having each square of the paper represent 1 square foot of landscape space. For larger areas, the class might use a different scale.

As the students draw an object in the mapped area, have them measure its distance from three spots on the map. These spots can be the corners of the area they are surveying, or landmarks such as buildings.

Design Principles

Ask the gardeners if they have ever seen a vacant lot covered with grass and weeds. Then ask them to try to picture what that same area would look like if it had green grass and big trees. Have them imagine flower beds full of bushy shrubs, brightly colored blooms all along the edges and even a small pond with a few orange fish swimming among the long, green leaves poking out of the water. Would they like to design an area to look like that? People who are landscape designers know tricks to making outside areas more beautiful. This section will teach the gardeners a landscape designer's secrets.

ACTIVITIES
❀ Nature Wheels

Objectives: To build a color wheel from items found in nature and to understand the relationships between the colors.
Time: 45 minutes.
Materials: White poster board, marker, color wheel diagrams in the JMG Handbook, glue.

Have the gardeners call out the colors they've seen in nature, and list them on a poster or chalkboard. Explain that green is common in nature. Remind them that the green in plants comes from chlorophyll. Tell them that a color wheel is a circle that shows the main colors seen by people. Then display a color wheel and have the group name the colors on the wheel and those

not on it. Make the color wheel available throughout the activity so the gardeners can refer to it. Create a group color wheel on poster board, but leave the sections white where the colors go.

Tell the group that they will go outside and find natural items. Their task will be to collect natural items to represent colors in the color wheel, such as bark, flowers, stems, leaves, etc. Remind the group to use only natural items. Break the JMG'ers into three groups. Assign one group to be the blues, one to be the reds and one to be the yellows. Each group should select only items that contain the color from its section of the color wheel.

Let the gardeners know that some colors may be unavailable at some times of the year. More natural materials and colors may be available in mid to late spring, depending on the area and what flowers are in bloom.

After the gardeners have collected materials, have them attach their finds to the group color wheel. Have the color groups discuss where they found their colors, as well as which colors were easiest and hardest to find. Tell them that when landscape designers choose plants for a landscape, they usually try to choose plants with colors that look good together.

Some colors that look good together are called "complementary" colors. Explain that they can tell what colors are complementary by where they are placed on the color wheel. Complementary colors are opposite each other. For example, blue and orange are complementary. Tell the group that colors that are next-door neighbors on the color wheel are called analogous. The colors green and green-blue are analogous colors; they are next to one another on the wheel. Have the JMG'ers point to two colors of plants on the color wheel that are complementary and two that are analogous.

Iñ the Classroom
Explain that climates and topography differ dramatically across the nation. Because all plants have different needs, a JMG group in another area may have a completely different set of plants and other natural materials to represent colors on its color wheel.

❧ Texture Collection

Objective: To understand how texture, a design element, is used to create visual interest
               in a landscape.
Time: 45 minutes.
Materials: Sandpaper, cake pans, poster or chalkboard, markers or chalk, piece of plastic,
               plants with different types of leaves, natural materials of different textures.

Have the gardeners close their eyes. Tell them that you will have them rub their fingers across two mystery objects and that you want them to describe how each feels. Allow each child to feel the rough sandpaper and smooth plastic. Have the gardeners open their eyes and ask them to call out words that describe what they felt. Write those words on the chalkboard or poster.

Tell the group that these words describe the objects' textures. Explain that the word "texture" means how something feels. Textures can range from very smooth or fine to very rough or coarse. Tell them that sometimes we can know how something feels just by looking at it. Show the gardeners the plastic to let the group see what smooth looks like compared to the coarse appearance of the sandpaper. Have them look around the room and call out words to describe the texture of different objects they see. They may include such words as slick, bumpy, pointy, soft, sharp, silky. Explain that temperature and color words do not describe texture.

Send the gardeners out on a scavenger hunt to find natural materials of at least three different textures. Tell them to think of a word to describe the texture of each item they bring back. Choose several of the items and challenge the group to put them in order from less to more coarse. Explain that landscape designers place plants with differing textures together to make a landscape more interesting.

Iñ the Classroom

Pair up the students and give one cake pan to each group. Tell the groups they have been hired to design a mini landscape. Each group will create a 3-D model to present to a client, using at least seven different textured materials. The base of the design could be made of sand or other suitable media found outside during the scavenger hunt. The designs can include paths, berms and other landscape features. Remind the groups to use only plants and other natural materials to embellish their designs.

Have the students write descriptions of their mini landscapes, making sure to include texture words.

✿ Same Sides

Objective: To understand balance, a design element, using symmetrical and asymmetrical visuals.

Time: 25 minutes.

Materials: One-Legged Table and Butterfly Symmetry activity pages (both in the Appendix), glue, paper, scissors, books, 2- by 4-inch piece of wood at least 6 feet long.

Hold up the Symmetry Butterfly page and ask the gardeners what is special about the wings of the butterfly. Guide them to notice that the wings on both sides have exactly the same pattern, just on opposite sides. Explain that this is called symmetry and that the butterfly is symmetrical. Fold the butterfly in half and hold it up to the light to show them that all the shapes and designs line up on top of each other.

Explain that landscape and flower designers sometimes use symmetry to make sure the items in a landscape or the flowers in a container are balanced. Have your group practice using symmetry by completing the One-Legged Table activity page.

Balance a wooden board on a few books on the floor so that it creates a seesaw. Have two students who are about the same size stand on the ends of the board so that it balances. Ask the group: If you drew a line midway between the two children, would the two sides be symmetrical? Ask if the board is balanced. Explain that when items in a flower bed or vase are balanced, they look nicer. Give the group this challenge: How can we balance the board without it having symmetry?

Stand on one end of the board and have your gardeners step one by one onto the other end until it balances. Then ask the group how the board was able to balance without both sides being the same. Tell the group that because the two sides of the board are not the same, it is asymmetrical. But it is still balanced. Explain that designers also can make things appear balanced without having the same-sized things on both sides. Point out that one large item can be balanced on the opposite side by a few smaller items.

Have the gardeners complete another One-Legged Table activity page, this time using asymmetrical balance. Explain that they must imagine how heavy one plant would be and balance it by placing other smaller plants on the opposite side. Encourage them to use all the plants on the page.

As they finish, have them show their table designs to the group.

❀ Does it Fit?

Objective: To demonstrate understanding of proportion, a design element.

Time: 30 minutes.

Materials: Small cup or mug, 2-liter soft drink bottle, a small flower, a small plant (about 8 to 10 inches tall) the size of each container, Does it Fit? activity pages (in the Appendix), scissors, paper, glue.

For this activity, you will need to plant a tall, thin plant in a small cup and place a small flower in a 2-liter bottle as a vase.

Show the group the two containers and ask them what's wrong with what you are showing them. Guide the gardeners to conclude that the bottle is too big for the flower and the cup is too small for the potted plant. Ask them if they think the potted plant looks as if it will fall over or if the flower looks as if it could be lost in the bottle.

Explain that landscape and floral designers pay close attention to how plants and other items fit together in their designs. One of the rules designers use to make sure plants and flowers fit in containers is that a plant should be about twice as tall as its container. For example, if a plant is 2 feet tall, the container should be about 1 foot tall.

Distribute copies of the Does it Fit? activity page to the group. Have them cut out the plants and containers from the page and then match the plant with the correct container. Have them measure to see if the plant is about twice as long as the container. Show the gardeners that they can also fold the plant in half to see if it is about the same size as the container. After they have finished matching, they can glue the pair together on a separate page.

Identification and Selection

Some plants grow well in some places but not in others. For example, some oak trees grow poorly in places that are very cold and get much snow; pansy flowers cannot live where it is very hot. Landscape designers must make good decisions about what kinds of plants to put in certain spots. To make those decisions, the designer must know which plants are which and what certain plants need so they can be healthy and look good. This section covers plant identification and the differences between plants.

ACTIVITIES

❀ Tearing Trees

Objective: To identify trees based on their classification and shape.

Time: 30 minutes.

Materials: My Tree Friend page (in the Appendix), Tree Shape ID page (in the Appendix), colored construction paper, glue, work sheet or 11- by 17- inch sheet of white paper, pencils or pen.

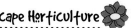

Have the gardeners close their eyes and think about what a tree looks like. Then ask them to open their eyes and try to illustrate the tree they imagined. As they finish, have them describe the shape of the top part of the tree containing the branches and leaves. Children often see trees only as having large sphere-shaped tops.

Take the gardeners outside and have each choose one tree nearby. Give each child a piece of construction paper. Tell the gardeners that their job is to tear away the edges of the construction paper until the paper has the same shape as the top of the tree they chose. Have each one glue the torn shape to the My Tree Friend page and draw in a trunk.

Tape the pages to a wall. Have the group look at each tree tearing and decide what each torn shape resembles—a circle, triangle, oval or some other shape. Explain that some tree shapes have symmetry (if they are folded in half, the edges match up), whereas others are asymmetrical.

Distribute copies of the Tree Shape ID page. From the six basic shapes shown (oval, pyramidal, round, columnar, rounded and V-shaped), have the gardeners decide which basic shape their tree resembles the most. Explain that although some trees have a few branches sticking out in odd directions, the basic outline of the tree will usually follow a recognizable symmetrical shape. Have them write the tree shape at the bottom of their tree pages.

In the Classroom

Your students could complete a research project on trees in your community. Use tree identification books and Internet resources to help your class learn about each tree, such as its common name, scientific name, the types of areas it grows in, its USDA zone, common pests and diseases that affect it, as well as other interesting facts about the tree. The JMG web site at *www.jmgkids.org* is a good source of helpful links for this activity.

❧ How Tall is that Tree?

Objective: To measure the height of a large tree.
Time: 20 minutes.
Materials: Pencil, measuring tape.

Take the group outside and have them find a tall tree. Ask the gardeners to guess how tall it is from the base to its top leaves. Have them take turns measuring each other and ask them how they think they might measure something as tall as a large tree. Pick two volunteers from the group to demonstrate an easy way to measure a tree's height.

Stand at a point where you can see the entire height of a tree, and have one of the gardeners hold a pencil at arm's length and look at the tree behind the pencil. The pencil should be pointing up and the tip of the pencil should "touch" the tip top of the tree. The gardener can then slide his or her thumb down the pencil until it "touches" the base of the truck.

Keeping the arm straight, the child should rotate his or her wrist so the pencil becomes horizontal and the child's thumb is still touching the tree's base. A second volunteer should now stand in the distance so that the point of the pencil is right on his or her toes. This gardener is now the same distance from the tree as the tree is tall! Using a tape measure, the group can measure the distance from the tree to the gardener standing at the pencil point. This measurement is the height of the tree.

Have the group choose partners and estimate and measure the heights of other trees. The group can then rank the trees from short to tall.

In the Classroom

Pose the following word problems for the gardeners to solve using the data they collected about trees in your area. Have them create additional problems for each other.

1. What is the difference between the height of the tallest and shortest trees?
2. How many trees are more than 20 feet tall?
3. What is the sum of the heights of the three tallest trees?
4. How many more trees are taller than 20 feet than are shorter than 20 feet?
5. What is the average height of all the trees measured?

❧ Learning your ABPs

Objective: To understand plant classifications of annuals, biennials and perennials.
Time: 20 minutes.
Materials: Pencil or pen, paper, clipboard (optional).

Ask the group if they know their ABPs. Explain that ABP represents the three main kinds of plants that people can put in their gardens: annuals, biennials and perennials. Write the three words on a poster or chalkboard. Ask the gardeners if they have any ideas about what the words mean. Give them a hint—underline the word "annual" and tell the group that it means "once a year." Tell them that when you are talking about plants, an annual plant is one that grows and dies all in one year. Some plants that are native to other areas may be grown as an annual in your area, but are perennial in their native environment.

Underline the prefix "bi" in biennial. Tell them the word bicycle also starts off with the prefix "bi" because it has two wheels, and explain that when we are talking about plants, a biennial is a plant that grows for two seasons instead of just one (like an annual).

Ask them how long they think a perennial lives. Tell the group that perennial plants are special because they live for many years. Explain that sometimes the top part of a perennial dies back if it gets too cold. When it does this, the bottom part of the plant continues to live and will grow a new set of stems and leaves when the weather warms again.

If possible, take the group to a nursery or other place that sells different types of plants, or arrange for a visit from someone from a nursery or your county Extension office. Ask that person to explain the differences among annuals, biennials and perennials. Have the group read plant tags to find out the common name, scientific name and classification. List the different annuals, perennials and biennials found in the nursery. Have the group look for similarities in the same types of plants.

❧ Great Green Grass

Objective:	To invent a new, improved variety of turfgrass.
Time:	40 minutes.
Materials:	Pen or pencil, paper, glue.

Take your group on a walk outside. Guide the gardeners to a grass-covered area and invite them to sit down. Ask them to try to think of any school yard, park, playground area or even backyard that isn't covered with grass. Ask them why they think people plant grass around so many buildings, park areas and play areas. Explain that many people use grass because it is prettier than bare ground or concrete; it's soft to walk and play on; and it stays pretty short so it doesn't hinder us as we walk over it.

Tell them that although grass is very popular for landscaping, it can also be expensive and hard work to keep it looking good. Have the group list some of the drawbacks of having grass (expensive to install, must be watered often, grows quickly and must be mowed regularly, can stain clothes if you slip on it, etc.).

Tell the gardeners that they will be research scientists whose job is to develop a new variety of grass with all the benefits of grass and none of its drawbacks. They can even create super varieties of their grass. Divide them into groups of two or three and have them list their ideas about their new Great Green Grass. Encourage them to be creative. Ask questions to spur ideas, such as:

1. What would make a grass prettier?
2. Can something be done about the grass needing so much water?
3. Sometimes grass gets worn out if it's walked on a lot—can that be improved?
4. What could be done so it wouldn't have to be mowed so often?
5. What about the problem of grass stains?
6. Does it always have to be green?

Have the gardeners make a rough sketch of their new grass and all the new "features" it offers. Ask them to label each improvement.

If time allows, have the group redraw their Great Green Grass, paying close attention to neatness, color and details. When all the groups have completed their work, have them present their new varieties of Great Green Grass to the rest of the class.

Installation

After you make a design and acquire plants for a landscape, the next step is to plant, or install, them in the ground. This section's activities will help the gardeners learn the best ways and times to install plants in a landscape. If the plants are put in the ground correctly, they will be healthier and the landscape will be even more beautiful.

❧ Arbor Day

Objective: To understand that trees are an important natural resource and that people have ways to celebrate their friend, the tree.

Time: Variable.

Materials: Internet, library, pen or pencil, paper, notebook.

This activity could be done in conjunction with the "Do it Right" activity.

Arbor Day is a national holiday first celebrated April 10, 1872, to encourage tree planting and to educate people about proper tree care. It was established in Nebraska to urge settlers and homesteaders in that prairie state to plant trees. The lawmakers knew that planting more trees would provide food, shelter, fuel and even cooling shade while adding beauty to the plains.

Today, National Arbor Day is held in communities all over the United States and is always the last Friday in April.

Ask the gardeners to imagine what our world would be like without trees. Have them think about the benefits we get from trees. List their ideas as they call them out. Explain that trees are so important to our lives and the environment that a national holiday was started more than 100 years ago to celebrate trees. Discuss the history of Arbor Day.

Have the gardeners help to plan a special event to celebrate Arbor Day. Have them write letters to local businesses about the upcoming Arbor Day celebration the JMG group is organizing. The JMG group could ask for donations to support tree planting in your area. As a part of the special day, the gardeners could sponsor a poster contest about trees and Arbor Day, give a short presentation about the history of Arbor Day, demonstrate the proper way to plant a tree, hold a tree-planting event and a special dedication for new or existing trees, or do anything else your group can think of to have fun while promoting trees.

For more information on Arbor Day, proper tree planting techniques, trees to plant in your area and when to plant them, contact the county Extension agent or check the Leaders' Links at the JMG Web site at *www.jmgkids.org*

Discussion Questions

1. What does arbor mean?
2. Do we need trees?
3. What are some reasons we need trees?
4. What is Arbor Day?
5. When is Arbor Day?
6. How do people celebrate this day?

✿ "Do It Right"

Objective:	To demonstrate through creative dramatics the proper way to plant a tree.
Time:	30 minutes.
Materials:	JMG Handbook, poster board, watering can.

This activity could be done in conjunction with the Arbor Day activity.

Ask the gardeners how they get dressed in the morning. Does order matter when they are putting on their clothes? Have volunteers list the order in which they put on clothes. Explain that some tasks must be done in sequence to ensure that the end product is a success. Turn the attention to trees. How do you plant a tree? Use the illustration in the JMG Handbook showing the proper way to plant a tree. As you detail the process, list each step on the board. You also could take the group outside to look at different trees. Discuss the requirements of one selected tree. Use the P-L-A-N-T-S acronym to remind the gardeners of a tree's requirements. (P = place; L = light, A = air, N = nutrients, T = thirst, S = soil).

Discuss each step of planting a tree. Ask for JMG volunteers to demonstrate tree planting. One volunteer can be the tree, and a few other volunteers can demonstrate the steps in planting the tree. A sheet of poster board cut lengthwise and placed around a student's feet can act as a container. The legs represent the roots; the torso represents the trunk; arms, the branches; and fingers, smaller branches or twigs. Use a table top and the ground surface to serve as a stage.

Have the gardeners act out the steps on the next page. Afterward, have the JMG group plant a tree in a local park, school or neighborhood.

1. Till the soil of the bed you are planting.

2. Dig a hole larger than the root ball you are planting.

(The root ball is the roots of your plant and the soil around the roots.)

3. Refill the sides of the hole with the soil you dug up.

4. Pack down the soil gently with your foot.

5. Water the soil around the plant.

In the Classroom

Have the students write the steps of tree planting in a how-to paper. After they have completed a rough draft, ask volunteers to read it to you as you follow their directions and pretend to "plant" a student.

As you follow their directions, be literal and pretend you have no knowledge of tree planting. For example, if a student writes, "Put the tree in the hole," plant the tree "head first," because the directions weren't specific. Explain that details are important when writing how-to instructions; they should assume the reader knows nothing about the subject.

❧ Seed, Sod and Plugs

Objective: To learn different ways to establish a lawn.
Time: Variable.
Materials: Seed, Sod and Plugs Interview page (in the Appendix), pencils.

Invite a visitor or take a trip to a seed, sod and plug farm or another facility that sells turfgrass. Have the group prepare to interview a sod expert. They can use questions from the Seed, Sod and Plugs interview page to record the information, or conduct a "live interview" with the sod expert in front of a listening audience.

After visiting the sod farm, have the JMG group discuss the different types of turfgrass seen on their trip. Compare the different types and the benefits of each. Remind the gardeners that during dry seasons, lawns use 25 to 60 percent of the water a household uses. Ask them which lawn method they would recommend to their client in establishing a lawn.

Questions from the interview page

1. What is sod?
2. When sod is used, how long must you wait to have a lawn?
3. How often and how long each time do you have to water the sod?
4. What types of turfgrass seed do you sell?
5. How long does it take before a lawn comes up when you plant with grass seed?
6. How often and how long each time do you have to water the seed?
7. What are plugs?
8. How often and how long each time do you have to water the plugs?
9. What type of grass grows best in this area?
10. Which grass has the most disease and pest problems?
11. Which type of grass must be mowed most often?

In the Classroom

Students can write a newspaper article from the information gleaned from their interview. Explain how commas and quotation marks can be used to include other people's words and make an article more informative and interesting.

Caring For Your Landscape

People spend a lot of time and money putting in a landscape. This is why it is important to take care of our trees and plants. Caring for them helps them grow and stay beautiful for a long time.

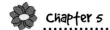

ACTIVITIES

❧ An Inch of Water

Objective: To understand landscape water use, water conservation and money savings by using irrigation systems properly.

Time: 50 minutes.

Materials: Inch of Water experiment page (in the Appendix), at least five tin pie pans, ruler, pencil or pen, paper, waterproof marker, graph paper, tape measure.

For this activity, you need an area with an irrigation system. Get permission to use it so the gardeners can research water usage in the landscape.

Lawn care and maintenance are expensive. For most homeowners, 25 to 60 percent of their water is used for their lawns. The higher amount (60 percent) occurs during the hot summer months.

Help the JMG'ers use a waterproof marker to mark the inside of each pie pan in one-half, one-quarter, or one-eighth inch increments to measure water levels. Have them number each pan. Place the pans in various areas of the sprinkler area, spacing them evenly. Before turning on the water, ask the group what they expect to happen. Ask them how long it will take for the pans to fill. Will all the pans receive the same amount of water?

Allow the sprinkler system to run for 5 minutes and have the group check each pan's water level, recording the amount on the Inch of Water experiment page. Have the group check the pans' water level every 5 minutes and record the data until the sprinkler has run for 30 minutes. Have the group complete the rest of the experiment page. Wind and rain will affect the results.

This experiment often shows that sprinkler systems water areas unevenly. Ask the gardeners if the amount of water in the pans was what they expected. Ask them to identify possible reasons for the differences in amounts of water collected from pan to pan (differences in types of sprinkler heads, overlapping areas, poorly designed layouts of the sprinkler system). Ask how nonuniform watering can affect grass, shrubs and trees (some areas may get too much water, other areas too little).

Walk the group around the area to see where water was lost to run-off, such as a sidewalk or a parking lot. Explain that water that flows off is wasted; ask the group for ways to prevent run-off (water for shorter periods).

🌿 Pruning Places

Objective: To learn proper pruning techniques and reasons to prune plants.
Time: 25 minutes.
Materials: Pruning shears, live shrub and/or small tree.

for this activity, find a shrub or small tree with some area of damaged, diseased or dead wood to use to demonstrate pruning. Your group will learn about pruning specifically to maintain plant health.

Plants are pruned to:
✓ Maintain plant health;
✓ Train the plant;
✓ Improve flowering, fruiting or branching; and
✓ Restrict plant growth.

When to prune
Generally, the best time of year to prune is during the dormant season, usually late winter/early spring.

How to prune
1. Start with a plan.
2. Use clean, sharp shears.
3. Make 45-degree cuts.
4. Cut stems back to a bud or branch.
5. Make your cut ½ inch from a bud or branch. This allows the plant to better heal itself, because the ½-inch area can die back while the rest of the plant is sealed off from the dead area.

For more information on pruning, visit the JMG website at *www.jmgkids.org* and click on Teacher/Leaders, then Level One, then Landscape Horticulture.

As plants grow, some branches or stems may become damaged or diseased or may die. To maintain plant health, it is important to remove these portions. This will help prevent the disease and damage from harming more of the plant.

Ask the group what would happen if a doctor performed surgery on a patient with a dull, dirty or rusty knife. Explain that when people have surgery, doctors use very clean, very sharp instruments so the wounds can heal quickly. We prune with clean, sharp instruments for the same reason. Tell the gardeners the reasons we prune plants.

Ask the gardeners what would happen if they were sent on a trip without knowing where they were going. (They could get lost, get into trouble, wander around aimlessly, take longer than needed.) How could this be avoided? (Make a plan.) Explain that when pruning any living plant, it is important to start with a plan. As plants grow, some branches or stems may become damaged or

diseased or may die. It is important to remove these areas to keep the plant healthy—pruning helps prevent the disease and damage from spreading. Explain that for this activity, they will prune only to maintain plant health.

Take the gardeners to the plant needing pruning. Show them how to examine the whole plant for areas that need to be removed, and then plan what to cut first. Explain that when you prune, plan to remove the largest area first.

Explain the steps for pruning. As you prune, ask volunteers to predict how the plant will respond to each cut after pruning. Take the JMG group to check the plant after 1 week, 1 month, and if possible, 1 year to observe how the plant responded to the cuts.

✿ More Mulch, More Moist

Objective: To study the effects of mulch on conserving water.
Time: 30 minutes.
Observation: 3 days.
Materials: 10-inch pots, plants, soilless potting media, mulch, paper, pencil, scale.

Tell the JMG'ers that they will conduct an experiment to save money and water and to grow healthier plants. Remind them that mulch is a layer of wood chips, compost, grass clippings, newspaper or other materials spread around the base of plants. Explain that many gardeners use mulch around their plants; one reason is to save water. Ask the gardeners how laying mulch over the ground could save water.

Have the JMG'ers plant two identical plants in two identical containers (at least 10-inch pots). Leave 4 inches of space at the top of each of the pots. Have the group water both pots with equal amounts of water until it saturates each container. Weigh the containers. Add 2 inches of mulch to one of the pots.

The gardeners should then place both pots in the same location under the same conditions. Have them predict which pot will contain more water after 3 days. The children should weigh both pots each day for 3 days. Have them remove the mulch each time before they weigh.

Ask them why they think the container with the mulch was heavier (the mulch helped to reduce the amount of water evaporating from the soil). Ask them to explain how mulch can help to save money.

The group can also experiment with different types of mulch, such as comparing pine bark mulch to cedar mulch, black plastic to clear plastic, or black plastic to a natural mulch, etc.

❧ Queen Bud

Objectives:	To learn the difference between terminal buds and lateral buds, and to know their effects on plants.
Time:	25 minutes.
Materials:	6-inch pots, plants, soilless potting media, mulch, paper, pencil.

All plants with branches have growing tips at the ends of the shoots. This growing tip is called the terminal bud (because it is at the end of the shoot). Beneath the terminal buds are lateral buds that grow very little unless the terminal bud is removed. To encourage some plants to bush out, gardeners prune the terminal bud.

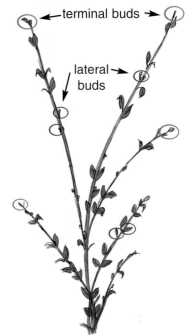

terminal buds

lateral buds

Tell the gardeners they will play a game in which they will all be special parts of a "royal plant." Choose one gardener to be the royal plant's Queen Bud. Next, choose a few more gardeners to serve as the princes and princesses.

Have the Queen Bud sit on a chair with a few of her princes and princesses, the next in line for the throne, sitting around her on other chairs. A few more of the princes and princesses should sit on the floor. Point to the queen and tell the group that this is Queen Bud of the royal plant. Explain that she is called the TERMINAL BUD because she sits atop the end tip of the plant and is the only part allowed to grow up. Have her rise slowly to a standing position on the chair to demonstrate growth. Explain that the princes and princesses are also buds, but because they are just LATERAL BUDS, they just sit near the queen, following her and waiting to grow someday. Tell the princes and princesses that they must just sit there, hardly growing at all until something happens to Queen Bud. Explain that if something were to happen to the Queen Bud, the lateral buds closest to the terminal bud would then become the new terminal buds and take the queen's place of growth.

Pretend that your arms are giant clippers, and "dethrone" the queen by "clipping" her off the royal plant. Inform the lateral buds on the chairs that they are now terminal buds and have them begin to rise as if growing. Then cut off the new terminal buds to allow those on the floor to become terminal buds next. Explain to the group that gardeners sometimes prune off a single terminal bud to cause more lateral buds to start growing. The lateral buds closest to the terminal buds are the ones that grow if the terminal bud is removed. Ask the gardeners why a gardener would want to do this (to make the plant more bushy). If possible, take your group outside to a plant and demonstrate pruning a terminal bud.

LEADERSHIP/SERVICE LEARNING PROJECTS

Below are projects to complete with your JMG group. The group should choose at least one to complete.

❀ Plant a Bed

Almost anyplace will look more beautiful with flowers. Ask permission to plant a flower bed somewhere in your neighborhood or at your school. Good places would be around the flagpole at your school or in front of a nursing home. People at those places might even be willing to donate money for the project. Your group will need to:

1. Get permission

2. Interview the client and find out what he or she would like

3. Conduct a site survey

4. Prepare the soil

5. Add organic matter

6. Choose plants

7. Make a design of how the bed will be planted

8. Dig holes larger than the plants' root balls

9. Put root balls in the ground and fill in with the soil you dug up

10. Press down soil to fill in air spaces

11. Water the plants

12. Maintain the area or show the client how to do this

❀ Neighborhood or School Tree Book
There are probably dozens of different types of trees around your school and community. Your group could be the first to write a book to tell all about them. Each page could include a picture of the tree, a leaf, and information about the tree. You could include the scientific name, where the tree normally grows, how tall it gets, and any other information you find.

If you want to make more than one book, you can scan your pages with a computer scanner or have color copies made at a copy store. The group can design a cover and have it copied, too. The copy store could even bind the book for you. Then you could give copies of the book to local schools or city libraries.

❀ Annual Business
If your group wants to raise money, you could have an Annual Business. Annuals are plants that grow, bloom and die all in the same season. The group can buy seeds and grow them to sell for the business. Your group will have to buy seeds, soil and containers. The amount they spend will determine the price they charge for the plants. The money your group raises can be donated to a charity or used to help your group do more projects.

❀ Wildflower Meadow
One very easy way to make a large area more beautiful is to spread wildflower seed. Your group will need to choose an area that will not be mowed regularly. Most wildflower seeds can be spread just by throwing them out and lightly tapping them into the soil with your foot. Be sure to give the seeds some water so they will start to grow. By spreading seeds, the group can beautify a large area for years to come.

❀ Create Your Own
Your JMG group can have fun creating its own unique leadership/service learning project.

For a child to be certified as a Junior Master Gardener, one individual and one group activity should be completed for each section/teaching concept in this chapter. Your JMG group should also select one leadership/service learning project for this chapter to complete.

Facts and History
GROUP ACTIVITIES

INDIVIDUAL ACTIVITIES
Mr. Appleseed
Prized Peanuts
Pomanders
Global Fruit
JMG Web

Products
GROUP ACTIVITIES

INDIVIDUAL ACTIVITIES
Jammin' Juice
Grape Bake
A Better Butter
Journal
JMG Web

Growth, Development and Growing Techniques
GROUP ACTIVITIES

INDIVIDUAL ACTIVITIES
Making Peanuts
Ripening Wrap
Designer Apples
Avocado Seed Soak
Attractive Snacks
Journal
JMG Web

Leadership/Service Learning Projectss

fruits and Nuts

facts and History

Although you have probably raised vegetables, it is a little harder to grow fruits and nuts. Fruits and nuts differ from vegetables in that most vegetable plants grow in one season, then die after they produce vegetables; the plants that grow fruits and nuts need to grow more than one season before they can produce edible food.

Plants that die after one season are called annuals. Plants that can live and grow year after year are called perennials. Most fruits and nuts are perennials. Some fruit trees, such as apple trees, must be a few years old before they can make fruit. This section covers fruits and nuts, their growth and the products made from them. It also explains how to plant trees as Johnny Appleseed did, make your own peanut butter, and create designer apples.

ACTIVITIES

❧ Dr. Fruit

Objective:	To research the origins and relevant information about fruits and nuts.
Time:	45 minutes.
Materials:	Reference materials, Dr. Fruit page (in the Appendix)

List the following foods for the junior gardeners and ask how many of them have eaten apples. Write the number beside the word Apple. Have a volunteer child continue to poll the group to find out how many of the gardeners have eaten each fruit.

✓ Apple	✓ Avocado
✓ Banana	✓ Blackberry
✓ Blueberry	✓ Cherry
✓ Fig	✓ Grape
✓ Grapefruit	✓ Orange
✓ Kiwi	✓ Lemon
✓ Lime	✓ Mango
✓ Papaya	✓ Peach
✓ Peanut	✓ Plum
✓ Pear	✓ Pecan
✓ Raspberry	✓ Strawberry
✓ Walnut	

Assign each gardener to become an expert on one of the fruits or nuts listed. Distribute copies of the Dr. Fruit page. Have each gardener choose a different fruit or nut to research and complete the page using the reference materials. The students may also check the JMG web site at *www.jmgkids.org* for more information on the fruits and nuts listed on the previous page. Have them create a poster, mobile or some other presentation method and share the information they learned with the JMG group.

In the Classroom

Have the students use the information they learned from their poll to create a graph of the five "Most Commonly Tasted Fruits and Nuts," "Least Commonly Tasted Fruits and Nuts" or any other data they want their graph to represent. The children could also poll the group again for other information to graph, such as Most Popular, Least Popular, Most Commonly Eaten in the Past Week, Sweetest, etc.

Linnaeus' World Wide Names

Objective: To understand the origin of scientific names.
Time: 45 minutes.
Materials: Linnaeus Name It page (in the Appendix).

Ask the gardeners if any have ever heard someone speak in another language. Make a list of all of the different languages they can think of (English, French, German, Chinese, Spanish, Japanese, Portuguese, etc.). Ask them if they could talk with someone from another country if they did not speak the language.

Tell the gardeners that one thing that stays the same in any country they might visit is their own name. Have them write down their full formal names. Under their names, have them write names that different people call them, such as nicknames. Have them underline their last name and explain that their last name refers to a group of people who are alike because they are related.

Explain that more than 200 years ago, a scientist named Carolus Linnaeus began giving names to all the plants and animals in the world. He came up with a way to create names that would be the same everywhere in the world. Tell the gardeners that Linnaeus gave things a name with more than one part, just as they have a name with different parts: a first, last, and sometimes a middle name. He put into groups plants or animals that were related and gave them a special name for being in that group. For example, watermelons, squash, and cucumbers are all in the Cucurbita group because they all grow on a vine and have similar flowers and leaves. The names Linnaeus created can have seven or more main parts, but most people use only the last two as the plant's name.

Tell the gardeners that they will group and name things the way Linnaeus did. Distribute copies of the Linnaeus Name It page. They should cut out the pictures and look for something in the groups of images that can split the group in half. Have them think of a name that describes each group (for example: rounds and corners.) Next, have them create another category to break each group into smaller groups (round dots and round lines, corner stars and corner crisscrosses). Finally, have the gardeners break the last group into even smaller groups and add the last name part. See the example below.

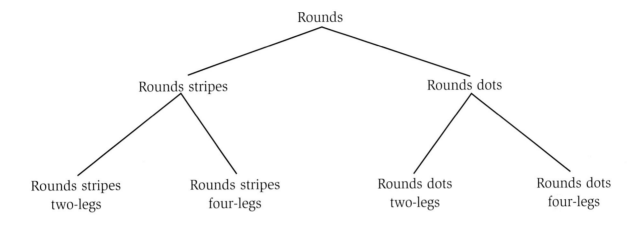

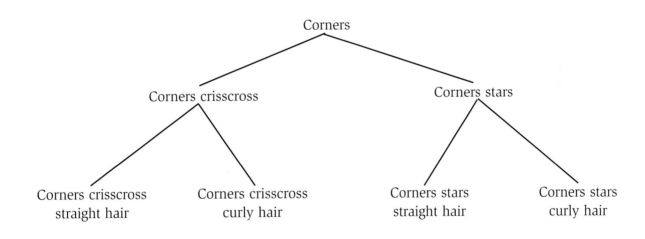

Explain that when Linnaeus gave something a name, the first part of the name included more relatives; the next name included fewer relatives. Show them that "Rounds" includes more relatives, while the name "Round Stripes Two-Legs" has more name parts and includes just two members.

❧ Botanical Wood Prints

Objective: To make a replica of a historical wood press.
Time: 1 hour.
Materials: Potatoes, plastic knife and spoon, ink pad or paint.

Ask the gardeners what they would do if they drew a wonderful picture and wanted to copy it for other people. (They could redraw it or use a copy machine.) Tell them that about 500 years ago, before printers or copy machines were invented, people had to think of other ways to make copies. Explain that one of the first ways to make copies was by using presses, which worked like rubber stamps. (You might show them a rubber stamp, and how it is inked and then pressed on paper to make a picture.) Tell them that the first stamps were carved from wood and that some of the these first presses depicted plants. These are called botanical wood presses; the pictures they made are called botanical wood prints.

Tell the gardeners they will make a print, but because it takes special tools to carve wood, they will carve their presses from potatoes! Ask each gardener to choose a fruit or nut to make a print of. Each should make a simple sketch of what the print will look like. Cut the potatoes in half length-wise and give each student one half. Have each student use a plastic knife and spoon to carve away the flat side of the potato to create an image.

Have the students press their potatoes into the ink and then onto blank sheets of paper. To make the wood print even more authentic, have the gardeners look for the scientific name of the fruit or nut to label under the print.

❧ A Bushel and a Peck

Objective: To gain an understanding of nontraditional measurements.
Time: 45 minutes.
Materials: Pencils, crayons, paper.

Ask the gardeners if they have ever followed a recipe. Ask them what part of the recipe tells how much of an ingredient to add. Have them call out different measurements they might see in a recipe (cups, quarts, tablespoons, pints). Explain that when you measure something by filling up a container, the amount is called the volume.

Tell the gardeners that when fruit is sold to stores or restaurants, it can't be transported in cups or quarts, because those containers are too small. Fruit is sold in big basket-sized amounts called bushels. Stores that don't want a whole bushel can buy a smaller amount, called a peck.

Explain that it takes four pecks to equal one bushel. Have the children create an illustration that shows a basket full of apples, oranges, avocados or some other fruit. The basket should be labeled with the word BUSHEL; beside that, they should draw four smaller containers and label each with the word PECK.

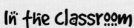

In the classroom

For an extended lesson on measurement, have the students practice converting measurements, including bushels and pecks. Have them use the information on the Bushel and a Peck conversion page (in the Appendix) to convert measurements of bushels, pecks, quarts, pints and cups.

🌾 Fruit and Veggie Lab

Objectives: To learn what a fruit is and to explore the difference between technical definitions and social customs.

Time: 1 hour.

Materials: A variety of of fruits and vegetables, paper plates, a knife for the leader to use to cut produce.

Ask the gardeners to list all the vegetables they can think of; write them on the board or on a chart. Make a second list of all the fruits they can name. Ask children how they know what a fruit or vegetable is. What makes a fruit a fruit, and a vegetable a vegetable?

In botanical terms, a fruit is the reproductive part of the plant that develops from the ovary of a flower and produces seeds. These seeds produce the next generation of plants. Many plant parts that we eat and commonly call "vegetables" are really fruits. A true vegetable is a food that comes from any part of the plant other than the flower, such as the roots (carrots and radishes), developing shoots (asparagus), stems (celery), or leaves (cabbage and lettuce).

Activity: Is it a fruit or Veggie?

Show the gardeners some produce items from the grocery store or garden. For each one, ask whether, in botanical terms, it is really a fruit or vegetable. (If you can cut it open and see seeds inside, as with tomatoes, cucumbers, squash and eggplant, it is a fruit. If it has no seeds, it comes from a part of the plant other than the flower and is a true vegetable.) Tell the gardeners that when they eat broccoli and cauliflower, they are actually eating flower buds before they have a chance to develop into fruits. So, what are they—a fruit, vegetable, or something in between?

On the vegetable chart, mark all the vegetables listed that are really fruits. The children may be surprised at the number of "fruits" they eat, botanically speaking. When all the produce has been labeled, cut it up and serve it as snacks while you lead the follow-up discussion below.

Follow-up Discussion: Customs

Ask the gardeners why they think many fruits are called vegetables. The distinction is based on social customs. Over time, people disregard some rules and distinctions, and use social preferences instead. As people become more accustomed to the social preference and less aware of the technical rule, the social preference gradually becomes a new rule, or custom, even though it may not be based in fact.

Chapter 6

The vegetable/fruit question has several explanations, depending on whom you ask. According to fruit and vegetable growers, the difference is based on how a crop is grown. Vegetables are annuals—which means they are planted, grown and harvested all in one year—and are planted in rows in fields. Fruits are perennials—which means they grow and produce fruit over many years, rather than just one—and are grown on trees. The only exception is strawberries, which are perennials like fruits, but are normally grown in fields like vegetables.

Another explanation of the distinction between fruits and vegetables concerns when the item is eaten. According to social customs, vegetables are foods eaten with a main meal, whereas fruits are sweet treats to be eaten for dessert. Therefore, tomatoes, squash and eggplants are considered vegetables because they are eaten as part of the main meal.

In 1893, the discussion of fruits versus vegetables even went to the Supreme Court. The case concerned tomatoes. As vegetables, they were taxed at a lower rate than fruits, which were considered a luxury item. The Supreme Court apparently thought social customs were more important than botanical distinctions, because they decided that tomatoes were vegetables. The line between fruits and vegetables has been fuzzy ever since.

The exact time and reason why many fruits began to be called vegetables is unclear, but one thing is for sure: A lot of fruits are masquerading as vegetables on our dinner tables! Tell the gardeners that the next time someone tells them to eat their veggies, they may need to look again to see if they are really fruits!

Products

Think of all the wonderful foods we get from fruits and nuts. What would the world be like without raisins, juice or peanut butter and jelly? Fruits and nuts give us many tasty, healthful snacks that we enjoy every day. This section explains how to make some of these products.

ACTIVITIES

✿ Snooty Fruit

Objective: To identify various fruits and nuts using the sense of smell.
Time: 15 minutes.
Materials: Various fruits and nuts cut or shelled, paper, pencil.

Hold up several fruits and ask the children to identify them. Challenge them to accomplish a more difficult task: to identify fruits using just their sense of smell.

Have the gardeners number from 1 to 5 on a blank sheet of paper. They should close their eyes as you hold a fruit or nut under their noses. Next, have them try to guess what it is they smell and write the name of the fruit beside that number. Also, have them rate the smell as good or bad by putting another number, from 1 to 5, beside their guess. They should rate the smells that really appeal to them with a higher number.

When the children have finished, have them call out their guesses before you show them each fruit they smelled. Ask them if they were surprised by some of the smells and guesses they made.

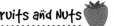

❧ Apple-ing Appearance

Objectives: To create an instrument to evaluate apples by two visual characteristics, and to contrast the results with an evaluation based on taste.

Time: 15 minutes.

Materials: Apples of at least two colors and three varieties, knife, paper, crayons.

Before this activity, cut the apples into bite-sized chunks (enough for each child to sample each type) and store them in three separate numbered containers. It might be helpful to fill the containers with water to preserve the apples' color.

Ask the gardeners to describe an apple. List some of the words they suggest. Now ask them to describe the shape of an apple; list some of those words as well. Have the gardeners draw a picture of a perfect apple.

Tell the students they will judge apples today. Tell them you will show them different apples, and they should decide which is the best. Ask the group to come up with three ways to look at an apple to find the best one. For example, an apple could be judged on color, shape, size, shine, lack of blemishes, or whatever else they decide. Write the three characteristics they choose on a chalkboard or poster.

Have the children fold a piece of paper into fourths. In three of the sections, they should write all three judging characteristics. Place three types of apples on a table and have the gardeners judge each type, one at a time. Each apple is judged in one section of the paper. The children should draw stars beside each characteristic to rate each apple: one star if it is poor, two stars if it is good, and three stars if it is excellent. After they all have finished rating the apples, have them count the total number of stars they gave to each apple. Poll the group to find out which apple was judged the best.

Discuss with the children what made that apple receive the highest score. Next, have them predict which apple they think would taste best. In the fourth box on their papers, have them write the numbers 1 to 3. Distribute the chunks of the three varieties and tell the gardeners to rate each apple's flavor. After they have finished, poll the group to find out which apple the gardeners thought tasted the best.

Often, gardeners choose red apples as the most attractive and predict that those will also have the best taste. But the green apples are usually rated as tasting best. If this happens with your group, explain that when we choose fruits and vegetables, we base our decisions on appearance. Tell them to be open to tasting new fruits and vegetables, even those that do not look as if they will taste good.

In the classroom

When children are thinking of descriptive words for apples, use this opportunity to teach them about adjectives. The students could be asked to think of at least three adjectives to describe something in their classroom or garden area. They could write down those words and have the rest of the class try to guess what each child is describing. Each child could reveal his or her adjectives one word at a time to narrow down what is being described as the others guess.

Taste Test

Objective: To evaluate fruits based on color, texture, taste and smell.
Time: 15 minutes.
Materials: Fruit Taste Test page (in the Appendix), five plates, five containers, five kinds of fruit.

Before this activity, cut up each of the five types of fruit into bite-sized chunks (enough for each child to sample each type) and store them in five separate containers.

On the chalkboard or poster, write these words: color, texture, taste and smell. Tell the gardeners that they will evaluate several different fruits. See the Veggie Taste Test activity on page 176 for instructions on the terms and how they will rate the food. Explain that texture is how the fruits feel in your mouth and against your tongue. Ask the gardeners if they have ever eaten foods with a smooth texture, and ask for an example. Do the same for crunchy, grainy, lumpy, sticky and other textures.

Have five plates of different fruits. Put a label beside each plate, such as A, B, C, D, E, so that the children do not know what the fruits are. Distribute the Fruit Taste Test page. Explain that the children should circle a number beside each characteristic to give it a "grade." One is the lowest score and five is the highest.

After the gardeners have finished tasting and rating each fruit, they should find which had the highest ranking. Have them try to guess what fruit was on each plate before you reveal the answer. Ask the children if any fruits were rated high that they did not know they liked.

❧ JMG Jam

Objective:	To make homemade jam.
Time:	30 minutes.
Observation:	One week.
Materials:	Crushed berries, sugar, 1 package of powdered pectin, freezer containers or canning jars.

Strawberries, blackberries and raspberries work best for this activity. They should be at room temperature before mixing. The jam is best when eaten within a few days after it's made, but it will keep for 2 to 3 weeks in the refrigerator or for up to a year in the freezer. Discuss with the children the rules of kitchen safety. Have them take turns helping to follow the JMG Jam recipe.

JMG Jam

2 cups berries
4 cups sugar
1 package powdered pectin
Cold water

Rinse and drain the berries. Remove the stems from the berries and crush the berries in a large mixing bowl. Add the sugar, mix well, and let the mixture stand for 10 minutes. Stir occasionally.

Dissolve the pectin in cold water. Bring the solution to a boil and boil it for 1 minute, stirring constantly. Add the pectin solution to the jam mixture and stir for 3 minutes.

Pour the jam into three plastic containers, leaving ½ inch of space at the top of the container to allow for the jam to expand. Cover the containers and let them stand at room temperature for 24 hours. This makes about 5 cups of jam.

If the jam does not set, allow it to cool further in a refrigerator. Point out to the gardeners that the jam's consistency changes in the cooking and cooling process.

❧ Johnny's Appleslop

Objective:	To create homemade applesauce.
Time:	15 minutes.
Materials:	Johnny Appleseed story, several apples, cinnamon, brown sugar, knife, slow cooker.

Ask the gardeners if they have ever heard of Johnny Appleseed. Have them tell you what they know about the story. Ask them if they think Johnny Appleseed was a real person or just a legend.

There are many children's book versions of the Johnny Appleseed story. Read one aloud and have the gardeners describe Johnny. Ask them again if they think Johnny Appleseed was a real person or just a legend. You can tell them that he was in fact a real person. Explain that Johnny Appleseed was his nickname because of his work. His real name was John Chapman and he was born September 26, 1774. Tell the gardeners there is more information about him in the JMG Handbook.

Explain that even though Johnny Appleseed was a real person, some of the stories about him are made up. As stories are retold, details are often added or exaggerated to make them more interesting. John Chapman is considered a folk hero.

Tell the gardeners that one thing you have heard is that Johnny not only liked to plant apple seeds, but he also liked to eat apples. One of his favorite treats was called Appleslop. Ask the gardeners if they would like to make some today.

Tell them that stories tell of Johnny wearing a burlap sack as a shirt and an old pot as a hat. That pot is what he would use to simmer Appleslop in. Help the children follow the recipe below.

As Johnny traveled along the countryside, he could carry only a little with him, including just a few basic cooking items. Rather than use measuring spoons and cups, he just threw in a little of this and a little of that. Follow the recipe as best as you can. It's easy to make this dish, which is like applesauce, only better.

Johnny's Appleslop

Several apples cut into quarters with the core removed
   (leave the skins on—Johnny liked it that way)
A couple handfuls of brown sugar
A few sprinkles of cinammon
A splash of water

Simmer all the ingredients in a slow cooker for 2 hours on a low setting and 2 hours on high. Stir it a few times while it cooks. Serve it while it is still warm.

While you are cooking, the room will be filled with the aroma that Johnny loved. Sometimes Johnny stirred in honey, or nuts. For an extra-special treat, he would spoon his appleslop over some homemade vanilla ice cream. Be creative and add your favorite ingredients.

Growth, Development and Growing Techniques

Fruit starts out as a flower. When pollen from a flower touches the pistil of a flower, it could make new seeds. As the new seeds form, fruit grows around them to protect them. The seeds in that fruit could grow to make a new plant, which can grow seeds of its own. People who want to grow their own fruit or nuts must know the secrets to help those plants grow. This section will help the gardeners learn how fruit and nuts grow and what to do to help them.

ACTIVITIES
❧ A Fruit's Life Rhyme

Objective: To understand the life cycle of plants.
Time: 15 minutes.
Materials: Rhythm sheet (in the JMG Handbook and Appendix).

The fruit we get from plants
all start as flowers.
Big or small, short or tall,
all have attracting power.

Flowers attract a visit
from a bird, bug or bee.
They buzz around from flower to flower
all for a nectar fee.

A flower's job is to make a seed
to grow a baby plant.
Without help, it won't do that job;
by itself, the flower just can't.

The pollen from the flower
must be carried to a mother.
It takes a bug to move it there,
or a bird, wind or others.

When the pollen gets to the pistil
it can become a brand-new seed.
How can the seed find a place to grow?
it becomes animal feed!

Seeds can grow a thick coat—
bright colors, reds and blues.
The color covering those little seeds
is yummy, juicy fruit.

The fruit can be eaten
or just fall to the ground.
Either way it ends up in the soil,
to the new home it's found.

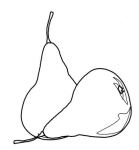

Then it sprouts to become a new plant
and grows a new flower.
Could be big or small, short or tall,
but will have attracting power.

❧ Fruit Frenzy

Objective: To become familiar with how fruits develop around seeds.
Time: 30 minutes.
Materials: Several fruits, knife, Fruit Frenzy! page (in the Appendix), paper.

This is an explorative activity. It can be messy, but fun. It is a good idea to choose fruits that form seeds in different ways and are different colors.

Distribute copies of the Fruit Frenzy! page. Hold up a piece of fruit that has a single seed, such as an avocado or peach. Have the gardeners draw an outline shape of the fruit in the first box on the Fruit Frenzy! page. Tell them that in the middle of almost all fruit grows a seed. Have them predict how many seeds are in the fruit and write it in the Guess circle.

Cut the fruit in half and show the gardeners the half with the seed. Have them draw the seed in the outline. Ask them how many seeds were in that fruit and if all fruits have the same number of seeds. They should write the number of seeds in the Actual circle.

Explain that their job is to open a fruit, look at it, draw a picture of the seeds in the remaining boxes on their page and predict the number of seeds each will contain, just as they did in the first box. Divide the children into groups of three and give them enough fruits to complete their pages. Help the gardeners by beginning a cut into the fruit and allowing them to tear it open with their hands. Have them count the seeds and record the number on the Fruit Frenzy! page. As they complete the page, they should spread the seeds on newspapers and allow them to dry for future use.

❧ The Zones

Objective: To identify the appropriate plants for a particular temperature zone.
Time: 40 minutes.
Materials: United States or state map, globe, Temperature Zone Map (in the Appendix).

Ask the gardeners to tell you what country and state they live in. Have them point it out on a map. Explain that on that map, north is at the top. Distribute the zone maps. Have the gardeners label north at the top of the map. Ask if they know the other main directions. They should also label east, south and west.

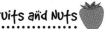

Arborday.org Hardiness Zones

Zone	Avg. Annual Low
2	-40° through -50°
3	-30° through -40°
4	-20° through -30°
5	-10° through -20°
6	0° through -10°
7	10° through 0°
8	20° through 10°
9	30° through 20°
10	40° through 30°

©National Arbor Day Foundation 2002

Ask the gardeners to show you the North Pole and South Pole on the globe. Explain that those are the coldest places on our planet. Show them that the line circling the middle of the globe, called the equator, marks the warmest places on Earth.

Then ask the gardeners to describe a cactus—what it looks like and what conditions it grows in. Ask them what would happen if a cactus were taken to a cold, wet place to grow. Introduce the idea that different kinds of plants like to grow in certain places.

Explain that some plants die if they get too hot, others when they get too cold. On the Temperature Zone Maps, have the gardeners find the zone they live in and then check the key to find the coldest it usually gets there. Point out that the zones farther north on the map get much colder than those to the south. Explain that this information is very important when choosing plants and trees to grow in their area.

In the Classroom

Take the group outside in the morning and have the students note the position of the sun in the sky. Have a child hold a compass to locate north. Share with the students that there are secrets to finding the main directions outside, such as the fact that the sun rises in the east. Have the students point in the direction of the rising sun, and then check their compass to see how close it is. Explain that as the sun passes through the sky, it heads west and finally sets in the western sky. Tell the gardeners to "Never Eat Soggy Worms" as a way to remember the main directions (N, E, S, W).

Play a direction game, in which you call out directions quickly and the students point in that direction as fast as they can. Try calling out several directions in a row. As the children gain their sense of direction, try calling out intermediate directions: northeast, northwest, southeast, southwest.

Chapter 6

🌿 Just Chill

Objective: To simulate a winter environment to provide the chilling requirement for an apple seed.

Time: Initial activity: 20 minutes.

Materials: Apples, knife, paper towel, sealable plastic bags.

Explain to the gardeners that different fruits and nuts grow in different places in the world. Citrus fruits, such as oranges, grapefruit and limes, grow in warmer parts of the world; other fruits, such as apples, must grow in places that have cold winters.

Tell the gardeners they will begin an experiment that will take months to finish. Bring in apple halves for the kids to enjoy. As they finish eating, have them save the seeds and allow them to dry.

Explain that some fruit trees that normally grow in areas with long, cold winters must have a certain number of hours of cold temperature before they sprout—these are called the chilling hours. Apple seeds need between 1,000 and 1,600 chilling hours before they can germinate. Ask the gardeners how they can fool the apple seeds so the seeds will "think" they have been through a cold, damp winter and begin to germinate. Have the gardeners fold two paper towels into squares and dampen them. Several seeds should then be placed between the towels. The towels and seeds can then be sealed in a plastic bag and placed in a refrigerator. Every couple of weeks, the seeds should be checked to see if they've sprouted. Once the sprouts begin to form roots, they can be planted in a large pot. These apple seedlings can be cared for by the gardeners or given away in remembrance of Johnny Appleseed.

Ask the gardeners how many hours are in a day. Have the older gardeners divide 24 hours into the 1,600 chilling hours required to find the number of chilling days that would be.

🌿 Fruit Factory

Objective: To use reference materials to choose a fruit or nut tree to plant or transplant.
Time: 20 minutes.
Materials: Poster, markers, Temperature Zone Map (in the Appendix), JMG Handbook.

When asked, many children will say that fruits and vegetables come "from the store." Tell the gardeners that you know how they can make their fruit right outside at a fruit "factory." They will help give a gift to other JMG'ers and people in the community for the future. This activity gives them an opportunity to select a fruit or nut tree appropriate for their area and plant it.

Their job is to choose a fruit or nut that they would like to grow, but that probably will not begin making fruit for some time. On the board or a poster, list all the fruits or nuts the gardeners would like to grow. Have them find out the growing area for each. This might be obtained from the gardeners' previous research information, reference materials, or the county Extension office. Have the children eliminate the trees that cannot grow in their area, and then vote on which tree to plant.

If money is available to buy a tree, learn more about its planting requirements from a county Extension agent or a local nursery that will sell (or possibly donate) it before obtaining one. If you cannot acquire a tree, have the group start a "factory" from scratch by planting and nurturing a seed.

Remind the gardeners that this tree is not for them; it's for the community. If they make sure it gets a good start, that tree could be living when they are their grandparents' age.

LEADERSHIP/SERVICE LEARNING PROJECTS

Your group should choose at least one of the following activities to complete.

❀ **Share and Care Fruit Basket**
Your JMG group can create a fruit basket featuring fruits and nuts from your state and deliver it to someone in need.

❀ **Create Your Own**
Your JMG group can have fun creating its own unique leadership/service learning project.

For a child to be certified as a Junior Master Gardener, one individual and one group activity should be completed for each section/teaching concept in this chapter. Your JMG group should also select one leadership/service learning project for this chapter to complete.

Vegetables and Herbs

Planning the Garden

If any JMG'ers in your group have ever worked in a garden, they probably know that the area didn't just become a garden by itself. It took a lot of planning and work. They may have had to pick the right spot and decide what to plant. They may also have had to decide where the plants would grow in the garden. The work you do with your JMG group in this section will help them plan ahead and make their garden a success.

ACTIVITIES

❧ Home Sweet Home

Objectives: To understand the criteria for selecting a good garden site and to choose an appropriate site based on those criteria.

Time: 30 minutes.

Materials: Site Evaluation form (in the Appendix), pencils or pens, clipboards if available.

When selecting a garden site, it is important to consider several factors. A garden should:

✓ Be easily accessible from where the group will be working

✓ Receive 6 to 8 hours of bright sunlight each day

✓ Be located near a water source

✓ Have loose, well-drained soil

✓ Have nearby access to space to store tools.

     The better a site meets these criteria, the fewer problems you will face later.

Have the gardeners tell you what they like about their house. Ask them what makes it a comfortable place to live. Write the letters P L A N T on the board (from Chapter 1) and tell them that each letter represents something plants need to survive (place, light, air, nutrients, thirsty). Ask them what kind of place a plant would want to live in.

Distribute copies of the Site Evaluation form. Take the group outside and stand in the shade of a tree. Ask them if it would be a good spot for a garden. If possible, take them to where water stands or near a ditch and ask them what they think about that location. Next, take the group to an area more isolated or distant from the work area and ask them if that is a good place. Discuss the pros and cons of each site.

Review with the gardeners that the garden location should be sunny, the ground well-drained, and the location easy to get to. Tell them to consider two other factors:
✓ Is there a place nearby to get water?
✓ Is there a place to store tools?

Give the group three possible locations to consider and have the members evaluate each site using the Site Evaluation forms.

Discussion Questions

1. Which site is most suitable for your group garden? Why?
2. Did everyone in your group recommend the same site? What were some of the other gardeners' reasons for recommending other sites?

Preparing an area for planting requires help from adults. Whether you use landscape timbers to raise the bed above the soil level or 5-gallon buckets to create cylinder gardens, adults will be needed to move heavy materials and work with the JMG'ers in the garden.

A successful JMG garden project should instill a sense of ownership in the gardeners as well as in parents and other community members. People develop a sense of ownership by contributing to the initial stages of a project. Incorporate a few work days into your schedule, and invite the gardeners' parents and other adults from the neighborhood to help with the project. This provides an excellent way to cultivate relationships with the gardeners in your group as well as with their parents. It will also enhance the shared feeling of ownership—the beginnings of any successful team.

❧ Make Your Pick

Objective: To select appropriate crops for planting based on the season.
Time: 20 minutes.
Materials: Planting Charts (in the Appendix).

Before this activity, gather information about the planting dates for the vegetables listed in the Planting Chart, because planting dates of different vegetables vary with each location. You can get information from your county Extension agent, seed packets, reference materials and on-line information.

Ask the gardeners if they have ever eaten a slice of watermelon in December. Explain that some plants grow better at certain times of the year. Divide the gardeners into pairs. Distribute copies of the Planting Chart from the Appendix.

Point out the column listing planting dates for each vegetable. Mention that the column under Planting Date is blank, and explain that even within their state, the planting times for each vegetable differ depending on the location. Distribute the planting dates you have gathered and have them fill in the boxes with planting dates for each vegetable. Have them cross out any vegetable with a planting date more than 2 weeks before today's date. Explain that planting these vegetables too early or too late may not leave enough time to produce a crop before it gets too cold or too hot. Some vegetables tolerate cold better than others. These vegetables are better suited for fall and winter gardens. Vegetables that grow best in warm weather, such as watermelon and peppers, are better suited for spring and summer gardens.

Explain that some vegetables (and other types of plants, too) grow best when planted as seeds; others grow best from already-growing plants called transplants. Have each pair of gardeners select two crops from the planting chart, one planted by seeds and one planted by transplants (listed as a T under Planting Depth on the chart).

In the Classroom
Have each student research one of the vegetables he or she will plant. The students could use reference materials to learn about the crop (Veggie Research page in the Appendix) and make a collage about it. For example, the collage could include magazine pictures of the plant, its products, the season it grows in, what continent it originated from, etc.

One Community Service project your group might do is to "Plant a Row." See the Leadership/ Service Learning Projects section at the end of this chapter.

Chapter 7

❧ Small and Large

Objective: To understand space considerations when planting seeds.
Time: 45 minutes.
Materials: Seeded paper towels (from Paper Towel Gardening on page 165), measuring tape, masking tape.

After the gardeners have decided what seeds and transplants to plant in the group vegetable garden, ask them how the garden should be arranged. Ask what will happen if all of the seeds are planted very close together. Guide them in a discussion to help them remember from the PLANT activity that plants need a place to grow. If plants are planted too close in that place, they might not all get enough light or water. Tell them that small plants such as radishes and carrots can be planted closer together than larger plants such as tomatoes or beans.

Ask four gardeners to volunteer to be plants. They will be radishes. Have them sit on the floor beside each other in a square, stretch out their arms and spread their fingers as if they are growing toward the light. Ask six other gardeners to be tomato plants and crowd around the radish plants. Have the tomatoes stretch their arms up and grow, too. Ask the radishes how they feel. Are they getting enough light? Explain that roots from the tomato plants will probably grow all around the radishes, soaking up their water. Ask the rest of the group to suggest ways to rearrange the tomatoes and radishes so that they have enough space, but not so much space that weeds can grow.

Next, add a few more gardeners to the plant group. They will be medium-size spinach plants. Have the class help rearrange the plants again. After the gardeners have decided on an appropriate arrangement and spacing for the plants, ask them which side of the garden is the front. Explain that gardens are arranged for visual appeal as well as vegetable spacing and shading. Taller plants are usually planted at the back, medium-size plants in the middle, and shorter plants in the front. Have them rearrange one last time with these considerations in mind.

Take the gardeners out to the garden site. Have them measure the length and width of the garden and then return inside to recreate the space with masking tape on the floor. (Hint: One standard-size floor tile is 12 inches square.) Next, have them take their seeded paper towels and place them within the area of the tape. Explain that this will be a garden jigsaw puzzle. Have the gardeners work together to arrange the paper towels as they will be laid out in the garden.

Remind them to use the information they just learned: Smaller plants are grouped together in the front, medium-size plants in the middle, and taller plants along the back edge. Once the gardeners have decided on a layout, have them make a map on paper recording the order and pattern of the towels. They can then use the map as a guide to plant the towels outdoors in the garden plot.

When planting the seed mats in the garden, have the gardeners practice their mapping skills by following the map they made inside. One by one, have each place a paper towel seed mat in the garden and cover it carefully with a shallow layer of soil so that the seeds are planted at their correct depth as specified in the Planting Chart in the Appendix. (The planting depth will vary from $\frac{1}{8}$ inch to 1 inch, depending on the type of seed being planted. In general, seeds are planted two to four times as deep as they are wide. It is very important to plant seeds at the correct depth. If planted too deep, the seeds may not sprout.)

In the classroom

After the students have measured the garden area, have them use graph paper and sketch the garden area to scale. The easiest method is to allow 1 square foot of garden space to equal one square on the graph paper. The students can draw the shape of the garden on their papers, then draw in the grid for each paper towel. They could create symbols to represent the different plants and include a key on the side of the map to show which symbols go with which plants.

Your group could use a compass to find north and have the garden map include the cardinal directions.

🌾 Rules are Rules

Objective: To establish rules for the garden that make it a safer place to learn.
Time: 45 minutes.
Materials: Poster board or construction paper, markers.

As the garden is being developed, ask the JMG'ers to compile a list of garden rules to make the garden a safer place for people and plants. Brainstorm rules with the gardeners. Pose the following situations to guide them in developing rules for their garden.

Garden Situations
✓ Someone is running through the garden and accidentally runs over and crushes a plant.
✓ A girl is playing with a shovel by spinning it in the air and hits another student in the back.
✓ A student is walking on the timbers edging the garden, and stumbles and falls into some plants.
✓ The JMG group arrives at the garden to find that the tools were left out all night. The wheelbarrow has been stolen and some of the other tools are beginning to rust.
✓ A boy is pulling weeds and raking the soil. In order to pull up a weed, he lays the rake down with the sharp tines pointed up. A girl walks by and steps on the rake. The tines stick into her sandals and cut her foot.
✓ A team is watering the garden. They are talking to each other while the leader is telling them how much plant food to put in the watering can. The group is not listening and puts too much plant food on the plants. Some of the plants die.

Try to keep the garden rules to six or seven or fewer. Have the gardeners decide on the most important rules from their lists, and have them work in partners to make a Garden Rules poster. Encourage the gardeners to make their posters colorful and to include illustrations if they'd like.

Discussion Questions
1. What happens if you are an adult and you break a rule such as running a stop sign in your car?
2. Why do we have rules?
3. Do you think our garden would work as well if we had no rules?

Chapter 7

❀ Schedule It

Objective: To establish a schedule so all gardeners help water and weed the garden.
Time   20 minutes.
Materials: Monthly calendar, markers, pen.

For this activity, the gardeners must have access to water regularly. Gardeners can water a small garden by hand. To water it by hand, the JMG'ers can fill half-gallon or gallon jugs at a sink or hose and carry them back and forth to the garden. If the water must be carried far or from inside, use a cart or wagon to take several jugs at a time. Show the gardeners how to water slowly at the base of the stem and water the plants one by one. Soaker hoses are also effective ways to irrigate. Made of spongy, porous material, they release water slowly along the length of the hose. The hose can be laid alongside a row of plants and the spigot turned on until the water soaks into the soil thoroughly.

Discuss with the JMG'ers the garden's maintenance needs. Do their plants need care every day? Will their garden need to be watered and weeded every day? Explain that even though the garden probably will not need care daily, it is a good idea to check the plants often for weeds or signs of drying.

Tell the gardeners they will make a schedule to make sure that everyone helps take care of the garden regularly. Divide the gardeners into groups, and have each group choose a name for itself. These will be the garden maintenance teams that take turns caring for the garden.

Show the gardeners a calendar to be used as a master schedule. Prompt the gardeners to list tasks that are most needed—watering, fertilizing and weeding. Tell them they will need to check the plants every other day to see if they need watering. The best way to check for watering needs is to stick a finger into the dirt about 1 inch deep (about the length from the tip of the finger to the first knuckle). If the soil is dry at that depth, it needs to be watered. Have a student draw in a blue water drop on every Monday, Wednesday and Friday to signify a watering day. Next, have a member of each team take turns and write his or her team's name by a watering day. That team will be responsible for watering on these days.

Mark one of the watering days each week as a fertilizer day also. Have each group sign up to fertilize 1 day each week by marking a symbol to represent fertilizer on the schedule. An easy way to fertilize is to use a water-soluble fertilizer. It can be spooned easily into jugs as the gardeners fill them, and the plants will be fertilized as they are being hand-watered.

Granular fertilizer worked into the soil does not need to be applied every week. If you use it, read the label carefully and schedule applications according to the directions.

The last task to be added to the schedule is weeding. To keep ahead of weeds, this needs to be done once or twice a week. Explain that weeds steal the water, food, light and space that the vegetables need. Decide on a symbol for weeding and pick a day of the week to do it. Have the groups again take turns signing up for weeding times. Demonstrate how to pull a weed, and explain that they should try to pull up all the weed's roots when they pull up the plant. Caution the gardeners to avoid mistaking weeds for the plant seedlings they are trying to grow.

In the Classroom

Have the class use a calendar to answer the following questions:

1. How many months are in a year? Name them.
2. How many weeks are in a year?
3. How many days are in a year?
4. How many watering days are in a year?
5. How many weeding days are in a year?
6. How many fertilizing days are in a year?

Some Like It Hot

Objective: To distinguish between warm- and cool-season crops.
Time: 30 minutes.
Materials: Some Like It Hot pages (in the Appendix).

Before this activity, reproduce the Some Like It Hot pages, front and back, to create learner cards. A heavy paper or tagboard works best.

Remind the gardeners that plants like to live in certain conditions, and just as the children could not live outside in a cold winter, some plants cannot live and grow where it is too hot or too cold. Distribute the Some Like It Hot pages. Have the gardeners divide into partner groups and cut out the cards from the pages. They should read the descriptions for each plant and sort them into two piles: WARM SEASON PLANTS and COOL SEASON PLANTS. Next, have them shuffle the cards and put them into one pile, picture side up. The learners should then take turns drawing a card, looking at the picture and stating whether it is a cool- or warm-season plant. If the child is correct, the card may be kept. If not, reinsert it into the pile. When all cards are drawn, the gardener with the most cards knows which like it hot and which like it cold.

Growing Techniques

Many of your gardeners have heard others talk about having a green thumb. They should know that it means those people are good at growing plants and know how to keep their plants happy and healthy. The JMG'ers have already learned some of these concepts in earlier sections of the Junior Master Gardener program. In this section you will help them learn more ways to make their thumbs green.

ACTIVITIES

❀ Cylinder Gardening

Objective: To grow vegetables and herbs successfully in containers.
Time: 30 minutes.
Materials: Five 5-gallon plastic buckets (buckets that once contained food or cleaning products often can be obtained for free), soilless potting mix, seeds/transplants, fertilizer, brown paper bags or newspaper (four to five layers).

Before this activity, have the plastic buckets cut into cylinders. Parents, Master Gardeners or other volunteers can help prepare the buckets. Have the volunteers remove the handles from the buckets and cut off the bottoms. (A bow saw, saber saw or hand saw works well.) The buckets should then be cut in half to create two 7-inch-long cylinders.

Tell the gardeners that even people without garden space can plant a garden. Explain that vegetables and herbs can be grown even in the parking lot. Show them the cylinders. Explain that cylinder gardening is a way to garden without the hard work of digging the soil.

Have the gardeners find an area that is flat and receives at least 6 to 8 hours of sunlight each day. Place the 10 cylinders in two rows, 3 feet apart to allow the plants to grow to full size and to give the gardeners room to work. If you place the cylinders on concrete, lay brown paper bags or newspapers on the ground and set the cylinders on them, with the wider ends on the ground.

Have the gardeners fill each cylinder with soil. Mix 3 tablespoons of slow-release fertilizer with the soil. Plant the seeds and transplants.

Be sure to have the gardeners check the cylinders so they don't dry out, because plants growing in cylinders are less likely to retain moisture than those growing in the ground. Refer to the information on seed packets or a planting chart (in the Appendix) for more information on when to plant. Also have them check the plants for signs of insect damage and keep the area free of weeds.

In the Classroom

Review variables and constants with the students. Discuss with the class ways to experiment with variables using cylinder gardening. Remind them that a variable is a single thing done differently in one plant or group of plants than in the others, to see if plants grow better because of the different treatment. The students should decide which variable to study. They could try using different amounts of soil, using different amounts of water, adding mulch, or using slow-release fertilizer versus weekly feeding.

Explain that scientists who study plants learn much about how to grow plants better just by experimenting with different techniques. Tell the students that two seeds from the same seed packet might grow differently, because each new plant is unique, just as each person is unique. Sometimes a plant grows taller just because it is a taller growing plant from the beginning. It is a good idea to have more than one cylinder testing a variable.

🌸 Paper Towel Gardening

Objective: To create seed mats and transplant templates to help organize and lay out the garden.

Time: 30 minutes.

Materials: Paper towels that are about 1 foot square, seed, school glue, markers, masking tape, Planting Charts (in the Appendix).

Team up the gardeners and give two paper towels to each pair. Help them choose two plants to grow from their planting charts. Encourage them to choose one plant started by seed and one plant started by transplant. They will use the paper towels as spacing and layout guides when they plant in the garden. Have the partners write their names, their plant's name, and the word short, medium or tall to describe the plant's height on each towel. Tell them they will plant their seed in a mini-garden the size of the paper towel, and ask them how many plants can grow in that little space.

Ask the gardeners why they cannot grow many plants in a small space. What problems might the plants have? Have the gardeners locate their vegetable in the Planting Chart in the Appendix and determine how many plants can be grown in the space the size of a single paper towel.

The directions that follow apply to both seeds and transplants. If the gardeners are planting seeds, they can glue them directly to the paper towel. If they are planting transplants, they can use the paper towel as a template and mark a spot or cut a hole in the towel to show them where to plant when they are in the garden later.

If the chart shows one seed per towel, the gardeners should paste a single seed (or make a mark) in the very center of the towel. If the chart shows four seeds per towel, the gardeners should fold their towels in quarters to make four equal sections. A seed can then be pasted in the middle of each of the four sections. If a plant calls for nine seeds per towel, the gardeners should fold the paper towel into thirds and then into thirds again, and paste a seed into the middle of each of the nine sections that result. (The children may have difficulty folding the towel into thirds, and may require some help.)

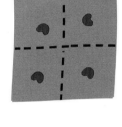
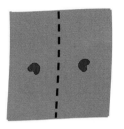
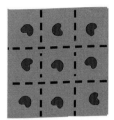
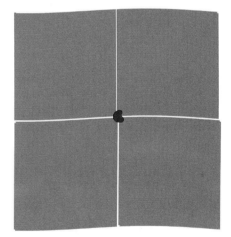

Explain that some seeds just don't germinate. It is a good idea to glue 1 or 2 extra seeds in each spot. If all the seeds do come up, all but one can be picked away. Explain that this is called THINNING. In this way we choose the strongest looking plant to keep growing. When the gardeners remove the extra plants, have them pinch off each seedling at the base so the roots of others aren't disturbed as when pulling the plant out.

Some plants such as squash grow large enough to require four squares, or towels, of space. Gardeners who choose crops that need this much space should tape four towels together to make a larger square (or a full sheet of newspaper can be substituted for this large square) and then paste the seed in the center. It is a good idea to use a paper tape, such as masking tape, and not glue the seed directly over the tape. If the garden space is small, you may need to limit the number of gardeners who choose plants requiring four paper towels.

In the Classroom

This would be a good activity for introducing fractions. Have the students fold a piece of paper in half and use a light color crayon to shade one half. Ask them to tell how many sections are on that piece of paper (two). Tell them to write the number 2 in the middle of each section. Now ask them how many of those sections are colored (one). They should write the number 1 above the 2 on the colored section. Explain that this is called a fraction. The bottom number is how many pieces there are in all; the top number is the number of pieces you are talking about.

Repeat the folding and coloring on other sheets to represent fourths, sixteenths, thirds and ninths. Have them write the fraction on each section of their folded papers.

❧ Tender Transplants

Objective: To understand the benefits and practice techniques of transplanting.
Time: 30 minutes.
Materials One flat of purchased transplants (these can be vegetable transplants for the garden, or flowers such as marigolds or pansies), spoons or trowels for digging.

Explain that some garden plants grow more successfully if they are planted as already-growing plants, or transplants. They may be difficult to grow from seed because they require special conditions for sprouting, or they may simply take a long time to grow. Some vegetables, such as tomatoes and peppers, are best grown from transplants. This allows the gardener to grow and harvest a crop before the weather gets too hot or too cold. Ask the gardeners if there are any other ways plants can get into a garden. (How do weeds get there?) Tell them that, just as people can move to live in a new home, plants can, too.

Cut up the flat so that everyone has a plant in a small plastic container. Tell the gardeners that the plants are very fragile, so they must be handled very gently, as if each were a small kitten or puppy. (Young stems are especially fragile. If crushed, they cannot transport water and nutrients from the roots to the leaves and fruit, and the plant will die.)

There are just four steps in transplanting a plant into the garden. Take the gardeners out to the garden, and demonstrate the steps for them before they transplant their own plants.

1. Dig a hole.

The hole should be about twice the size of the container. It is easier to work with the soil if it is slightly moist when it's time to transplant.

Chapter 7

2. Remove the plant from its container.

Make a V with your fingers and gently slide them around the base of the plant, cupping the root ball. Turn the plant upside down and pat the bottom of the container. The root ball should slide out of the container. If it does not, gently squeeze the container. Continue patting and squeezing until the plant roots loosen and slide out. (If the seedling is growing in a "plantable" pot made of peat, both the pot and the seedling are planted in the new container.)

If the plant is very root-bound—that is, if the roots have formed a solid white mat around the edges of the container—you will need to break up the mat by pulling or slicing the roots on each side of the container. This allows new roots to form and grow into the surrounding soil. (Plants that are root-bound have outgrown their pots and should have been transplanted sooner. This is common with purchased transplants because they grow quickly.)

3. Plant it.

Plants should be planted at about the same depth in the soil as they were in their original container. The root ball should not stick up out of the soil, nor should it be sunk down into the soil so that the stem is buried. However, do cover the root ball with a shallow layer of soil—about ¼ inch—to keep the root ball from being exposed and drying out. Fill in around the roots with soil, and gently pat down the soil (don't pack too hard) to remove air pockets.

4. Water it.

Water the newly planted transplants using a gentle spray. Thoroughly soak the soil several inches deep, so that the water reaches the roots of the transplant. (Demonstrate that a light sprinkle only dampens the surface and doesn't reach the roots where it is needed. Deep watering is important.)

Check the young plants daily for the first week to make sure they do not wilt or dry out.

In the Classroom

Have the students fold a sheet of notebook paper into fourths. They should number each box. Have them write the steps to transplanting a plant. Tell them to be very specific. When they have finished, have volunteers read to you the steps as you follow their directions. Follow them as if you have never transplanted before. For example, if they say "dig a hole," intentionally dig a hole the wrong size or if they say "water it," sprinkle a few drops of water on the leaves. Have the students go back and add information to their steps. Challenge them to be so specific that anyone could follow their directions.

✿ Weed Mats

Objective: To create a natural form of weed control.
Time: 25 minutes.
Materials: Newspapers, scissors, soil.

Ask the gardeners what makes a plant a weed. Explain that a weed is just an unwanted plant—what some people view as a weed, others might consider to be a beautiful garden plant. Tell them that people have different opinions about what a weed is, but if their vegetable garden has too many extra plants, the vegetables will not have enough water, sunlight and space to grow well. Ask them how to keep weeds out of a garden. List the gardeners' ideas (pulling the weeds, spraying weed killer, etc.) and discuss the pros and cons of each idea.

Have the gardeners tell you what plants need. Remind them that weeds have those same needs. Explain that the best way to get rid of weeds is to prevent them from growing in the first place. Tell them that they will cover the soil with something to keep weeds from getting some of what they need and to keep them from growing. Ask them for their ideas.

Tell the gardeners that they will place weed mats in the garden to help keep weeds out. The weed mats are sheets of newspaper. Have each JMG'er take a few sheets of newspaper to the garden. They can cut a slit in the side of the sheet to slide the paper around a plant stem. The paper can then be anchored down by sprinkling it with water and then putting a thin layer of soil over the paper. Tell the gardeners that eventually the newspaper will break down and become part of the soil. Explain that sometimes people put a plastic weed mat down over the soil in the garden and cut small openings for the vegetables. They might want to experiment to see which is most effective.

In the Classroom

Hold up a picture of a flower. Ask the students to raise their hands if they think it is a flower. Tell them everyone knows this is a flower, and you could look it up in the dictionary to prove that it is a flower. In other words, it is a fact that it is a flower. Now ask the students what is the most beautiful flower they have ever seen. Ask if anyone can prove that the flower he's thinking of is the most beautiful flower in the world. Tell them that different people sometimes think differently about some things. These ideas are called opinions.

Ask the students to think of things they have learned about plants—facts they could prove. List several of the suggestions they make. Go through the list and have them decide if each is truly a fact or not. Next, have them do the same with flowers, vegetables or anything else. Distribute the Plant Fact and Opinion page (in the Appendix) and have the students complete it independently.

🌿 Season Extenders

Objective: To create an environment for plants.
Time: 25 minutes.
Materials: Pencils, markers, drawing paper.

Remind the gardeners that certain plants grow well only when it's cool, and others only when it's warm. So what happens if they have a warm-season plant that is doing well, but a cold front is coming?

Tell the gardeners that they will be inventors. Their job is to invent something to help a warm-season plant continue to grow even after the weather starts to cool. Ideally, your gardeners have a particular warm-season plant, such as a tomato or pepper, to use as the model for their invention.

Remind the gardeners of a plant's needs and allow them time individually to sketch ideas with pencils and paper. Encourage them to be creative with their sketches and design their inventions using any materials they like. As they are working on their creations, allow them to team up with a partner for several minutes and share their ideas. Allow them to decide whether to continue working by themselves or with partners. Have them include more details and label the parts and materials of their finished products. Give the gardeners as much time as they need to complete diagrams of their inventions.

Once all the gardeners have finished, have them share their inventions with the rest of the group and invite feedback from the others on whether all the plant's needs are met and if the plant is protected from the cold. Have the gardeners vote on one or two designs that might work best and ask them if they would like to gather the materials and actually create their inventions to extend the season.

Explain that plants can also be fooled into getting a head start on the season by planting seeds indoors a few weeks before the weather outside begins to warm. This allows the plant to grow and mature more quickly and produce more vegetables for their table.

Harvesting

When a gardener or farmer works hard to grow the fresh vegetables and herbs that will end up in your kitchen, the work isn't over until the food is harvested. How does a gardener know when to harvest vegetables? How do we know which vegetables at the grocery store are fresh and ready to eat? The work you do with your JMG group will help them learn how vegetables and herbs are harvested and how they can choose the best ones at the grocery store.

ACTIVITIES
❧ Garden to the Table

Objective:	To determine harvest time of various garden vegetables.
Time:	Variable.
Materials:	Variable.

One of the most exciting times for any gardener is the harvest. As your vegetables near harvest time, ask your JMG'ers how they will know when it is time to pick them. The length of time from planting to harvest varies, depending on the crops grown. The guide below will help your group know when to harvest.

Vegetable	When to Harvest
Carrot	The orange tops start showing
Radish	Radishes are quarter-sized
Lettuce	Any time before it flowers
Cabbage	Head is at least softball-sized and firm
Broccoli	Head is tight green buds
Cauliflower	Head is tight and white, not separated
Potato	Plants begin to turn yellow and wither
Green beans (to harvest pods)	Beans are 3 to 4 inches long and crisp
Green beans (to harvest seeds)	Seeds in the pods are hard and dry
Tomato	The fruit develops its full color
Summer squash	Fruit is 5 to 8 inches long
Peppers	Anytime
Pumpkins/gourds	Ground-spot or "belly" is orange-yellow
Okra	Okra pods are 3 to 5 inches long
Greens	At any usable size
Eggplant	Fruit turns from shiny purple to dull purple
Peas	Pods are plump and the seeds are almost full-size
Southern peas	Pods change color and seeds are full-size
Onions	Thumb-size for green onions, baseball size for bulb onions
Cantaloupe	Fruit "slips" from the vine
Melons	Fruit produces a hollow, dull sound when thumped

Be sure to discuss proper washing and preparation methods for vegetables. Washing vegetables thoroughly is a good habit to develop. In general, soak greens in water for a few minutes to remove soil particles and any small organisms living deep in the leaves. Rinse fruit and root crops, and scrub them lightly with a vegetable scrubber if needed.

Beauty Contest

Objective: To rank vegetables based on appearance.
Time: 25 minutes.
Materials: Fresh vegetables.

Before this activity, put the gardeners into groups of four and assign them to bring a particular vegetable to the meeting on the day of this activity. One group might bring tomatoes, another eggplants and another onions. Any vegetable will work, as long as it is available in stores and the gardeners have access to them.

Ask the gardeners if they or their parents have ever judged a beauty contest. Next, ask if they or their parents have ever bought fresh vegetables. If they say they have, tell them that they probably decided whether or not to buy the vegetable based on how it looked.

Explain that their job is to look at the vegetables the groups brought and rank them from first to fourth place. Have the gardeners give each vegetable a name. Allow them to pick up and examine a vegetable closely before ranking it.

As they rank the vegetables, they should write a reason for placing one over another. They might state that one was larger, had better color, had fewer blemishes or any other criterion. Once everyone has decided on the ranking, have each gardener share his or her decision with the rest of the group to see if all agreed. Those who came to different conclusions should explain their criteria, and the group should decide together on an order for first through fourth. Have members from each group share their prize-winning vegetable and its beautiful qualities with the rest of the class.

Seed Bank

Objective: To collect seeds from various fruits and vegetables.
Time: Ongoing.
Materials: Seeds from vegetables, paper towel, airtight containers.

After the beds are in place, one ongoing gardening expense is to buy plants and seeds each season. Your JMG'ers can create their own "bank" of seeds to collect a variety for their home or JMG garden.

Tell them that they will begin a JMG Seed Bank. Explain that a seed bank is like a regular bank—they can't just take seeds out, they also must put seeds in. Saving seeds is a way to collect seeds that cost nothing. Most people throw away the seeds of vegetables they eat.

Instruct the gardeners to keep some seeds next time they eat veggies or fruits with seeds inside, such as tomatoes, peppers and watermelons. The steps: Remove the seeds from the food and allow them to dry on a paper towel. Label and store the seeds in an airtight container in a cool, dry place (a refrigerator is perfect). Seeds encased in a fleshy pulp, such as tomatoes, require a little more effort but work very well. Squeeze the tomato pulp into a jar half-full of water. Then shake the jar vigorously to help separate the seeds from the pulp. Place the mixture in a strainer and spray it repeatedly with water to further remove the pulp. After the pulp is removed, the tomato seed can be allowed to dry on a paper towel also.

Explain to the gardeners that the seeds are offspring of the parent plants. They will be similar to the parents just as people are similar to their parents. Soon the group will have a large assortment of seeds to trade and use in gardens.

Nutrition in the Garden

"You are what you eat!" is another saying your gardeners may have heard before. They will learn that it doesn't mean if they eat a tomato they will become a tomato—it just means that if they eat healthful foods, their bodies will be healthy. In this section they will learn about the foods they eat and ways to be healthy.

ACTIVITIES
✿ The Pyramid

    Objective: To use the Food Guide Pyramid to plan balanced meals.
    Time: 25 minutes.
    Materials: Food Guide Pyramid (in the Appendix), Pyramid Menu page (in the JMG Handbook).

Ask the gardeners if they have ever seen a pyramid. Tell them that the most famous pyramids in the world are in Egypt and they are believed to be more than 4,000 years old. Have them describe the shape of a pyramid. Explain that the reason the pyramids have lasted for so long is that pyramids are built with such a wide base. This wide base is what provides such a strong foundation. Ask them if they have ever heard of the Food Guide Pyramid. Have them turn to the Food Guide Pyramid in their handbook. Then ask what the food pyramid tells them. Use the following questions to lead a discussion of how to "read" the Food Guide Pyramid:

I. What is in the largest section of the pyramid?
2. What is in the smallest section at the top of the Food Guide Pyramid?
3. Why do you think that certain foods are in big sections and some are in the smaller sections? (The bigger sections show foods that we should eat more of; the smaller sections show foods we should eat less of.)
4. What are examples of foods from each group?

5. Who should follow the Food Guide Pyramid carefully?
   (All people should follow the Food Guide Pyramid, but those who have to work their bodies hard, such as athletes, must be even more careful to put the right foods in their bodies.)
6. Fruits and vegetables have their own sections on the Food Guide Pyramid. Where are nuts?
7. How do we know how much of each food group to eat?

Distribute copies of the Pyramid Menu page. Assign the gardeners to make a menu including all the recommended servings for a full day. The gardeners can create a list, make a restaurant-style menu containing the meals, or cut pictures from magazines or newspapers and glue them on paper plates. They can complete the assignment either with the group or at home with their parents.

🌺 Food Safety

Objective: To understand and practice food safety rules.
Time: 30 minutes.
Materials: Cutting board, stickers.

Ask the gardeners these questions
1. What should you do before crossing the street?
2. What should you do if a stranger asks you to go with him or her to look for a lost puppy?
3. What should you do if you see a small child playing with matches?

Have a JMG'er tell you what the word "safety" means. Ask the gardeners why they want to be safe. Explain that if they are being safe, they are protecting themselves from danger. Next ask if they should be safe with their food.

Explain that being safe with food means doing things to make sure their food isn't dangerous and doesn't make them sick.

Share with them the saying:
J ust clean the surface.
M ake sure to wash your hands.
G arden veggies should be rinsed—gets rid of soil, bugs and sand.

Explain that if germs such as bacteria and other organisms such as fungi end up on food, they can make people sick. Tell them that germs are everywhere and that the best way to be safe is to make sure that whatever goes into their mouths is very clean. Ask them to list everything they have touched that day—desk, books, doorknobs, dishes, countertops, sinks, playground ball, etc. Ask if they would want to touch their mouth to any of those items. Explain that because we often eat food with our hands, germs from all those items they listed might end up in their mouths. Stress that washing hands is vital in preventing illness.

Ask them why it is important to wash the vegetables they grow or even vegetables from the store. They probably have had to throw away a piece of candy because it fell on the ground; the vegetables from the earth have been on the ground for quite some time. Washing and sometimes scrubbing helps remove all sorts of things—soil, insects, tiny organisms too small to be seen and even some chemicals such as pesticides and fertilizer.

Hold up a cutting board and ask the gardeners to tell you what it is. Explain that a cutting board is one of the best hiding places for germs. Tell them that sometimes people use the same board to cut up both raw meat and fresh vegetables. Explain that it's a good idea to use different cutting boards for meats and vegetables. Have the JMG'ers learn the safety saying on the previous page and repeat it to each other.

Distribute stickers. When the gardeners go home, their job is to place those stickers on areas where germs could be hiding and that must be cleaned regularly. Have them make a list of the items they put stickers on and bring that list to the next meeting to share.

Label Reader

Objectives: To learn the importance of eating breakfast and how to make healthful food choices by using information from food labels.

Time: 30 minutes.

Materials: Label Reader page (in the Appendix), samples of food labels from breakfast-type foods (such as cereal, breakfast bars, toaster pastries, fruit juice, eggs and milk), sample labels for fruits (apricots, grapefruit, kiwifruit, mangoes, raspberries)(in the Appendix), Food Labeling page (in the Appendix).

Ask the gardeners if they have ever heard the saying, "Breakfast is the most important meal of the day." Then have them explain why breakfast is the most important meal of the day.

Next, ask the group to tell you what makes a car run. The obvious answer should be gas or fuel. Ask what happens if you forget to put gas in the car. The car eventually runs out of gas and won't run anymore.

Explain that breakfast means "to break the fast." Think about the time that passes between when a person goes to sleep and wakes up the next morning. Point out that for some people, that may be 6 to 10 hours—or even longer. Even though the person was sleeping, his or her body was still working. As a result, the person's "fuel" or energy levels get low. Explain that if you don't re-fuel your body with food when you wake up, you may be running on empty. Ask, "Does a car run on empty?" Ask if a person can run on empty (maybe, but not very well).

Next ask the JMG'ers the following questions: "What if I don't have any gas to put in the car? Can I put other things in a gas tank to get the car to run?" The answer is no. If you don't put the right fuel in the car, the car won't run.

Explain that one difference between people and cars is that people can run on different types of fuels or foods. Still, some types of fuel or food help us run better than others.

Next show different types of foods commonly eaten at breakfast (cereal and milk, juice, eggs, etc.).

Chapter 7

Ask the students, "If I have many different fuels to choose from, how can I decide which helps my body run at its best?"

Distribute a sample of a food label and identify its components. Explain to the group that food labels tell people what they are eating. The labels explain how much fuel and nutrition are in the food. Have the group look at the percentages of each nutrient on the label. The percentages tell us how much of a certain nutrient is found in a serving. Try to select foods that provide more than 20 percent of calcium, iron, vitamin A, vitamin C and fiber. If you eat these foods, over a day's time you are likely to meet the goal of 100 percent. Fat, cholesterol and sodium play important roles in the body, but should be eaten in smaller amounts.

Now, have group members look at the breakfast labels you brought. Have them use the labels to rank the nutrients from highest to lowest daily percentage.

JMG'er home activity: Have each child choose five foods commonly found at his or her home. Using the Food Labeling Chart provided in the Appendix, rank the foods in order of highest to lowest for each nutrient, based on the food label. Bring the list back next time to share with the group.

❀ Veggie Taste Test

Objective: To evaluate vegetables based on color, texture, taste and smell.
Time: 15 minutes.
Materials: Veggie Taste Test page (in the Appendix), various vegetables.

Before this activity, cut up five types of vegetables into bite-sized chunks (enough for each gardener to sample each type) and store them in five separate containers.

Write the words COLOR, TEXTURE, TASTE and SMELL on a chalkboard or poster. Tell them they will evaluate several veggies. Make sure the gardeners understand each of the terms and how to rate the food. Explain that texture refers to how a vegetable feels in their mouths and against their tongues. Ask the gardeners if they have ever eaten foods with a smooth texture, and ask for an example. Do the same for crunchy, grainy, lumpy, sticky and other textures.

Have five plates, each with a different vegetable. Put a label beside each plate that does not show what the vegetable is, such as A, B, C, D, E. Distribute copies of the Veggie Taste Test page. Instruct the gardeners to circle a number beside each characteristic to give each veggie a grade. One is the lowest score, five the highest.

After the gardeners have finished tasting and rating each veggie, they should add everyone's scores to find which had the highest ranking. Have them try to guess what was on each plate before you reveal it. Ask if any vegetables were rated high that they did not know they liked.

✿ Junk Food Blues

Objective: To understand the value of healthful eating habits by learning a song.
Time: 15 minutes.
Materials: Song sheets (in the Appendix and JMG Handbook).

Sing the song first so the students can pick up its rhythm. Have the gardeners join in. Challenge them to create additional verses. The group could also perform the song for a younger group of children.

Junk Food Blues

I had a big hunger, wanted a tasty treat.
Grabbed some soda and chips—started to eat.
I ate the whole bag of chips, drank a can of soda, too.
Now I ache somethin' awful—I got the low-down junk food blues.

Chorus:
I'm tired, my stomach hurts, my head and body ache.
I'm eatin' too much junk food, too many fries and sugar flakes.
Now I want some good food—something my body really needs.
Payin' attention to what I eat—each time before I feed.

Now I forgot my own song, when I fixed today's lunch.
I packed some nachos, cookies and candy bar that crunched.
Same thing happened when I ate, 'cause healthy food I did not choose.
I got that achy, tired feelin'—the low-down junk food blues.

I'm tired, my stomach hurts, my head and body ache.
I'm eatin' too much junk food, too many fries and sugar flakes.
Now I want some good food—something my body really needs.
Payin' attention to what I eat—each time before I feed.

Gotta big game today, playing the Mighty Bears.
Eatin' some candy, lots of sugar, my plan to get prepared.
Wanna be fast and win against this other guy named Fred.
But the candy didn't work, I lost, my face is sweaty and red.

I'm tired, my stomach hurts, my head and body ache.
I'm eatin' too much junk food, too many fries and sugar flakes.
Now I want some good food—something my body really needs.
Payin' attention to what I eat—each time before I feed.

The game was over and they had won, they were happy but I felt sick.
Saw Fred munchin' on some grapes and some orange carrot sticks.
Then I knew it was my fault, I finally got a clue,
'Cause all the junk that I ate before, gave me the low-down junk food blues.

Vegetable Products

Most people think vegetables are just for food. Fresh, canned and frozen vegetables are probably a part of most of your meals, but veggies also have other uses. Vegetables come from many different parts of the world. Vegetable products keep people clean, make them prettier, provide decorations for their homes, and make their soft drinks taste better. Vegetables are even used in pepper sprays that police use to catch criminals.

ACTIVITIES
✿ Garden Veggie Casserole

Objective: To make a casserole with vegetables from your garden.
Time: 30 minutes.
Materials: 2 yellow squash, 1 white onion, 2 tablespoons Parmesan cheese (grated), ½ teaspoon basil, 1 zucchini, 1 tomato, ½ teaspoon seasoned salt, ½ teaspoon thyme.

Have your JMG'ers create a special treat while teaching them how to prepare a healthful dish. Ideally, they could use vegetables harvested from the JMG garden or bring in ingredients from home. Although the younger students might be unable to slice the vegetables, they can help by cleaning them and measuring the other ingredients.

Slice all the vegetables. Have the students place the sliced vegetables in an oven-safe pan and mix in all other ingredients. They should then toss the mixture lightly and cover it. Bake it in the oven for 20 to 25 minutes at 350 °F.

In the Classroom

Pose this question to the class: "What if we needed twice as much of the casserole because we had invited many people to eat with us? How much of each ingredient would we need to include?" Have the students double the recipe. Have them calculate the ingredient amounts for half as much.

If the students have trouble visualizing that ¼ is half of ½ teaspoon, have them see how many ¼ teaspoons it takes to fill up the ½ teaspoon. You may further challenge them by having them convert measurements to answer the questions below:

✓ How many ¼ teaspoons are in 2 teaspoons?
✓ How many ¼ teaspoons are in 4 teaspoons?
✓ How many ½ teaspoons are in 2 teaspoons?
✓ How many ¼ teaspoons are in 3 teaspoons?
✓ How many ¼ teaspoons are in 2 half-teaspoons?
✓ How many teaspoons are in 2 tablespoons?
✓ How many ½ teaspoons are in 1 tablespoon?

🌿 Veggie Pizza

Objective: To make a pizza using vegetables from your garden.
Time   25 minutes.
Materials: Vegetables, basil, cheese, oven, pizza crust, sauce and pan. Optional: sauté pan, oil.

One of the most popular foods for children is pizza. This activity takes advantage of pizza's popularity by allowing the JMG'ers to make their own pizzas topped primarily with veggies. You can buy pre-made pizza crust or the gardeners may make their own (pizza crust recipe below).

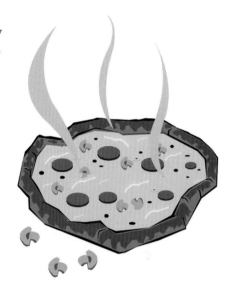

Have the gardeners cover the crust with sauce and sprinkle it with chopped basil and sliced vegetables. Then top it with cheese. Allow them to choose how to prepare the pizza. Although some vegetables are typically part of a pizza, your JMG'ers might also try zucchini, carrots, broccoli or anything else they are growing or like. They might also make individual pizza crusts and pizzas and decorate them with funny faces. Allow them to be creative in exploring these healthful foods.

Bake at 425 °F until the cheese is bubbly. If your group prefers that the vegetable toppings be less crisp and crunchy, sauté them for several minutes in a lightly oiled pan.

Pizza crust

2 cups all-purpose flour
1 cup whole-wheat flour
1 package active dry yeast
1 cup warm water (120 to 130 °F)
2 teaspoons cornmeal

Combine 1 cup of the all-purpose flour, 1/4 cup of the whole-wheat flour and the yeast. Add warm (not hot) water. Beat with an electric mixer for 1 minute, while scraping the bowl. Beat on high speed for 3 more minutes. Stir in the remaining wheat flour. Then stir in the rest of the all-purpose flour. Knead the dough for several minutes on a floured surface.

Preheat the oven to 425 °F. Divide the dough and let sit for 10 minutes. Lightly oil two 12-inch pizza pans and sprinkle each lightly with cornmeal. Roll dough into circles slightly larger than the pan. Place dough in pans and roll in edges. Bake 10 to 12 minutes or until golden brown. Then top with ingredients and bake.

In the Classroom

Before your students begin topping their pizzas, have them plan what they will look like. Distribute paper plates and have the students decorate them to look like their veggie pizzas. Encourage them to include the colors and shapes of the cheese, veggies and crust. On a separate sheet of paper, have each student list names of family or friends they would like to invite over for pizza if they could. Have them count the total number of people, including themselves.

Their task is to divide the pizza into that many pieces. It is a good idea for the children to use a pencil to sketch the lines of cuts on the uncolored side of the plate. They might need to erase and adjust the lines to make each slice the same size. Then the students can cut the paper-plate pizzas into that number of slices, glue them to a large sheet of construction paper and label what fraction the slices are cut into.

Party Confetti Salad

Objective: To make a salad using vegetables.
Time   25 minutes.
Materials: Various vegetables, salad dressing, crackers.

Plan a day for the JMG'ers to bring a couple of their favorite veggies to add to a group salad. Allow them to show what vegetables they brought and tell why they were chosen. As a different vegetable is introduced, explain how it is usually prepared or cut in making a salad. For example, bell pepper must have the insides removed and it can be cut into chunks, slices or rings.

Spend some time discussing the importance of rinsing fruits and vegetables to remove insects, soil, chemicals and tiny organisms. Some people say potatoes should even be scrubbed to remove soil clinging to the skin. Have the gardeners clean their vegetables before preparing the salad.

Allow the gardeners whose vegetables can be cut with a butter knife to do so. After all the produce is prepared, have each pick up a bowl and add all the ingredients desired to his or her salad. Bring crackers and different salad dressings to complement the JMG salad supper.

In the classroom
Make a class graph of the vegetables the students brought. Depending on the grade level, students can create simple picture or bar graphs, or a more complicated pie graph. Assign each student to be the teacher and to list questions they might ask of other students when reading the graph. Compile a list of questions from several students and write them up for the class to answer based on the information in the graph.

Cultural Cooking

Objective: To plan, plant and harvest a theme garden to grow ingredients for a recipe from a different culture.
Time: Variable.
Materials: Garden space, seeds or transplants.

Youth gardens can be built around specific themes. The JMG group can design and create a cultural garden built around a dish from a particular country or region of the world. For example, the gardeners could grow a salsa garden, including tomatoes, onions, cilantro, peppers and garlic. Or they might grow a stir-fry garden of broccoli, red peppers, onion, garlic, peanuts and green beans. As the JMG'ers are designing the garden, its shape can be a part of the theme, too. The stir-fry garden might take the circular shape of a bowl with two lines of bricks coming into the "bowl" to represent chopsticks. When it's time to harvest, the group can prepare the dish for which the garden was grown. For more ideas on theme gardens, visit the JMG web page at *www.jmgkids.org.*

Garden Sponges

Objective: To grow and harvest a crop of loofa sponges.
Time: Initial planting time, 15 minutes.
Materials: Loofa seeds, garden space with area to climb.

Loofas grow in the summer. If your gardeners do not meet over the summer, they might start them at the end of the school year for the new group coming in the fall. You must make sure the loofas receive plenty of water during the summer.

Chapter 7

Tell the JMG'ers that they will grow sponges in their garden. Have them make illustrations of what the sponge plant will look like. After they have drawn their plants and shared the pictures with each other, explain that there really is a sponge plant they can grow; it's called a loofa. It is a vining plant with large yellow blooms.

Explain that vining plants have long stems that grow along the ground or climb up objects such as fences, buildings or even other plants. Loofa seeds can be bought at nurseries or through seed catalogs. For information on seed companies, check out the JMG Web at *www.jmgkids.org*.

The loofa fruit will grow to resemble a very large zucchini. After it has grown to about 12 inches long, your group can remove the loofa and allow it to dry, or let it dry on the vine itself. Once it is dry, have the gardeners pull the skin off the sponge and remove the seeds. The seeds can be traded among your JMG'ers or saved for next season.

Herbal Products

Herbs are plants that have been used for thousands of years for medicines, for seasoning dishes and for their great aromas. Around the world, people from different cultures have planted herbs that can grow well in their area. That's why certain foods from some countries have a special flavor. For example, many Mexican foods include the herb cilantro, which has a unique flavor that makes pico de gallo, salsas and other dishes so delicious.

ACTIVITIES
❧ Touch and Smell

Objective:	To identify herbs based on the senses of touch and smell.
Time:	25 minutes.
Materials:	Paper bags, fresh herbs, paper, pencils.

Herbs are treasured for their diverse scents and flavors. Collect several different fresh herbs. Hold them up to show your group what each is called and allow the students to smell them all. Place each herb in a separate paper bag and number each bag. Have the gardeners write the numbers on a sheet of paper.

Challenge them to put their hands in a bag without looking and go back and write down what they think the herb is. Have them repeat the process, except this time they should close their eyes and smell the herb.

After all the gardeners have written down their guesses, pull out each herb and identify it to let them check their answers.

❧ Herbal Vinegar

Objective: To make and bottle herbal vinegar.
Time: 25 minutes.
Materials: Vinegar, herbs, nonmetallic container, plastic sandwich bags, decorative bottles.

To complete this activity, your JMG'ers must have a source of fresh or dried herbs. The best herbs are those grown in the group's garden. Most herbs grow readily from transplants.

Herbal vinegars have become popular to use in cooking and to sprinkle on salads with a little oil. To make herbal vinegar, your gardeners should harvest some herbs and bruise them by placing them in a plastic bag, then squeezing and twisting the bag. Have them put herbs in a nonmetallic container such as a jar with a plastic lid. An adult should heat and pour hot (but not boiling) vinegar over the herbs. Have the gardeners cover the container and allow the vinegar to steep in a warm, dark place for 3 weeks. Explain that this allows the herbs to flavor the vinegar.

Next, have the group strain the vinegar through two coffee filters. They can do this by putting the filter in a small strainer or a funnel and slowly pouring the vinegar through the filter. They should repeat this process until the vinegar is clear. The vinegar should then be poured into clean bottles that can be corked. Insert a fresh sprig of the herb into the bottle to serve as a decoration. Herbal vinegar can be sent home with students, given as gifts to volunteers who have helped with the garden, or sold as part of a business for your JMG group.

❧ Herbal Bath Salts

Objective: To prepare herbal bath salt wraps.
Time: 25 minutes.
Materials: ½ cup thyme, 1 cup baking soda, 1 cup Epsom salts, 1 cup of your favorite herb, cheesecloth, string.

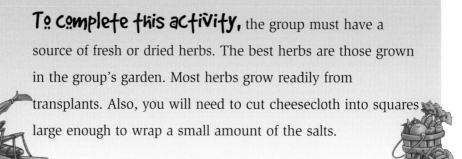

To complete this activity, the group must have a source of fresh or dried herbs. The best herbs are those grown in the group's garden. Most herbs grow readily from transplants. Also, you will need to cut cheesecloth into squares large enough to wrap a small amount of the salts.

Ask the gardeners if they have ever taken a bubble bath; then ask if they have taken a salt bath. Tell them that herbal bath salts added to bathwater are popular because they make a soothing bath and smell wonderful. Explain that special salt called Epsom salt is used to make bath salts.

Have the gardeners place all the ingredients in a large bowl and mix them well. Next, they should measure 2 tablespoons of the mixture and spoon it into the middle of each cheesecloth square. The cloth should then be gathered around the bath salts and tied with string.

These bags will be placed in bathwater or under the faucet while the tub is being filled. This makes a nice, calming bath in which to relax. The salts can be sent home with students, given as gifts to volunteers who have helped with the garden, or sold as part of a business for your JMG group.

Herb Sachets

Objective: To create herbal sachets from dried herbs.
Time: 25 minutes.
Materials: Fabric, needles, thread, dried herbs.

To complete this activity, the gardeners must have a source of fresh or dried herbs. The best herbs are those grown in the group's garden. Most herbs grow readily from transplants. Herbs that work especially well are lavender, rosemary, rose-scented geranium and lemon verbena.

This activity is a good first experience with sewing. For many children this age—both boys and girls—it is a challenge to use needle and thread to create stitches. This is a good way for the JMG'ers to develop their fine motor skills as well as their patience. Because this may be the first time your gardeners sew, it is a good idea to plan to have a few adults to help so that you have one adult for every four to six children.

Tell the gardeners that they will make natural air fresheners. Have them measure and cut a 4- by 6-inch rectangle of muslin. They should fold the fabric and sew the two long sides together. Then have them sew the two short sides, except for a small area in one corner, and turn the pocket inside out. Next, have them fill the pocket with the dried herbs and then stitch it closed. Sachets make small places such as closets and drawers smell nice.

In the Classroom

After the students have measured and cut out the material, have them place notch marks on the fabric at every inch along the length and width. Ask them how many inches long the fabric is and how they measured it. Next, ask them how many square inches it is.

Explain that they can tell how many square inches something is by drawing straight lines across it at every notch mark. Show them how to lightly draw lines across the material to make a grid. Have them count the number of squares to find the number of square inches. Explain that the number of square inches of the fabric is called the area. When they have finished, explain that the shortcut to finding the area of square inches, feet, or anything else is to multiply the length times the width.

LEADERSHIP/SERVICE LEARNING PROJECTS

Your group should choose at least one of the following activities to complete.

❀ JMG Cookbook

In this chapter your JMG group learned about eating more healthful foods. Each JMG'er should find one or two healthful recipes that use vegetables. Parents, grandparents and friends may have special recipes to share. Neatly write or type the recipes. Gather all of the group's recipe pages together and copy them. Also make a table of contents and an illustrated cover and copy them. Bind the book by stapling the pages. Cover the stapled edge with colored tape. Books could be given as gifts from the JMG group or sold as a fund-raiser. The members might give the money they earn to a local charity or use it to buy supplies for the group.

❀ Cafeteria Consultants

Is your group's school cafeteria serving healthful foods? Does the school cafeteria manager want to know what the students' favorite and least favorite meals are? Have the gardeners make a list of several foods the cafeteria serves. They can visit classes and ask students to vote for their favorite foods and least favorite foods. Create a graph to show these foods. Invite your school's cafeteria manager to visit your JMG group to tell you how he or she chooses what foods to serve. Show the graph to the cafeteria manager. If the school serves food that students like and eat, that means less food is thrown away and wasted!

❀ Veggie Fair

Many fairs across the country have competitions for home-grown vegetables. Your JMG group could do the same. Prizes awarded include: Largest, Best Color, Best Shape, Oddest, Fewest Blemishes, or any other award your group can think of. Your group could also hold a fair for recipes. Invite other students from your school or people from the community to be voters for your fair.

Plant a Row

Many people in your community are hungry because they may not have enough money to buy the food they need. You can help them. Your group could contact a food bank in your area and find out what fresh foods they need. Plant a special section in your garden just for the food bank. As vegetables are harvested, clean them and take them to the food bank to help eliminate hunger in your community.

Pyramid Presentation

You know there are some foods you should eat more of and some foods you should eat less of. The Food Guide Pyramid helps us to see how much of each kind of food we should eat. Your group can make a large Food Guide Pyramid poster using bright colors on poster board or bulletin board paper. Explain it to a group of younger children. You might lead an activity in which they cut out food pictures from magazines and decide where they belong on the pyramid.

Harvest Fest

The group can plan and conduct a special harvest festival to celebrate harvest time in your group garden. Activities could include garden tours, taste tests, and scarecrow making.

Create Your Own

Your JMG group can have fun creating its own unique leadership/service learning project.

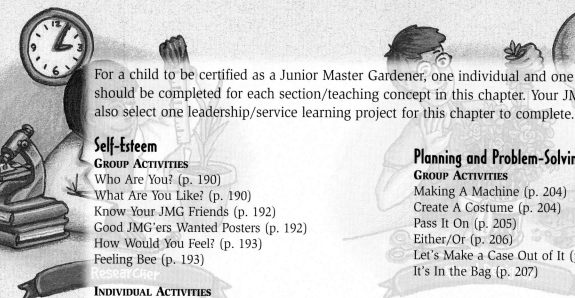

For a child to be certified as a Junior Master Gardener, one individual and one group activity should be completed for each section/teaching concept in this chapter. Your JMG group should also select one leadership/service learning project for this chapter to complete.

Life Skills and Career Exploration

Self-Esteem

A wise old Greek man named Socrates used to walk the streets of Athens saying, "Know thyself." He had learned that if people did not understand themselves, they probably could not understand other people.

Learning about ourselves and others is interesting. Each of us has a different personality, characteristics, experiences, family and ethnic background. It is important to explore these differences.

Understanding ourselves is not easy. Our total self comprises many parts:
✓ A Physical Self, which includes body skills and how we look, such as weight, height, age, color of eyes and hair, etc.;
✓ A Psychological Self, including our feelings, emotions, values and personality traits; and
✓ A Social Self, including how we act and feel with others.

These three aspects combine to make each person an individual. Each of us is uniquely different from any other person.

To be effective in life, we must not only understand but also accept ourselves and others. All people need to feel that they are "okay." We need to feel accepted, important and able to do many things in ways approved of by others.

A positive and realistic self-image involves understanding and accepting one's self.

Ground rules

In Self Esteem lessons, always give the gardeners the option of not answering a question, or not sharing with the group. Never force children to reveal what they do not want to reveal, or ask them about very personal family matters. At the same time, children often can clarify their thoughts and understand themselves better by writing or expressing their ideas and feelings.

There are no right or wrong answers; both the leader and the group should offer positive acceptance as each child explains personal feelings.

ACTIVITIES
❀ Who are you?

Objectives:	To understand the many roles we have in life and begin to understand that each person is unique and special.
Time:	20 to 30 minutes.
Materials:	Paper and pencils.

When someone asks, "Who are you?" our first answer is typically our name. That is because we identify each other by our names. But our names are just one little part of ourselves. We play many roles: brothers, sisters, classmates, children, students, cousins, aunts, uncles and so on. In each of those roles we act differently. For example, we obey our parents and teachers, but we might not obey our classmates.

This activity will help the children recognize all the different roles they play. Although we are alike in many ways, each of us is different from every other person in the world. Ask your group to name some of the ways we are alike or different. Is it good that everyone is different? Why?

Ask everyone to write the numbers 1 through 10 on a piece of paper. Each child should then find a partner, and have one of them ask the question "Who are you?" to the other JMG'er 10 times. Have the gardeners write down their partners' 10 answers. Each "Who are you?" is to be answered with only one statement, starting with the roles they play. Then they can include adjectives describing themselves.

Have the partners switch roles and let the other partner ask the question. Once everyone has finished, have the members introduce their partners to the group using the list of 10 items.

After the activity is finished, give the children their lists.

In the Classroom
Instruct the students to write a descriptive paragraph about their partners. This activity can be used to introduce the word "biography," which is a nonfiction story about a real person written by another.

❀ What Are You Like?

Objective:	To help members examine their feelings, self-concepts and values as they make choices.
Time:	20 to 25 minutes.
Materials:	Typing paper or small pieces of poster board, marker to prepare signs before the meeting.

During the activity, ask such questions as "Are you more like the sun or moon?" The students should decide which one they identify with most and stand next to that word. Ask one student from each side why he or she picked that word. Then have everyone return to the center of the room for another "What are you like?" choice. Members can again choose between the alternatives by moving to the appropriate side of the room. This may be repeated for all the word pairs on the work sheet. Be sure to pick a new student to explain the choice each time.

Sample Choices

1. Are you more like the sun or the moon?
2. Are you more like a roller skate or a pogo stick?
3. Are you more like a Ping-Pong paddle or a Ping-Pong ball?
4. Are you more like a mountain or a valley?
5. Are you more like breakfast or dinner?
6. Are you more like summer or winter?
7. Are you more like a president or a secretary?
8. Are you more like a follower or a leader?

In the Classroom

Have the students create a Venn diagram about one of the pairs of words. They should draw two circles that overlap in the middle. Each circle represents one of the words. In the part that overlaps, they should write words that describe what the two things have in common. In the non-overlapping sections, they should write characteristics that are unique to each word.

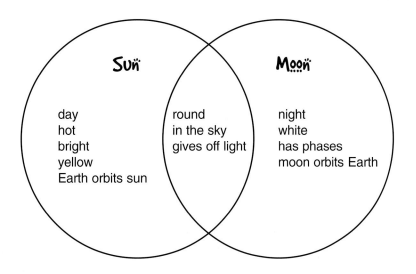

🌼 Know Your JMG Friends

Objective: To accept fellow students and recognize their positive attributes.
Time: 25 to 35 minutes.
Materials: Know Your JMG Friends work sheet (in the Appendix), pencil.

Distribute copies of the Know Your JMG Friends work sheet. Have the gardeners fill out their sheets with information about every other person in their group. Allow them to work on the sheets for 5 minutes. Then ask them to share their responses with each other. Each child should be called on to share a response with the group. If desired, you can post the work sheets.

🌼 Good JMG'ers Wanted Posters

Objective: To confirm each student's uniqueness by having each take his or her own fingerprints.
Time: 20 to 30 minutes.
Materials: Official JMG Group Fingerprint Card work sheet (in the Appendix), ink pads, paper towels, magnifying glasses (optional).

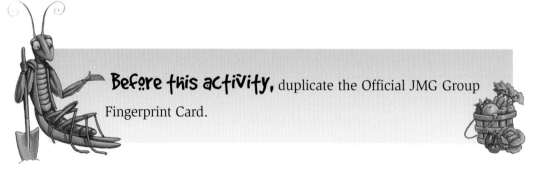

Before this activity, duplicate the Official JMG Group Fingerprint Card.

Show the gardeners how to make a fingerprint by pressing a finger onto an ink pad and then onto a sheet of scratch paper.

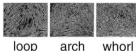

loop   arch   whorl

Have the gardeners work in pairs to complete their fingerprint cards. Provide paper towels so they can wipe the ink off their fingers.

Distribute magnifying glasses and encourage the gardeners to examine their fingerprints more closely. Have them compare their fingerprints and note differences and similarities.

In the Classroom

Have each child make a thumbprint on a large unblown balloon. Have the children blow up their balloons so that the thumbprints enlarge. Fingerprints are characterized by loops, arches or whorls. Have the students evaluate all the fingerprints and classify each into one of these groups.

Students can also learn about how scientists and forensic experts use fingerprints to help in identification and in police work.

❀ How Would You Feel?

Objective: To understand that the way you treat other people is very important.
Time: 20 to 25 minutes.
Materials: How Would You Feel? work sheet (in the Appendix).

This activity will help the children think about how they treat others. They should learn to treat everyone kindly because it's not fun to be treated badly or ignored.

Cut out the instruction cards from the How Would You Feel? work sheet. Tape a card on each child's forehead. Remind the gardeners not to talk at all until directions are given. Separate the class into small groups of four or five children. Give each group a scenario to talk about for 10 to 15 minutes. An example of a scenario might be to have the children plan a container garden. Tell them to decide what types of plants and soil to use, make a schedule of who will care for the garden for a week, and then decide how to divide the crop (vegetables, herbs, or flowers) at harvest.

Once the children have separated into groups, they should read each other's cards and then treat each person as the card indicates. Remind them not to tell each other what the cards say. Have them discuss all the questions that were asked for the scenario.

Reassemble the children and have them discuss how they felt. How did it feel when people ignored you? Did you like bossing someone around? Would you like to be bossed around? Did you like doing all the work? These are just a few of the many questions you could ask after this activity.

Explain that it is very important for the gardeners to consider what they do and say to others. They should always treat others as they would want to be treated.

❀ Feeling Bee

Objectives: To understand that different people have some of the same feelings in certain situations and to express an accepting attitude toward themselves and others.
Time: 20 to 30 minutes.
Materials: Feeling Bee work sheet (in the Appendix), two chairs.

Divide the group into two teams. You may have one gardener keep score on the board. Let the first person on each team sit in the "feelings" chairs. The leader says a word from the Feeling Bee work sheet and the two players think of a situation in which they felt that way (such as: Happy, "I felt happy when I passed my test."). The first person answering gets to remain in the chair. The gardener on other team leaves the chair and is replaced by another teammate. If a team gets loud, give the other team a point. If a youth repeats a situation over and over, you may have to rule that twice is the limit.

In the Classroom
Have the students write a paragraph using five Feeling Bee words. Or, divide the children in groups of four or five and have each group find pictures in magazines or newspapers that describe the words in the Feeling Bee.

In the Classroom
Another activity would be to glue a picture on a sheet of construction paper and have the JMG'ers use the Feeling Bee work sheet to cut out words describing the picture. They could then paste the words next to the picture. Explain that several words that mean the same thing are called synonyms. Then have them find words from the work sheet that have opposite meanings and glue them to the back of the paper. Explain that two words with opposite meanings are called antonyms.

Relating to Others

Making and keeping friends is fun. It can be a challenge, too! It takes time and practice to learn how to be a true friend. Discuss with your group the aspects of friendship below.

When you and your friends get together you usually have fun. Why? Because friends are special people:
✓ Friends care about you and what you do.
✓ Friends enjoy doing things with you.
✓ You can share your ideas, feelings and activities with friends.
✓ You can play games with friends.

Most boys and girls enjoy being with friends. They feel close to their friends and enjoy their companionship. A friend is someone you can talk to, someone who listens to you and is interested in what you have to say.

Friends also try to understand you. They are concerned about how you act and feel. Your friends want you to understand how they feel, too. A friend is someone you like and respect. That friend also respects you. You can trust a friend to:
✓ Help you   ✓ Keep a promise   ✓ Tell you the truth
✓ Treat you fairly   ✓ Stand beside you

Friends also help you learn how to get along with others. When you and your friends get together, you learn how to act in different situations. You learn to share, cooperate and take turns as you play together.

Friendship requires give and take. A friend must learn to share and cooperate with others. You will not always get your way. Try to be understanding of others' feelings in sharing situations. Making friends and getting along with others takes time, practice and patience.

ACTIVITIES
❀ Where's My Fruit?

Objective:	To demonstrate the importance of sharing with friends.
Time:	20 to 30 minutes.
Materials	Several kinds of fruits (one fewer than the number of children).

Have the gardeners sit in a circle. Place the fruit in a bowl in front of you. Starting with one child, ask which fruit he or she wants. Then give him or her the chosen fruit. Of course, one child will get none. You might say, "Oh dear, Linda didn't get any fruit! We must start again." Collect the fruit and repeat the process starting with a different child each time. Do this until each child has been left out once. You might then say, "We have a real problem here. We are hungry and we all want fruit, but we don't have enough! What can we do?"

If none of the children comes up with the idea of sharing, you may have to prompt them. The next problem becomes how to share the fruit. Discuss some different options with the children. Example: All the people who want the apple can share it. However, with this option the "apple eaters" get less fruit than the others. Ask for the children's ideas. The desired result is a fruit salad so that the fruit is shared by all and everyone gets the same amount. After the solution is reached, make a fruit salad, eat and enjoy. Note: When making the salad, allow the gardeners to help as much as possible. Have them wash their hands first. They can easily cut banannas with table knives, break oranges into segments and pull grapes from the stems. Everyone can help put the fruit in a bowl, stir it and dish out a serving.

You can also use this idea to make a trail mix. Remember to have one less ingredient than the number of children, or the process won't work. Use equal amounts of dry cereals, coated candies, peanuts, raisins or anything else that tastes good. Follow the directions given above, mix it in a bowl, and dig in.

❧ Let's Build It

Objectives:	To learn that it is important to cooperate in groups and to discuss ways people can help others.
Time	20 to 25 minutes.
Materials:	Blocks (either a purchased set that you can write on or one homemade from wood scraps), markers.

Before you begin this activity, build a model from the blocks. This model can be as simple or elaborate as you want. Based on the complexity of the design, set a time limit for the JMG'ers to re-create the model. Place it behind a screen so that the children cannot see it from where they are sitting.

Divide the JMG'ers into two groups of four to five children. Allow both groups to select one person to be the "eyes" of the group. Explain that the "eyes" will direct the group in building a structure just like the model. Those two children will get to go behind the screen to see the model for up to 30 seconds. Once they return to their group, the gardeners begin building. One group will be allowed to talk during the building process; the other group will not. As soon as they touch the blocks, begin timing. The "eyes" can return once for another 30-second look during the building process.

Allow the other gardeners to watch the activity. After the structures are completed, ask them what was said and done to help each group cooperate in building its structure. Try the activity again with two new groups. Ask the last two groups to explain if they learned anything from the previous groups that helped them build their structure faster.

In the classroom

Give each child a block and a marker. Explain that just as individual students had to work together to build the structures, individual words must work together to form a complete sentence. Make sure the children know all parts of a complete sentence and all the parts of speech (nouns, pronouns, verbs, adjectives, adverbs, prepositions, conjunctions and interjections). Write the eight types of words on the board and have each child pick types of words to write on a block. For example, if they picked noun, adjective and adverb, they could write cat, cute and slowly. Do this until each side of the block has a word on it. Then put the children back into groups of four to five. Give the groups a time limit to create as many sentences as they can using their blocks. Have one student from each group write down each sentence made. After they finish, the groups can share their sentences with the class.

❧ JMG Cooperation Roster

Objectives: To understand the importance of cooperating in a group and to discuss ways people can help others.
Time: 20 to 25 minutes.
Materials: Chalkboard or large sheet of paper, chalk or marker.

Put a large sheet of paper on the board and have the gardeners tell how groups cooperate. Have them brainstorm ideas for different settings—classroom, sports team, club. Write down all the responses on the paper or board. Ask them if people cooperate differently in each setting. Encourage them to discuss the roles adults play in the school or clubs, as well as how children can cooperate to improve their school, JMG club or community.

🌿 Musical Chairs With a Twist

Objective: To understand that cooperating and sharing in a group is important.
Time: 20 to 25 minutes.
Materials: Chairs, pillows or carpet pads (one per child), music.

Place the chairs, pillows or carpet pads in a circle. Be sure each child in the group has a place to sit. Start the music and have the gardeners move around the circle. When the music stops, they sit.

Start the music again and remove one seat. Stop the music and ask the children to sit as quickly as they can. The child without a seat must sit in the lap of another child. Start the music again and remove another seat. Continue the game until only one seat remains and everyone is sitting on one person's lap. Now that's sharing! This is sure to produce lots of giggles and fun.

🌿 Over and Under

Objective: To understand group cooperation in a competitive situation.
Time   15 to 20 minutes.
Materials: Beanbags or small balls.

Form two teams of five to six players each. Give each team a beanbag or small ball. The first player on a team gives the beanbag or ball to the second player by passing it over his or her head. The second player passes it to the third player by passing it under his or her leg. The teams continue to pass the beanbag or ball over and under until it reaches the last player on the team. When the last player gets the beanbag or ball, he or she must run to the first player. The team finishing first wins.

A variation of this activity would be to have the group stand in a large circle and hold hands. Place a hula hoop on the arms of two people holding hands. The group must pass the hula hoop around the circle without dropping hands.

🌿 Cooperation Countdown

Objective: To demonstrate the importance of cooperating in a group.
Time: 15 to 20 minutes.
Materials: Cooperation Countdown work sheet (in the Appendix).

Divide the children into two teams. Give each team member a large card from the Cooperation Countdown work sheet with a number printed on it. These cards should be large enough to read the numbers from across the room. Call out a series of numbers, such as 5, 9, 2, 1, 10. The children holding these numbers must arrange themselves in numerical order. You can designate ascending or descending order. The first team to arrange itself correctly gets one point. The team with the most points at the end of the game wins.

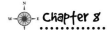

Communication Skills

Communication is the basis of understanding others. It is much more than just two people talking. It is what we say, how we say it, why we say it, when we say it, and what we do not say. It is the expressions on our faces, our posture, and the tone of our voices. Communication includes all the things we do with our bodies that let other people know how we feel or think.

Communication is the process of sending and receiving messages, or exchanging information. It requires two or more individuals and may be verbal (an exchange of words) or nonverbal (including body language, facial expression, tone of voice.)

Communication is vital to leadership; it is the basis for building understanding among individuals and members of a group. Saying what you feel and think about something that bothers you, rather than attacking the other person for it, contributes to sound communication.

Common mistakes made in communication include interrupting, arguing over the facts, blaming each other, attacking personalities, making the other person feel guilty, and sending mixed messages (saying one thing while your facial expressions or gestures indicate the opposite).

Good communication includes good listening, which requires considerable skill. We often think we are hearing the other person, when actually we are not. Almost everyone needs to improve his or her listening skills. You can become a better listener if you practice and want to improve. Communication includes not only listening, but also showing that you hear and understand what a person says.

It is important to remember that the goal of effective communication is not agreement, but understanding. You have communicated well if you have heard and been heard. Although being understood is different from being believed or agreed with, it is essential to communication, which is in turn essential to working out conflicts or disagreements.

Families communicate to handle disagreements, make decisions and set up rules. Communication plays a key role in drawing family members closer or in pushing them apart. People must learn to communicate well in order to get along. To communicate, you must understand others, their words as well as their body language.

ACTIVITIES
✿ Garden Shed

Objective: To develop listening/communication skills.
Time: 15 to 20 minutes.
Materials: None.

Have the gardeners form a circle. One person starts off by saying "In my garden shed I found a. . ." and he/she fills in the name of an object such as a rake.

The next person in the circle repeats what the first person said and adds another object. The gardeners continue repeating what the previous people have said until someone can no longer repeat the growing list.

❧ Who's On Our Team?

Objective: To identify and practice different methods of communication.
Time: 30 to 45 minutes.
Materials: Who's On Our Team? work sheet (in the Appendix), pencils or markers.

Pair up the gardeners to ensure that each interviews someone he or she does not already know well. Then give each a Who's On Our Team? work sheet; have one child interview his or her partner, asking the questions on the data sheet and recording the exact answers given. Then let the other partner interview. Allow each child to decorate his or her own data sheet. Have the children use the data sheets to introduce their partners. Finally, post the data sheets around the room so everyone can learn Who's On Our Team?

❧ Can You Follow Me?

Objective: To identify and practice different ways to communicate.
Time: 10 to 20 minutes.
Materials: Paper, pencils.

Tell the gardeners that listening closely to directions is a skill that can be developed or improved. Explain that this activity will challenge and test their listening skills. Have the JMG'ers get out a sheet of paper and a pen or pencil.

Read the directions for each item and give the participants time to follow directions and write the answer for each one. After they have completed the activity, have them discuss and evaluate their accuracy. Discuss successes and areas to improve.

Cooperation Countdown Items

1. Draw a triangle. Inside the triangle, draw a rectangle that touches each side of the triangle. Put an X inside the rectangle.
2. Give the wrong answer to this question: Are owls birds?
3. In the left margin, write the symbol used in comic books to show that someone is sleeping.
4. If 3 days before tomorrow was Wednesday, draw six diagonal lines.
5. Put in time order: childhood, old age, teens.
6. Write the initials of the United States of America.
7. Underline three times your answer to Question 4.
8. Print the name of your favorite vegetable.

❧ Plant A Seed

Objective: To demonstrate the importance of communicating clearly when speaking.
Time: 15 to 25 minutes.
Materials: Water container, potting soil, pot, hand trowel, seeds, watering can, water.

Explain that it is very important to have good communication skills. We must speak clearly so other people can understand us, and we must listen well to understand what others say. We should also think about what we are going to say and how to say it before we actually speak. When explaining something to someone, we should be as clear as we can.

This activity is an exercise in speaking and listening. It is most effective to have two volunteers complete this activity. Bring the two gardeners to the front of the room and have them sit back to back so each cannot see what the other is doing. Tell the students that one will be the "instruction giver" and the other the "doer." Tell them that they are going to plant some seeds. The "doer" must follow the directions exactly. If the directions are unclear, the "doer" should do what he or she thinks the "instruction giver" might be trying to say. For example, if the "instruction giver" simply says "put a seed in the pot," the "doer" should take the seed from the package any way he or she chooses and then put it in the pot with no soil.

Place these items on a desk: a small pot, a bag of soil, some seeds, a trowel and a container of water. Tell the gardeners to begin and let the group watch how the seed is planted.

After they have finished, ask if the task succeeded or failed. Was the seed planted as it should have been? Were any steps out of order? Will this seed germinate and grow? Then follow up with more questions on communication. How could we have made the instructions more clear? Is it important that we listen to instructions? What kinds of instructions should we pay special attention to? What are some good ways to give instructions?

In the Classroom
Have the students write a "how to" paper on planting a seed. They can use the information from the activity to help them write more descriptively.

Decision Making/Goal Setting

Goals set the directions for the actions of one's life. Everyone has goals. However, many children do not know why they behave as they do, nor do they consider how much they could accomplish if they were to set obtainable and positive goals for their future. This lesson covers what the goal-setting process is and how to use goal setting to enhance self-perceptions.

Research indicates that understanding one's values and goals is a critical first step. Values help a person decide what is important, where to stand on an issue and what to do. A person's values determine his or her goals. A goal is a dream upon which a child acts. Other aspects of goals:
✓ Goals must be reasonable, practical and obtainable for the child.
✓ Goals need to be clearly defined and understood.
✓ Goals should be expressed simply, in one or two sentences.
✓ Goals need to be listed in two categories: short- and long-term.
✓ Achievable time lines should be assigned to goals.
✓ Failure can be a positive step in the growth process.

Children's self-perceptions are affected by whether or not they achieve their goals. Failure can harm self-esteem. However, children who set realistic goals and who base their goals on their abilities are more likely to adjust and learn from their experiences.

Adults can help by encouraging and assisting in strategy planning. However, the child must feel that the goal is his or her own and that it has not been set by someone else. If children are to attain their goals, it is critical that they feel committed to them. Some younger children will have difficulty with long-term (1-year) goals because of their cognitive level.

ACTIVITIES
❧ Goal Search

Objective: To identify what a goal is.
Time: 15 to 25 minutes.
Materials: Magazines, scissors.

Explain that a goal is something you would like to have, to be, to learn or to do. Have the JMG'ers look through magazines and cut out pictures of something they would like to have or do. After everyone has found at least one picture, have each child share with the group one thing they would like to do. After everyone, including the leader, shares one picture, the gardeners may show another item.

In the Classroom
Encourage the students to list things they would like to learn about in school. Have each choose one item and write it in the center of a sheet of construction paper. Have each student identify three things they must do to reach their goal. Have the students write these steps, with arrows pointing toward their goals. Allow them to share their goals with others and post the goals in the classroom.

❧ Right On Target

Objectives: To demonstrate how to set goals and to identify personal goals.
Time: 10 to 20 minutes.
Materials: My JMG Targets for This Week work sheet (in the Appendix).

Distribute copies of the My JMG Targets for This Week work sheet to the JMG group. Have each child write in the center of a target one goal to "shoot" for during the week. Have them write in each of the target's outer rings things they must do to achieve that goal. Give an example so they will see the process of goal setting. For example:

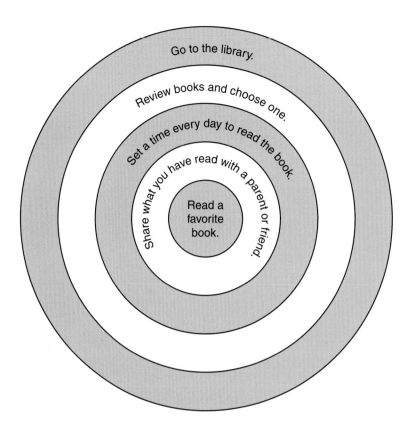

Have the gardeners color each ring of the target as they achieve that step toward their goal. At the end of the week, ask them how many targets they hit; that is, which goals they achieved. When a goal is completed, the entire target will be colored. Allow each child to share with the group one goal achieved.

In the Classroom
Have the students make a large target to post in the classroom. Help them identify a goal they want to achieve. Perhaps this could be a test score, leadership project, achieving a reading goal, etc. Put that goal in the bull's-eye. Encourage the students to identify what they must do to reach this goal. Have them identify the steps each must do individually for the group to reach its goal.

❧ The Class/Club Chronicle

Objective: To write group short-term goals.
Time: 20 to 25 minutes.
Materials: Chalkboard, chalk, pencil, paper, Class/Club Chronicle work sheets (in the Appendix).

Encourage the JMG'ers to discuss events that have happened during the week. On the board have them list all the group goals accomplished in the past week. On a separate list, have the gardeners brainstorm and identify new group goals for the next week. It is important that they choose the goal(s) themselves. You may offer suggestions to help them accomplish their goals.

Using this list, have the children fill in the Class/Club Chronicle work sheets. You can send these sheets home with the children for their parents to read. This will help you assess the success and impact of various activities on the children.

❧ Watch Me Grow

> Objective: To identify two types of goals: long- and short-term.
> Time: 20 to 30 minutes.
> Materials: Pencils, pens, My Growing Season work sheet (in the Appendix).

This is a good activity in which to involve parents. Invite parents to attend a "goal-setting" party. Start by allowing each gardener to explain his or her projects and group activities. This is a great time for students to highlight produce and plants grown, projects completed, etc. Then allow the children and parents to break into small groups to share individual accomplishments and identify areas for self-improvement. It is important that both children and parents participate, not merely observe.

Give each child a My Growing Season work sheet to complete. Explain to the JMG'ers and their parents that this activity will help them set goals. Have the children fill out the work sheets independently and then share them with their families. Keep a copy of the goal sheet for each JMG youth.

Encourage the gardeners to evaluate and update their goals during the year. Set a date with the JMG'ers and their parents to share what they have learned in the JMG program and to evaluate their My Growing Season work sheets. Ask the children to share the goals they have achieved and have them discuss the goals they had to change.

Planning and Problem-Solving Skills

Children and adults face problems and must make decisions every day. All people must make their own decisions and solve their own problems. Learning to make wise decisions and to take positive action in solving problems is an important part of growing up. Some of the most critical life skills are making decisions and solving problems effectively.

Some decisions and problems are easy; others are difficult. However, no matter what decision must be made or problem must be solved, several common elements are involved. People base every action or decision on their values, beliefs, information and attitudes. Children's values are affected by their experiences, family, friends, school, church, community and nation. Once they have clearly defined their beliefs, attitudes and values, children are better prepared to make wise choices.

People find it less complicated to make decisions and solve problems when they see clearly their values and goals. Children need to understand how their decisions and solutions can affect themselves and others and be willing to accept responsibility for their actions. When children understand and use the steps listed on the next page, they will be more effective decision makers and problem solvers.

1. Define the problem.
2. Gather information.
3. List the alternatives or choices.
4. Evaluate the alternatives.
5. Decide on an action plan.
6. Complete the action plan.
7. Evaluate the results.

Although people who use this process do not always succeed, they do achieve the desired results more frequently than when just "guessing" or letting someone else decide. People begin making decisions in infancy and continue throughout their lives. Parents and other significant adults can help children learn how better to make decisions and solve problems.

"Learning By Doing" is a 4-H slogan. Tell the gardeners that throughout 4-H and the JMG program, they are learning many new things. They are also gaining some skills for learning and sharing with others. We learn by doing things by ourselves and with others. We use all of our senses to learn—sight, sound, touch, taste and smell. We learn by observing or watching, by experimenting, by reading, by experiencing and by asking questions.

ACTIVITIES

❧ Making A Machine

Objective: To plan and cooperate within a group to solve problems.
Time: 25 to 40 minutes.
Materials: 10 slips of paper containing names of machines, box.

Place the slips of paper in a box. Tell the JMG'ers that machines are made of many moving parts. Examples include a lawn mower, vacuum cleaner, record player, etc. Divide the group into teams of five or more. Each group will draw a name of a machine to imitate together.

After selecting the machine, the group should decide which member or members will act out the various parts. Every member should have a part. One member might be a narrator to explain the working parts of the machine. If two or more groups are involved, one group can demonstrate the machine being imitated and the other groups can guess what machine it is. Repeat this process until each group has demonstrated its machine.

❧ Create A Costume

Objectives: To develop group planning and problem-solving techniques; to stimulate creative thinking; to implement the group decision-making process; and to develop a finished product.
Time: 30 to 40 minutes.
Materials: Many old newspapers, several rolls of masking or cellophane tape (at least one roll per group).

Pair the gardeners or divide them into groups of three to six members. Give each group an equal amount of newspaper and tape to make a costume with. It might help to give the group a category of costume to create, such as an alien, animal, insect, movie star, vegetable, etc.

Each group should select a member to be its model and wear the costume. The costume should include creative ideas such as a hat, jacket, gloves, shoes, paws, antennae, or whatever is appropriate for that category. Set a time limit for this activity. After the model is dressed and before time has expired, each team should choose a narrator to describe the costume to the other groups. At the end of the time limit, each group will have its model step forward in costume while the narrator describes it. Each team is allowed 1 minute to describe its costume.

Encourage the JMG'ers to share the decisions they had to make as a group. Examples: who would be the model, how to design a costume, and others. Explain that good ideas result from working together.

Pass It On

Objectives: To help group members get to know each other and to learn that it is important to plan.
Time: 15 to 20 minutes.
Materials: Drawing paper, timer, markers, crayons, colored pencils or paints.

Give each gardener a sheet of paper. Set the timer for 1 minute. Tell the JMG'ers to write their names on their papers and start a drawing. When time expires, have each pass his drawing to another person in the group. Then start the timer again and have each gardener work on the new drawing.

Pass the sheets eight to 10 times (depending on the size of the group.) Then have the gardeners evaluate and interpret the drawings they had at stopping time. Ask the person who started each drawing what his or her plans were for the drawing. Did it turn out that way?

Have the gardeners list the steps that could have been taken to ensure that the drawings turned out the way the original artist intended. Encourage them to list such steps as they would if giving good directions and telling others about the plan.

In the Classroom

Set a timer for 2 minutes and have each child begin writing a story on a sheet of paper. After the alarm sounds, have each student pass his or her story to the next person. Then have the students begin writing on the new story, trying to pick up where the author finished. Pass the stories four or five times. Then have several of the students share the stories with the class. Discuss how good story writers start with a plan or an outline. Start a class outline for a story and build a class story together. Afterward, students can choose partners to finish writing the story.

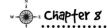

❧ Either/Or

Objective:	To understand the decision-making process.
Time:	20 to 25 minutes.
Materials:	Chalkboard and chalk or large piece of paper and markers, poster board with decision-making steps, magazines, crayons (optional).

Lead the children in a discussion on the importance of making good decisions. Ask the children such questions as: What would you need to decide if you were going to get a new pet? What information would you need to know before planting a garden? List their responses on a chalkboard or large sheet of paper. Show how their answers fit into the decision-making steps below:

1. Define the problem.
2. Gather information.
3. List the alternatives or choices.
4. Evaluate the alternatives.
5. Decide on an action plan.
6. Complete the action plan.
7. Evaluate the results.

Outline the decision-making process using other examples to illustrate the steps. A few examples might include buying a gift, handling matters when someone's lunch money is stolen, taking a trip, etc. Have the children think of one important decision they have made recently or will make soon. Older children can write down the steps they took to make their decision, using the list of steps in the process. Younger children can draw or cut out pictures from magazines to correspond to each step in the decision-making process.

❧ Let's Make A Case Out Of It

Objective:	To use the decision-making process to evaluate scenarios and reach a consensus on how to solve a problem.
Time:	20 minutes.
Materials:	List of seven steps to good decision making from previous activity, poster board or flip chart.

Explain to the gardeners that a case study is when a group is given a situation and asked to decide what should be done. Read a few case studies aloud and ask the gardeners what they would decide in each situation. Encourage them to use the seven decision-making steps. The gardeners may want to role-play the case studies.

Some examples:

1. You have homework to do, but your friend has invited you out for pizza with his or her family. Do you go or stay home?
2. Your family is planning a vacation. You and your mom want to go to the beach. Your sister and dad want to go to the mountains. Where does your family go on vacation?
3. It's your turn to fertilize the garden. You know that you are supposed to give each plant 1 teaspoon of plant food. You think that if 1 teaspoon helps them grow, then maybe 4 teaspoons would make them grow really fast. How much should you fertilize the plants?

4. You have won a pizza party for five people. You have six friends you would like to attend the party. Whom do you invite?

Ask the children to suggest other case studies.

❧ It's In the Bag

Objective: To gather information for making decisions and solving problems.
Time: 20 to 25 minutes.
Materials: Large paper bag or burlap sack, objects to identify.

Tell the group that they will be detectives in this activity. An object will be placed in a paper bag or burlap sack and the children have to guess what is inside, using different clues given. Put an object in the bag or sack (not letting the children see it). Give the bag to the first gardener, who will look into the bag and give clues to the others to identify the object inside. For example: "It's red. It's round. You throw it."

The clues are given one at a time, with a pause after each clue for guesses. If no one guesses the object on the first clue, the gardener gives another, and so on. Have the JMG'ers state the clues and guesses in complete sentences. Whoever guesses correctly becomes the next clue giver. Put a different object into the bag and give it to this gardener, and the activity continues.

In the Classroom
You can use the grab bag as a catalyst for a creative writing narrative story or paragraph. Place 15 to 20 random items in the bag. Have each student draw out three items and write the names of the items on a sheet of paper. After all students have drawn, have each write a creative story using the three items from the bag. For example, if the items were a flower, a key and a pencil, this story could be written:

A beautiful red flower was growing in my garden. I bent down to smell the flower and noticed a small key in the dirt. I picked up the key and brought it in the house. I put the key next to my rainbow pencil in my collection box.

Responsible Behavior

Children need to understand the responsibilities they have to themselves and others. They must learn that their attitudes and actions can influence what happens to them. Children need to develop internal control to direct their thoughts and behaviors, rather than relying on external controls. These may include fear of punishment or various rewards. Understanding the consequences of not following through with various responsibilities helps children realize the importance of being responsible.

Even at young ages, children can assume responsibility in several areas. They can be responsible for the safety and well being of themselves, their friends and their families. Responsibility is often learned by observation and experience. Children pay closer attention to what people do than to what they say. Be sure to set a good example for the gardeners to follow. Give them opportunities to make various contributions, such as completing tasks or activities.

Encourage the gardeners to develop respect for themselves, others and the law. As citizens, we have additional responsibilities that are often shared with members of our family, school and community. Learning to be responsible involves participation, practice and a lot of patience.

ACTIVITIES

❧ Shared Responsibility

Objective: To identify responsibilities, including responsibility to a group and its members.
Time: 15 to 20 minutes.
Materials: Situation slips.

Before this activity, write different situations on separate slips of paper. Sample situations:

✓ You need a design for your garden.
✓ Company is coming for dinner.
✓ A school play is being planned.
✓ You're planning a bake sale.

To begin the activity, discuss how two or more people often share responsibilities. Divide the gardeners into groups of four to six, and give each group a "situation slip." Have each group discuss the situation. Decide what tasks need to be done and who will be responsible for getting them done. Tell the gardeners that everyone in the group must have a responsibility. Then have the groups explain their situations and decisions to the other groups.

❧ Consequences

Objectives: To understand self-responsibility; to identify actions and related consequences.
Time: 20 to 25 minutes.
Materials: Poster board, large paper or writing board, markers.

Discuss the meaning of self-responsibility. Explain that it means to take responsibility for your attitudes and actions, whether they are good or bad. Responsible people admit their mistakes as well as their successes and live up to their personal standards regardless of what others think and do.

Present the gardeners with the following situation: A girl in your group has worked very little in your JMG garden. When it is time for harvest, everyone who has helped gets to take vegetables home. The girl wants to take home a share of the vegetables.

Ask the gardeners

1. Should the girl get to take her share of the vegetables?
2. Why didn't she help as much?
3. Could she do anything to make up for not helping earlier?

Tell the gardeners that we all must make decisions every day. Some are easy to make; others are difficult. Discuss the steps to good decision making. Apply these steps to the sample problem.

❧ Touchdown

Objectives: To set responsibility goals to work toward. To practice setting goals.
Time: 20 to 25 minutes.
Materials: Bulletin board or large piece of paper, construction paper, marker.

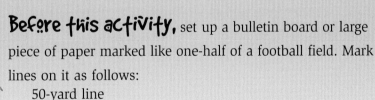

Before this activity, set up a bulletin board or large piece of paper marked like one-half of a football field. Mark lines on it as follows:

50-yard line
40-yard line
30-yard line
20-yard line
10-yard line
Touchdown
Team   Coach
Game Date

Have the JMG'ers list the responsibilities they have. For example: making their beds, taking out the trash, feeding pets, etc. Explain that to reach goals, each person must meet his or her individual responsibilities.

Have the group set goals to work toward for a period of time. Depending on the group, this could be weekly or monthly goals. Examples might be:

50-yard line   We will all be on time every day.

40-yard line   We will all have our JMG Handbook and all materials ready each time we meet.

30-yard line   We will identify our group project and be ready to work and listen.

20-yard line   We will all keep our garden and work areas clean.

10-yard line   We will help other gardeners in our group.

Touchdown   We will complete our JMG group project.

Have the gardeners make football players or footballs out of construction paper, each with a gardener's name on it. Use these to decorate the board. The team should be the JMG group, the coach is the teacher/volunteer and the game date is the time set for all goals to be reached.

If all goals are reached, the gardeners should be proud of themselves. A special award may be given, such as treats, a movie, a special time to do something of their choice, etc.

The gardeners can change their goals weekly or monthly to suit their needs.

Don't Stamp Me

Objectives: To learn that stereotypes influence how people act and respond to situations.
              To understand personal attitudes about stereotypes in a group or workplace.
Time   20 to 30 minutes.
Materials: Small pieces of paper, two containers.

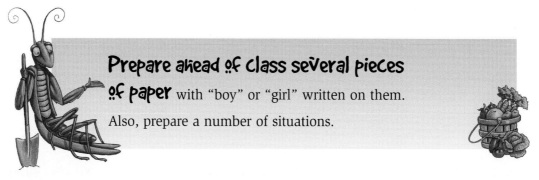

Prepare ahead of class several pieces of paper with "boy" or "girl" written on them. Also, prepare a number of situations.

This game is like charades. Each gardener draws two slips of paper. One slip tells the gardener to be a boy or girl. The other tells about a situation, such as: Two friends get into an argument. A friend is cheating on a test. You lost your baseball uniform. You make the honor roll.

Have the gardeners act out the ending of the situation they picked. The group tries to guess whether the actor is a boy or a girl and identify the situation.

After the gardeners have completed the game, have them discuss what happened. Was it easier to guess the situation or the gender they were portraying? Do boys and girls act differently in similar situations? Are boys and girls treated alike or differently in similar situations?

Career Awareness

The world of work has changed dramatically over the past decade. Technology plays an increasingly vital role in the workplace, and computer skills are essential for most occupations. The workplace itself is also constantly changing.

For example, workers need to be problem solvers who can integrate mathematical, written and oral skills. The structure of work has become more complex, with teams becoming an increasingly important component of many work environments. In short, the gardeners need exposure to and an opportunity to learn skills that will enable them to succeed in a highly technical, quickly changing and team-structured workplace.

ACTIVITIES
✿ Careers and School

Objectives:	To compare and contrast school and the world of work and to determine the relevance of school subjects to careers.
Time:	30 to 40 minutes.
Materials:	Subjects and Career Cards and Mobile Careers work sheets (in the Appendix), container, chalkboard, chalk.

Photocopy the Subject and careers cards work sheet for the group. Cut out the careers and put all the cards in a container.

Discuss how school is like the world of work, and list ideas on the board. For example: The group might say, "You have to write stories in school and at work you have to write letters." Have the gardeners draw cards with names of careers. Then ask them to list one or more school subjects relating to that career. Allow several children to share their answers and lists with the group. Discuss the reasons for their choices. Emphasize that all school subjects relate to certain careers and are even more relevant in higher grades.

Divide the JMG'ers into groups of four or five. Give each group a copy of the Mobile Careers work sheet. Have the group work together to answer the questions about each career listed. Once the groups have completed the work sheet, discuss each question together. Explain the answers and ask students about careers they are familiar with.

In the Classroom

Have the students research a particular career. Encourage each to learn about the career, the education needed for that career, special skills needed, and the people working in that career. Have the students write their findings in a descriptive paper.

Career Teams

Objective: To analyze various careers and identify different career opportunities and qualifications.
Time: 20 to 30 minutes.
Materials: Who Am I? and Career Helper Cards work sheets (in the Appendix), containers.

Before this activity, photocopy the Who Am I? work sheet, cut out the questions and put them in a container. Also copy the Career Helper Cards work sheet, cut out the statements and put them in a container.

Allow each gardener to draw a card and read it to the group. Encourage the group to identify the kind of person being described. Brainstorm by asking questions (Are you a helper? How do you help at home and at school? What happens to people who do not do their part? Did you ever think that, because of your help, you make life easier for your mom or dad or teacher?)

Relate working together as a family to people working in teams or groups in careers to do a better job. Discuss the idea that a job can be done better when people work as a group than when just one person does it. Encourage the gardeners to identify examples of JMG activities they have done that have worked out well because a team worked on the project.

Next, allow the gardeners to draw from the Career Helper cards one at a time. They need to decide whether the task can be done better by a group or by one person. Encourage them to notice as they observe people working whether they work alone or with others.

Discuss whether people must act a certain way to work well together, and if so, how. Compare working in a career to working in a family.

❧ When I Grow Up

Objectives: To learn about the choices one needs to make when choosing a career and to identify career options.

Time: 30 to 40 minutes.

Materials: 9- by-12-inch construction paper, scissors, glue or paste, magazines or catalogs, markers, crayons or pencils.

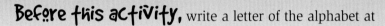

Before this activity, write a letter of the alphabet at the top of each sheet of construction paper.

Encourage the gardeners to name the different types of jobs adults have. List these on a piece of paper or the chalkboard. Let the JMG'ers share what kinds of work their parents do and what they'd like to do when they grow up. Give each gardener a sheet of construction paper, and have each cut out magazine photos or draw pictures of the various jobs that begin with that letter of the alphabet. The children can also list people they know or famous people who work in that career. Once completed, compile all the individual letters into a group JMG Career book.

Examples:

Aa	astronaut, actor	Nn	nurse, nutritionist
Bb	baker, banker, businessman	Oo	operator, optician
Cc	cowgirl, crane operator	Pp	pilot, paramedic
Dd	doctor, dentist	Qq	queen, quarterback
Ee	engineer, electrician	Rr	repairman, race car driver
Ff	factory worker, farmer	Ss	singer, secretary, soldier
Gg	gardener, geologist	Tt	typist, teacher, trainer
Hh	helicopter pilot, hairdresser	Uu	usher, undertaker
Ii	ice cream vendor	Vv	violinist, veterinarian
Jj	janitor, jockey, judge	Ww	word processor, waitress
Kk	king, karate instructor	Xx	X-ray technician
Ll	lifeguard, lawyer	Yy	youth minister, yoga instructor
Mm	mail carrier, mother	Zz	zookeeper

❧ Dream House

Objectives: To analyze personal decisions and demonstrate understanding of the purpose and nature of work. To identify the impacts of various careers on their world.

Time: 30 to 40 minutes.

Materials: Paper, pencils, assorted craft items.

Tell the group that almost everyone would like to design and build his or her own house. Well, it's their turn! Have each gardener draw a floor plan of his or her dream house, labeling each room. The JMG'ers should include driveways, walkways, patios, pools or any other extras they want. Encourage them to include really neat, fantasy features, such as robots, elevators and other items. The children can also use assorted craft items to build models of their dream houses.

After the children have drawn floor plans or built their dream house model, ask them to list the workers who would help build their houses. Example: architect, electrician, plumber, carpenter, etc.

Explain that workers assemble or put together the shell of the house, the electrical system, etc. Other items for the dream house will be assembled at the factory and then installed in the home. Name other pre-assembled items they will need to buy (such as a water heater, furniture, refrigerator, fireplace, etc.).

Allow the JMG'ers time to share their lists so they can learn from each other.

Have the group identify other things needed for the dream house. Will the yard need to be landscaped? Who will build the pool? What people would be involved to help?

Reinforce the concept that teams of people are often needed to complete a project.

✿ All For One

<table>
<tr><td>Objectives:</td><td>To learn that some careers involve group work, while other careers require individual work. To identify careers that require people to work independently and careers that require teams.</td></tr>
<tr><td>Time:</td><td>20 to 30 minutes.</td></tr>
<tr><td>Materials:</td><td>Paper, pencil, Group or Alone work sheet (in the Appendix).</td></tr>
</table>

Tell the JMG'ers that they will experience group and individual work processes during this activity. Explain that when job hunting, some people choose a career that involves working with many people, a group, or a team. For example, if you worked on an assembly line, or played in a rock group or on a football team, you would do your job with others. If you were an artist or writer, you might work alone.

Give each child a copy of the Group or Alone work sheet. Give the gardeners 5 minutes to list as many jobs as they can for each category. Now, form groups of four or five. On another work sheet, have them combine each separate list into one group list without repeating any jobs. Then ask them to add more jobs to the list.

Ask each child to answer individually the questions at the bottom of the Group or Alone work sheet.

Wrap up this activity by asking the following questions

1. What are some important rules for group members to follow?
2. Were you a leader or a listener as you worked in your group?
3. Is it good to know how you work best. . .in a group or alone?

LEADERSHIP/SERVICE LEARNING PROJECTS

Your group should choose at least one of the following activities to complete.

❊ **Career Display**
Have the group contact their school or local librarian and ask if they can make a display about the career opportunities that your JMG group studied.

❊ **Job Shadow**
Contact a person working in a career that your JMG group would like to learn more about. Make an appointment for the group to go and visit this person on the job.

❊ **Learning to Share**
The JMG members can teach a group of younger children one of the life skill/career activities that your JMG group completed.

❊ **Create Your Own**
Your JMG group can have fun creating its own unique leadership/service learning project.

Registration Packet

JMG® REGISTRATION PACKET

The forms described below are used in registering youths and leaders in the Junior Master Gardener program, and for ordering completion certificates.

I. *Junior Master Gardener Registration Agreement Form.* The JMG Registration Agreement Form registers a properly organized and functional JMG group. The registration serves as a permit for use of the 4-H and JMG service marks, names, logos and emblems. It allows a group to function with all the rights and privileges of 4-H/JMG membership.

2. *Junior Master Gardener Member Group Enrollment Form (JMG 1-5.061).* The JMG program is expected to reach hundreds of youths across Texas and the nation. To document each youth's participation in the program, the teacher and/or leader must complete form JMG 1-5.061 for each group. JMG 1-5.061 will provide statistical data for state and federal governments for future funding and civil rights documentation.

Use these guidelines when completing the Junior Master Gardener Member Group Enrollment Form:
County Name: County in which the JMG program is being conducted
JMG Group Name: This name can be created by the youths (something catchy, or related to region)
JMG Group Teacher/Leader: Name of classroom teacher and/or leader (A registration form must be included for each person named.)

SECTION I: Unit Information
The JMG program can be organized in several ways:

Community:	A community 4-H club having club officers, regular monthly meetings, a community service project, project meetings, a club manager, parental participation and project leaders.
Project:	Same as a community club, except that it concentrates on only one project and expands into other projects after the original one.
School:	Same as community club, except that it is organized and conducted in school; members may be divided into several clubs of different ages.
Community Partnership:	Has the same structure as a community club and can be delivered in a school setting. However, the lead volunteers managing the club come from at least two other distinct organizations whose goal or project is to work with youths (e.g., Lions Club, Key Club, etc.).
Special Interest:	Organized or coordinated by Extension personnel and directed and/or taught by volunteer adult or youth leaders. The meetings are conducted in informal classroom settings with members participating in at least 20- to 60-minute learning sessions with the total learning time of at least 2 hours.
Curriculum Enrichment:	A learning activity in a classroom setting, led by school faculty, a staff member or a volunteer. The project consists of at least six learning experiences, each 20 to 60 minutes long. It uses the 4-H clover, and promotes other delivery methods in which youths can participate.
Camping:	Youth program in a structured, informal setting ranging from 1 full day to overnight.

ENP-Y:	(Expanded Nutrition Program - Youth). Program designed to teach good nutrition and health. This program involves youth in all aspects of food production and consumption and can be delivered at schools as curriculum enrichment, in after-school programs orneighborhood groups, at recreation centers and summer day camps, and/or as displays at community health fairs.
Clover Kids (K-2):	Informal educational program for youths ages 5 to 8 in kindergarten, first and second grades. This program is an introductory 4-H program for boys and girls.

SECTION II - Distribution of Member by:

Record information in this section as accurately as possible. Make sure that each person in the project is accounted for and that the totals in all four boxes match. If the RACE AND GENDER Section reflects that all participants are of the same race, then please complete the two questions under the box. This will provide civil rights documentation concerning the setting of the project and its accessibility to all races and sexes.

3. *Junior Master Gardener Leader/Teacher Registration Form (JMG 2-1.056).* All teachers and volunteers must complete this form, which will be used to gather statistical information on all volunteers and teachers in the program. The back of the registration form is an optional volunteer screening process. After completing these forms, school teachers and officials are strongly encouraged to review the information about all volunteers before beginning the program.

The teachers and/or volunteer leaders should complete this form at the beginning of each new class of Junior Master Gardeners.

> You will receive from the JMG Program headquarters an official letter of registration for your group. A copy of your Registration Packet will be sent to your local Extension office for its records.

4. *JMG Completion Form.* Mail the completed JMG Publication Order Form plus your check or money order for the publications, to JMG Distribution. All other forms in the JMG Registration Packet should be mailed to the Junior Master Gardener headquarters.

Junior Master Gardener Headquarters
225 HFSB
Texas A&M University
College Station, Texas 77843-2134
(979) 845-8565
FAX (979) 845-8906
E-mail: jmg@tamu.edu

JMG Kids[SM]
4066 State Hwy 6 South
College Station, TX 77845
1-888-JMG-KIDS

When members of your group complete the JMG curriculum requirements, order JMG Certificates by completing the JMG Completion Form and mailing it to the JMG Program headquarters at Texas A&M University. Certificates will be returned promptly so you can present them to the newest Junior Master Gardeners!

Please complete and return the following 4 pages.

JMG® Junior Master Gardener® Registration Agreement Form

We request through this Registration Agreement Form to be an official JMG group. Our group has met all of the following criteria:

1. A minimum of five youths
2. One or more adult teacher/leader(s)
3. Suitable meeting facilities (classroom, garden area)
4. An official club or group name (JMG office reserves the right to modify name)

JMG group name desired _____

JMG site _____

County where JMG group is located _____

Designated JMG Teacher/Leader _____   Date _____

    Address _____   Telephone _____

    _____   e-mail _____
        City   State   ZIP
       (Notify of any address changes)

Submitting this form:

The group teacher/leader should complete this form and submit it to the JMG Program headquarters at Texas A&M University:

    Junior Master Gardener Program
    225 Horticulture/Forestry Science Building
    Texas A&M University
    College Station, Texas 77843-2134
    Phone: (979) 845-8565
    Fax: (979) 845-8906

Educational programs conducted by the Texas Cooperative Extension serve people of all ages regardless of socioeconomic level, race, color, sex, religion, disability, or national origin.

Check:

❏ I have read the JMG Management Guide and agree to follow the JMG guidelines.

❏ I agree to assist in protecting the service marks and copyright of the JMG program as described.

_____
JMG Teacher/Leader signature   Date

JMG® Junior Master Gardener® Leader/Teacher Registration Form

JMG 2-1.065

JMG Group Name _____

Unit/Club Number _____

Check (✔) preference   ☐ Mr.   ☐ Mrs.   ☐ Ms.   ☐ Dr.

Name _____
(Last)   (First)   (Middle Initial)

Mailing Address _____

City/Town _____   Zip Code _____

Phone Number: Home (___) _____   Work (___) _____

E-mail Address: _____   ☐ Male   ☐ Female
                                            ☐ Adult ☐ Youth

This information is requested to gather statistics for compliance with nondiscrimination requirements.

Check (✔) only one

☐ 1. American Indian or Alaskan Native
☐ 2. Asian or Pacific Islander
☐ 3. Black - not Hispanic origin
☐ 4. Hispanic
☐ 5. White - not of Hispanic origin

Code   Project Name

10089   Junior Master Gardener

Years as a 4-H Leader *(including this year)* _____

Residence
Check (✔) only one

☐ 1. Rural/Farm
☐ 2. Town less than 10,000
☐ 3. City between 10,000 and 50,000
☐ 4. Suburb of city more than 50,000
☐ 5. Central city more than 50,000

Type of 4-H Unit
Check (✔) only one

☐ 1. Community
☐ 2. Project
☐ 3. School
☐ 4. Community Partnership
☐ 5. Clover Kids (K-2)
☐ 6. Special Interest
☐ 7. Curriculum Enrichment
☐ 8. Camping
☐ 9. ENP-Y

Major Leadership Responsibility

☐ 1. Club Manager
☐ 2. Project Leader
☐ 3. Activity Leader
☐ 4. JMG Volunteer *(specify)*
_____
☐ 5. Other *(specify)*
_____

4-H Alumni: ☐ Yes   ☐ No

State _____
County _____

Do you work directly with youth?
☐ Yes   ☐ No

_____   _____
Date   Signature

The following information is requested in support of the Texas 4-H JMG Program's commitment to continually guarantee the safety of the members during 4-H participation.

Volunteer Interest *(To be completed by volunteers 18 years or older)*

Have you previously served as a 4-H volunteer?   ❏ Yes   ❏ No

If yes, where? _____ County _____ State

And how many years? _____

Personal Information

Do you have a current/valid driver's license?   ❏ Yes   ❏ No   If Yes, Driver's License # _____

Do you have automobile liability insurance?   ❏ Yes   ❏ No

Have you ever been convicted of a violation of any local, state or federal law, **other than minor traffic violations?** (This includes a plea of guilty or no contest.)   ❏ Yes   ❏ No   **If YES**, list all convictions below, from the oldest to the most recent.

Date of Conviction Month and Year	Mark appropriate box		Offense (Do not use abbreviations)
	Misdemeanor	Felony	

References

1. Name _____
   Address _____
   City _____ Zip _____
   Telephone _____

2. Name _____
   Address _____
   City _____ Zip _____
   Telephone _____

3. Name _____
   Address _____
   City _____ Zip _____
   Telephone _____

I certify that the statements made by me on this registration form are true, complete and correct to the best of my knowledge and belief and are made in good faith. I understand that any false statement made herein will void this registration form and any actions based upon it. I authorize the 4-H JMG Program or any of its components to make reference checks relating to my volunteer service. I understand that this application and all attachments are the property of the Texas 4-H & Youth Development Program.

_____   _____
Date   Volunteer Signature

JMG® Junior Master Gardener® Member Group Enrollment Form

JMG 1-5.061

County Name _____

JMG Group Name _____

JMG Group Teacher/Leader _____

Date _____ / _____ / _____

FOR OFFICE USE ONLY

County Number _____

Unit/Club Number _____

SECTION I - Unit Information: Type of 4-H organization (*Check only one*)

☐ 1. Community
☐ 2. Project
☐ 3. School
☐ 4. Community Partnership
☐ 5. Special Interest
☐ 6. Curriculum Enrichment
☐ 7. Camping
☐ 8. ENP-Y
☐ 9. Clover Kids (K-2)

SECTION II - Distribution of Members by: Totals in this section for age, residence and race and gender should all be the same.

RACE AND GENDER

	Males	Females	Totals
White - not of Hispanic origin			
Black - not of Hispanic origin			
American Indian or Alaskan Native			
Hispanic			
Asian or Pacific Islander			
Totals			

If all participants are of the same race, please answer the following questions:

Is this unit in a racially mixed community (at least two different racial groups)? ☐ Yes ☐ No

Is this unit integrated? ☐ Yes ☐ No

RESIDENCE

Residence	Number
Rural/Farm	
Town less than 10,000	
City between 10,000 and 50,000	
Suburb of city more than 50,000	
Central city more than 50,000	
Total	

JMG PROJECT CODE

Code	10089
Males	
Females	

AGE

Age	Number
Under 9	
9	
10	
11	
12	
13	
14	
15	
16	
17	
18	
19	

224

JMG® Junior Master Gardener® Completion Form
(For Certificates - Duplicate as Needed)

Upon completion of the JMG curriculum requirements, fill out this form to request JMG Certificates for your group members. Mail the completed form to Junior Master Gardener Program, 225 HFSB, Texas A&M University, College Station, Texas 77843-2134.

Date: _____ County: _____ JMG Group Name: _____

| NAME | ADDRESS | CITY/ZIP | PROGRAM COMPLETED | | UNIT(S) COMPLETED |
			JMG	GOLDEN RAY SERIES	

*Check One Below
_____ I certify that JMG group members have completed all the requirements to be certified as Junior Master Gardeners.
_____ I certify that JMG group members have completed all the requirements to receive Golden Ray Series Certification (list chapter/unit completed above).

Teacher/Leader Name: _____ Signature: _____ Date: _____

Certificates should be mailed to the following address: _____ City _____ State _____ Zip _____

Phone (___) _____

225

Looking for more FUN for your JMG kids?????

VISIT THE JMG GARDEN SHOP!

www.jmgkids.org
or call
Toll free 888 JMG KIDS

JMG...Cultivating youth and communities through gardening sm

Working with Young People

WORKING WITH YOUNG PEOPLE

This guide is part of the Junior Master Gardener program for youths ages 9 to 19. It uses enjoyable activities to teach horticulture, environmental science and leadership concepts.

The guide is designed to help you provide fun, educational activities that help youths develop critical thinking skills, identify community concerns, and take action to address those concerns through individual and group projects.

Preparation is Vital

For the activities in this handbook to work well, it is important that you prepare ahead of time. Review the whole handbook first to become acquainted with its contents, scope and sequence. Here is a checklist to help you get organized:

✓ **Resources Needed**
Note any resources you need for the activities and gather them before the meeting time. Some activities require paper, pencils and craft materials. Large sheets of poster board (or paper) and nontoxic markers may be useful for displaying ideas.

✓ **Number of Participants**
Make sure you know how many young people will be involved in each activity. Most of the activities are designed for between eight and 20 people. They can be adapted for smaller or larger groups, but you will need to determine the necessary logistical changes.

✓ **Small Groups**
For some activities, you will need to divide the participants into working groups of about three to five children. Think about the composition of your groups. Whenever possible, mix the participants in groups by gender, ethnicity, age, experience, etc.

✓ **Site/Classroom**
Check out the facility where you will conduct the activities. Some activities require you to make arrangements for work site visits; others need only a site big enough for all participants to work comfortably.

✓ **Work Space and Furniture Arrangements**
If the participants will be working in small groups, it is best to have a space divided into separate areas for each group, so you may need to rearrange furniture. In a classroom setting, push desks together to make tables. In a room where only chairs are available, place the chairs in small circles. If you are visiting a site, have the group gather around the person or object being observed, and make sure that all participants are close enough to hear and see what is happening.

✓ **Safety**
Before you begin, conduct a safety check. Do the participants know the safety procedures they must follow? Particularly when visiting work sites, plan to give safety instructions to the participants before the event.

Helping Young People Learn

Your role is to help young people "learn for themselves" by engaging them in activities in which they can acquire skills and knowledge. The ways the participants share information, answer questions or reach agreement about an issue will in itself be a learning experience. Many experiences will require them to reflect on their own interests and backgrounds, and how those relate to the activity at hand. People are successful in their careers partly because they have a high degree of self-awareness coupled with thoughtful decision making. A time to reflect and share experiences is an integral part of the Junior Master Gardener experience.

Individual Differences

Each participant will bring his or her own understanding to the activities outlined in this handbook. The group members may have quite wide differences in background, maturity, level of self awareness and prior knowledge. It is important to respect each person's knowledge, abilities, skills and talents and to acknowledge that everyone has something to contribute.

Your Role

In helping young people learn more about horticulture, careers and leadership skills that will prepare them for the world of work, your role is as a "facilitator of learning." As with participants, facilitators are also unique and diverse. Your sincere interest in preparing young people and your enthusiasm for providing programs will be a key source of inspiration for the participants.

When we think of our favorite teacher or others from whom we have learned, descriptive words such as "kind," "patient," "enthusiastic," "interested," "inspirational," "respectful" and "organized" come to mind. On the other hand, it is more difficult to learn from those who are overbearing, patronizing, inflexible, unenthusiastic, disorganized or frightening. Draw upon your own best memories and your own personality and talents to develop a style with which you are comfortable.

Above all, remember that you are also a learner in these situations, if not about content, then certainly about the participants themselves and their many ideas. Spend some time after each activity and reflect on how it went, including how you as a leader performed. Take note of any points to keep in mind for the next activity, and any general points to enhance your effectiveness.

Other Tips

✓ Be enthusiastic. Let the youths know that learning is fun.
✓ Gather all supplies before each lesson.
✓ Ask your county Extension personnel for help if you need it.
✓ Keep the sessions relaxed and casual.
✓ Encourage the young people to ask questions and share their ideas.
✓ Use the lesson outline and the activity sheets you select to guide your session. They will help you keep your place and make sure you haven't left anything out.
✓ Give youths plenty of positive feedback. Let them know they are doing a good job.
✓ Use the skills in the project yourself. Even adults need to brush up on skills once in a while.
✓ Personalize your activities for your group. Use examples that fit into the children's experiences or community.
✓ Celebrate. When your group completes the program, remember that certificates of completion are available.

Teaching Techniques

Young people will be more interested and active learners if you use a variety of teaching methods. The amount of information they retain varies with the methods used. Remember that "learn by doing" is a basic concept in 4-H, and is often the best way to retain knowledge. Below is a list of teaching methods you may want to adapt for your group. Experiment with other methods as well.

Demonstrations
A demonstration shows and tells how to do something; show each step by actually doing it and create the finished product to be displayed. An example may be a child showing the group how to make a snack or beverage, or the steps in planting a seed.

When children give demonstrations, they develop a positive self-concept, acquire more self-confidence in front of a group, learn to express their ideas clearly, and acquire subject matter knowledge.

Discussion Groups
Discussion groups stimulate the participants' thinking and understanding. Discussions are an excellent way to crystallize thought on a subject, and they give opportunities for the club members have their questions answered. The amount of direction needed depends on the members' ages and abilities. The following suggestions may help:
- ✓ Make sure the topics or questions for the discussion are stated clearly.
- ✓ For younger members, keep the list of topics or questions short. They lose interest and direction quickly.
- ✓ Differences of opinion will occur. Such conflict is good if the members can discuss their differences and reach some agreement.
- ✓ Try to elicit contributions from all the members. Avoid having a few members do all the talking.

Exhibits
4-H members learn by preparing a project or other kind of exhibit. They also learn by observing the exhibits of other 4-H members. Exhibits encourage 4-H members to complete their projects and to improve project quality. An exhibit provides a way for boys and girls to receive recognition for their work.

Members may want to create a group exhibit of their work for a group meeting, fair or information event. This gives them an opportunity to work as a group and to experience successful cooperative efforts.

Field Trips and Tours
Well-planned and organized field trips garner more interest in the program. New experiences are a vital part of each person's development. Young people are often interested in meeting new people and seeing different places. This is a popular teaching technique. To provide a meaningful learning experience, you will need to:
- ✓ Plan carefully; involve the young people.
- ✓ If possible, visit the location or person ahead of time.
- ✓ Provide transportation; this is one way to involve parents.
- ✓ Make sure the trip's purpose is clear.
- ✓ Tell the members enough of what to expect to arouse their interest.
- ✓ Evaluate the experience with the members soon afterward.
- ✓ Carry over the learning from the trip into project activities.

Reading Assignments

Researching and acquiring knowledge from bulletins, project guides, magazines and books can add greatly to the growth experience in a 4-H project. With this age group, assign topics or reading material only to those children who can read well. Remember that children in this age group would rather see, touch and feel actual objects than just hear about the subjects.

Boys and girls may find two or more articles related to their 4-H project. They may bring them to the project meetings and share ideas with other members. Some will be more interested than others in searching for additional information.

Young people retain about 10 percent of what they read. Reading printed project materials and other literature is an important way to acquire knowledge, but supplement this with other learning methods.

Skits and Role Playing

This activity adds much interest as a teaching method. Boys and girls can gain additional information about the project by preparing for and participating in the skit.

Always develop a purpose for the skit. Determine what needs to be done and why, based on what is to be taught. The task includes:
✓ Listing materials needed.
✓ Writing out the skit in detail.
✓ Determining who is going to do what.
✓ Summarizing the important points to learn.

Workshops

This method consists of showing the boys and girls how to do a job, then having them perform the same job under supervision. This method rates high because it incorporates other methods, such as talks and demonstrations.

Teaching Aids

Teaching aids add interest and help members visualize what they hear. Use only the teaching aids that are age appropriate and that lend themselves to extending the hands-on activities you have already planned. Teaching aids include:
✓ **Literature:** Bulletins, project guides, magazines, books, etc. Be sure the gardeners have the 4-H material that is available for their project or activity. Members can refer to it at home and whenever they need it for reference. Reading is an efficient way to learn.
✓ **Exhibits:** Excellent for arousing interest and creating a desire to do.
✓ **Pictures:** Can be used effectively to illustrate or emphasize a point or stimulate a discussion.
✓ **Slides:** Excellent for illustrating subject matter talks. Can be rearranged, added to or eliminated to fit various situations.
✓ **Videos:** Provide a wide range of knowledge and experience. Make possible to see things that are otherwise out of reach.
✓ **Flash cards:** Use as interest-getters and learning aids. Should be large, simple and easy to see and/or read at a glance.
✓ **Models:** Most effective if three-dimensional. Good for use when the real item is impractical or unavailable.
✓ **Computer programs:** Interactive learning through various project-related programs. Used in self-paced learning.

STAGES OF GROWTH/DEVELOPMENT

4-H is Developing Youths. . .Not Things

Understanding Boys and Girls

Certain characteristics are common to children at each age level. Although children develop at different rates, the order of the stages does not vary. Although it is extremely important to remember that every child is unique and special in his or her own right, some needs and interests are universal to all children.

Characteristics of 9- to 11-year-olds

Characteristics	Suggested Activities
Are quite active with boundless energy.	Emphasize active learning experiences.
Like group activity. Group and club membership is important.	Emphasize group learning experiences.
Like to be with members of own sex.	Encourage learning experiences to be done with members of the same sex.
Have interests that often change rapidly, jumping from one thing to another.	Encourage many brief learning experiences.
Usually do best when work is presented in small pieces.	Give simple, short directions.
Need guidance from adults to stay on task to achieve their best performance.	Work closely with this age group.
Admire and imitate older boys and girls.	Encourage apprenticing with older youths.
Are easily motivated and eager to try something new.	Provide a wide variety of learning experiences.
Dislike keeping records, and do not see the value in them.	Help and closely supervise them in completing records.
Like symbols, ceremonies and songs.	Hold initiation and installation ceremonies for new members and officers.
Are extremely curious. 9- to 11-year-olds constantly ask "why?"	Do not answer all their questions. They will learn by finding some answers on their own. Encourage a few to find answers and report to the group.
Enjoy cooperation.	Plan activities so that the youths work together sometimes.

Characteristics of 9- to 11-year-olds - continued

Characteristics	Suggested Activities
Show independence by disobedience, back-talk and rebelliousness.	When you notice these characteristics, allow the youths to show independence. Ask them which activities they would like to participate in, and give them individual attention.
Need recognition and praise for doing good work.	Recognize their work in front of peers and parents.
Have feelings of competence that enhance self-concept.	Provide activities to let the youths succeed. Recognize them for their accomplishments.
Dislike comparisons with others.	Instead of comparing youths to each other, compare an individual's present and past performance.
Can direct a single familiar activity.	Give adult support.
Have limited decision-making ability.	Guide them by helping them understand the steps in decision making and ways to compare choices.

Characteristics of 12- to 14-year-olds

Characteristics	Suggested Activities
Are concerned about physical development, being liked by friends, social graces and good grooming (even though they don't like to admit it).	Encourage learning experiences related to understanding oneself and getting along with others. Be willing to talk about physical changes.
Change at different rates, according to highly individual "clocks." Can be painfully self-conscious and critical. Are vulnerable to bouts of low self-esteem.	See that they have many varied opportunities to achieve and to have their competence recognized by others.
Are self-conscious, with many needing help to overcome inferiority complexes.	Concentrate on developing individual skills.
Have intense feelings related to sex and keen interest in their own bodies, especially sex and sex processes.	Help the youths discuss body development as a natural and normal process. Provide opportunities to discuss human sexuality to ease anxiety associated with a developing body.
Experience emotions that are on a roller coaster ride. Changes in hormones and in thinking contribute to mood swings.	Accept their feelings. Remember that adolescents are known for their drama, and their feelings may seem extreme at times.
Desire independence, yet want and need their parents' help.	Encourage the youths to work with adults and older teens to complete learning experiences. Provide opportunities for apprenticing.

Characteristics of 12- to 14-year-olds - continued

Characteristics	Suggested Activities
Like fan clubs. Many have older or adult idols.	Encourage the youths to work with or apprentice to older teens and adults.
Still depend on parental guidelines.	Involve youths in deciding on their own group rules. Give them parameters to follow.
Are beginning to question the authority and values of parents.	Be willing to spend time discussing values and morals.
Peer pressure mounts, first from the same sex, then from the opposite sex.	Use peer pressure as a positive influence. Use the group to encourage participation. Have the group encourage individuals.
Are interested in activities involving boys and girls.	Encourage learning experiences involving boys and girls.
Are interested in sports and active games.	Encourage active, fun learning experiences.
Are ready for in-depth, longer learning experiences.	Encourage deeper exploration of leadership roles; encourage them to keep more detailed records of leadership experiences.
Can take responsibility in planning and evaluating their own work.	Allow members to plan activities. Expect follow through. Help them evaluate the outcome. Let members have responsibility for group activity.
Can plan their own social and recreational activities.	Form planning committees to plan parties and other social activities. Give experience in working in groups.
May avoid difficult tasks.	Help the youths choose tasks at which they can succeed. Encourage them to participate in all tasks. Help them eliminate their fears and succeed in difficult tasks.
Want to get outside their own community to explore.	Provide learning experiences outside the community.
Are leaving the age of fantasy. Beginning to think of what they will do when they grow up but are often unclear of needs and values.	Relate life skills to career choices.
Gain skills in social relations with peers and adults.	Provide opportunities for interaction with peers and adults. Provide activities that foster social interaction.

Characteristics of 15- to 18-year-olds

Characteristics	Suggested Activities
Have high social needs and desires.	Put more emphasis on personal development (mental and social) whenever possible.
Want and need a strong voice in planning their own programs.	Provide suggestions and several alternatives rather than detailed instructions.
Need freedom from parental control to make decisions.	Make the youths aware that in these situations they are making decisions for themselves or a group like themselves.
Want adult leadership roles.	Emphasize guidance and counseling from adult leaders rather than directions. Recommend group discussion methods.
Quite interested in coeducational activities.	Plan coeducational and group-oriented projects or activities.
Strong desire for status in peer group.	Make sure the youths are encouraged by their peers. Help establish a climate that is conducive to encouragement.
Are restricting areas of interest; patterns of interest are becoming more definite.	Projects can have considerably more depth. May need to suggest related areas to give the youths a broader outlook.
Reach high levels of abstract thinking and problem solving. Can choose purposes, make and carry out plans, and evaluate the results.	Put the youths into real-life problem-solving situations. Allow them to fully discover ideas, make decisions and evaluate the outcomes.
Have widespread feelings of inferiority and inadequacy.	Counter their feelings of inferiority and inadequacy by encouraging the youths and helping them to see their positive worth.
Are beginning to know themselves as individuals. Personal philosophy begins to emerge.	Allow time for the youths to explore and express their own philosophies. Use activities that encourage this.
Are developing community consciousness.	Recommend civic projects that are a service to others.

Characteristics of 15- to 18-year-olds - continued

Characteristics	Suggested Activities
Are developing a growing concern for the well-being and progress of other individuals and groups.	Encourage interest in and discussion of community and world problems in which they express concern.
Need life planning guidance.	Include activities and information regarding life planning.
Are beginning to think of leaving home for college, employment, marriage, etc.	Emphasize consumer and financial management.
Many will leave the community for employment, and many who enter college will not return to their present communities after graduation.	Introduce the youths to other settings through tours and trips to state and interstate conferences.
Are interested in travel and adventure.	For incentives, provide trips rather than medals and ribbons.

Chapter 1 Work Sheets

PLANT PARTS PAGE

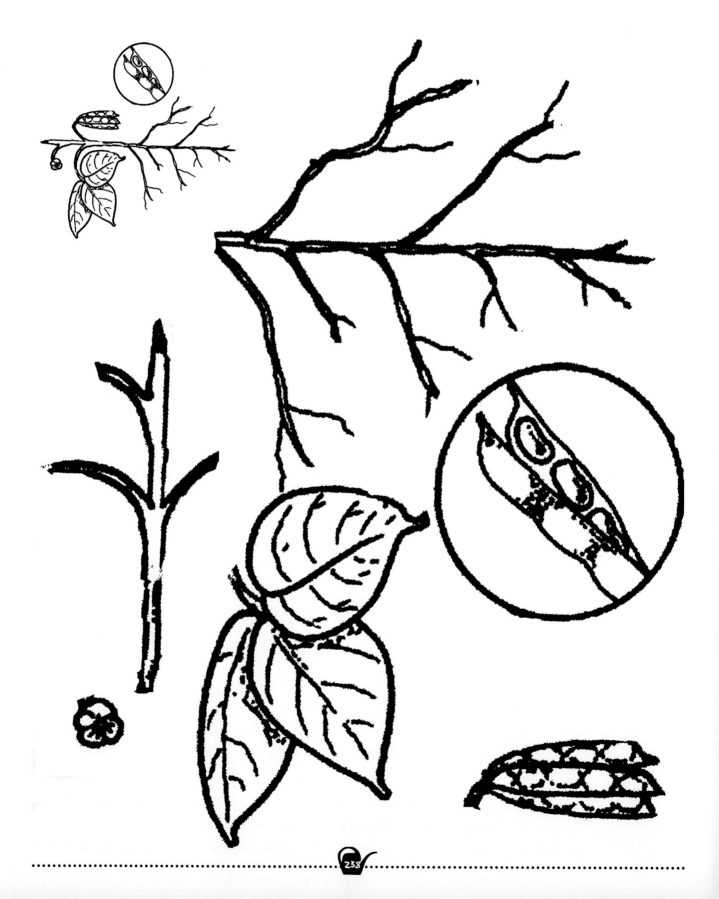

SEQUENCING TOPS AND BOTTOMS

Cut out the following boxes from this page. Glue them in order on another sheet of paper.

Mr. and Mrs. Hare open a vegetable stand.

The rabbits tell Bear that they will work for him.

Bear gets the tops of the carrots, radishes and beets.

Bear tells the rabbits that he wants the tops.

Rabbit loses a risky bet with a tortoise.

Bear tells the rabbits that he wants both tops and bottoms.

Mr. and Mrs. Hare come up with a plan.

Bear yells, "From now on I'll plant my own crops and take the tops, bottoms and middles!"

Bear only gets the roots of the plants from the rabbits.

Bear decides that he wants the bottoms.

The lazy bear's father gives his son his wealth.

Name _____ Date _____

SEED SCIENCE EXPERIMENT PAGE

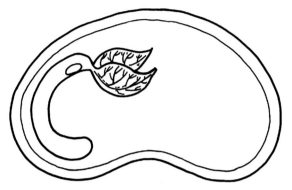

1. Draw a star on the **cotyledon** of this seed.

2. Draw a circle around the **embryo** of this seed.

3. What does the lunch box (called the cotyledon) do for the plant?

_____

_____

Question

4. What do you think would happen if we removed the cotyledon?

_____

5. Draw a picture of the plants in your bag. Make sure it shows one whole seed AND one seed with the cotyledons removed.

Hypothesis

6. Write what you think the two plants will look like in 1 week.

_____

7. Draw a picture of what you think it will look like.

Experiment

8. Draw a picture of the plants now.

Results

9. What happened to the seed without the cotyledons?

_____

Name _____ Date _____

PLANT PARTS DIAGRAM

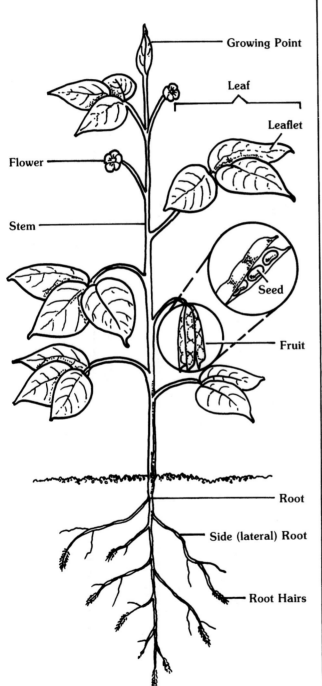

Growing Point

Leaf

Leaflet

Flower

Stem

Seed

Fruit

Root

Side (lateral) Root

Root Hairs

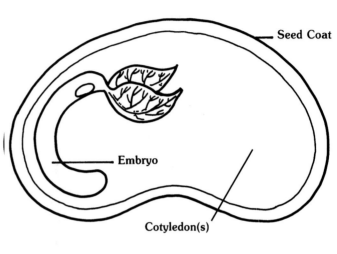

Seed Coat

Embryo

Cotyledon(s)

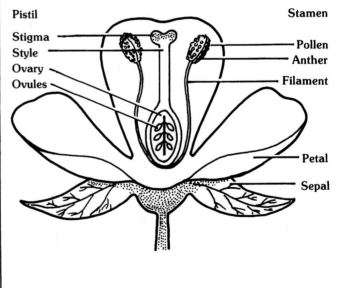

Pistil

Stamen

Stigma

Style

Ovary

Ovules

Pollen

Anther

Filament

Petal

Sepal

Name _____ Date _____

LIGHT VARIABLE LAB SHEET

✍ Draw a circle around the parts of the experiment below that are the same.

✍ Draw a box around the part of the experiment below that is different.

> *water*   *size of container*
>
> *soil*
>
> *light*   *number of seeds*

Question
Do you think the plants that have different light will grow differently? _____

Hypothesis
In the boxes below, draw your three plant containers. Draw in what you think the plants will look like after growing for 2 weeks.

```
┌──────────────┐   ┌──────────────┐   ┌──────────────┐
│              │   │              │   │              │
│              │   │              │   │              │
│              │   │              │   │              │
└──────────────┘   └──────────────┘   └──────────────┘
```

Experiment
List the three types of light your plant will grow in.

_____   _____   _____

Results
Finish this section in two weeks!
Did plants grow differently in different light? _____

Draw in the boxes below what each plant looks like.

```
┌──────────────┐   ┌──────────────┐   ┌──────────────┐
│              │   │              │   │              │
│              │   │              │   │              │
│              │   │              │   │              │
└──────────────┘   └──────────────┘   └──────────────┘
```

Name _____ Date _____

OXYGEN FACTORY

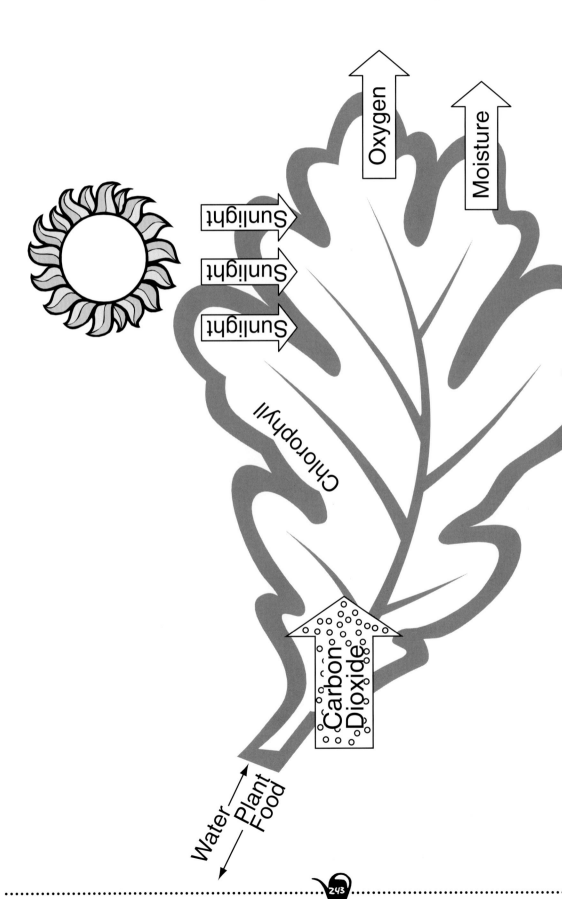

Oxygen

Moisture

Sunlight

Sunlight

Sunlight

Chlorophyll

Carbon Dioxide

Water — Plant Food

Chapter 2 Work Sheets

Name _____ Date _____

NUTRIENT VARIABLE LAB SHEET

✎ Draw a circle around the parts of the experiment below that are the same.

✎ Draw a box around the part of the experiment below that is different.

water   *size of container*
soil   *number of seeds*
light   *amount of fertilizer*

Question
Do you think the plants that have different amounts of fertilizer will grow differently? _____

Hypothesis
In the boxes below, draw your four plant containers. Draw in what you **think** the plants will look like after growing for 2 weeks.

water only- no fertilizer	recommended rate	3 times the recommended rate	4 times the recommended rate

Experiment
Keep the soil moist and measure the height of each plant every few days. Graph the height of each plant below. To record your measurements, use a different color of dot for each container. Then connect each container's dots with the same color of line.

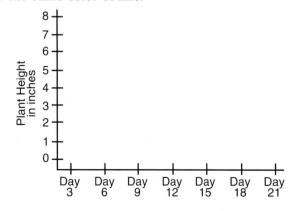

Results
On the back of this page, draw a picture of what each plant looks like after 3 weeks.

Name _____ Date _____

COMPOSTING CRITTER PAGE

Fill in each box with a critter that you find in your compost bin.

_____	_____
_____	_____

✓ Can you name what you found? If not, try looking in a reference book to identify them.

✓ Which organism do you think might eat the other things in the compost pile? _____

_____

Name _____ Date _____

EARTH APPLE GRID

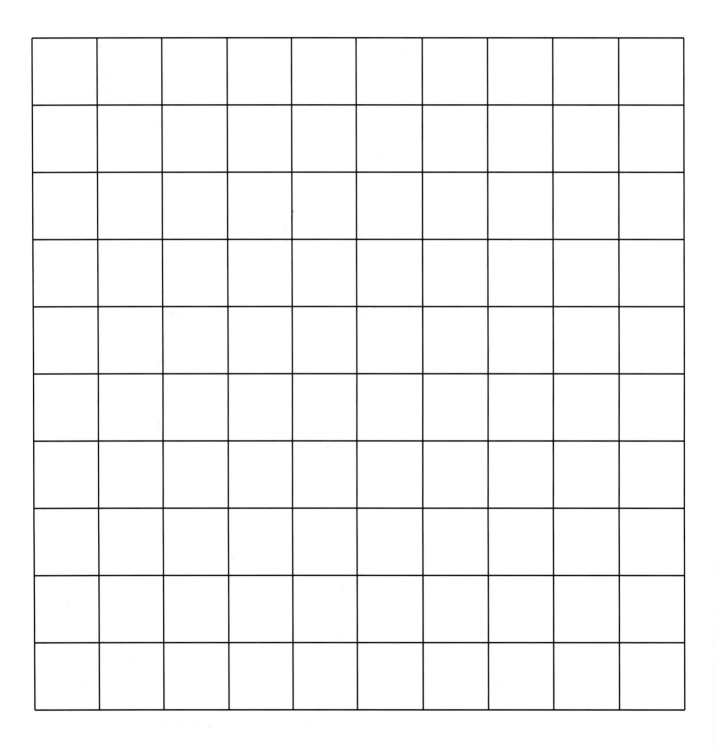

Chapter 3 Work Sheets

Name _____ Date _____
Person being interviewed _____

BACKYARD BUDDY CHECKLIST

Backyard Buddy Checklist	**Yes**	**No**
Do you maintain a water source for birds or other wildlife?	❏ (10 points)	❏ (0 points)
Do you maintain a food source for birds or other wildlife?	❏ (10 points)	❏ (0 points)
Do you provide a birdhouse or other habitat for wildlife?	❏ (10 points)	❏ (0 points)
Is a variety of plants available?	❏ (10 points)	❏ (0 points)

(If there is a variety of plants, pests and disease are less likely to invade the area.)

Does your area include flowering plants?	❏ (10 points)	❏ (0 points)

(Flowering plants attract helpful and beautiful pollinators.)

Can you distinguish harmful insects and other creatures from beneficial ones?	❏ (10 points)	❏ (0 points)

(Knowing the difference between those creatures that help us and those that cause damage keeps people from destroying the helpful ones!)

Can you name two of each? Name them.

_____Beneficial (2 points)   _____Beneficial (2 points)
_____Harmful (2 points)   _____Harmful (2 points)

Do you maintain a compost bin?	❏ (10 points)	❏ (0 points)

(A person who composts is recycling, and that's a good thing!)

When do you water your plants or lawn?
❏ early morning (10 points) ❏ midday (0 points) ❏ evening (5 points) ❏ any time of day (0 points)
(It is best to water early in the morning so that little water is lost to evaporation.)

Do you keep your yard area clear of dead plants and litter?	❏ (10 points)	❏ (0 points)

(Dead and dying plants attract pests and diseases; litter is unattractive.)

Do you apply pesticide?	❏ (0 points)	❏ (10 points)

When do you apply pesticide?
❏ morning (points) ❏ afternoon (5 points) ❏ evening (5 points) ❏ any time of day (0 points)
(Applying pesticide in the morning may harm helpful pollinators.)

Do you use mulch around your plants?	❏ (10 points)	❏ (0 points)

(Mulch helps soil keep its moisture, discourages weeds and keeps soil from becoming compacted.)

Does your area contain any native plants?	❏ (10 points)	❏ (0 points)

(Native plants are those that typically grow in an area naturally. They need less water and care.)

When you use chemicals, how carefully do you follow the label's directions?
❏ Very carefully (10 points)   ❏ Use more chemical if it's a big problem (0 points)
(When people use a chemical contrary to what the label recommends, it could be dangerous and pollute the environment.)

Backyard Buddy Award

presented to

_____

by the

Junior Master Gardener® Program

for using environmentally friendly practices in your community
and making the world a more beautiful place.

_____
JMG Leader

_____
Date

_____
Junior Master Gardener®

_____
JMG Group Name

Nature Masks

NATURE MASKS

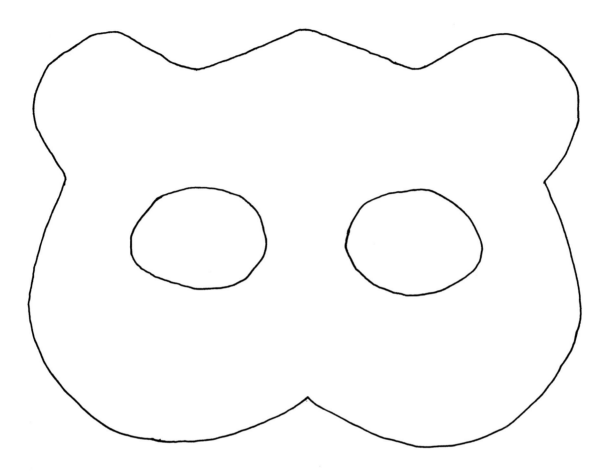

Nature Masks

Chapter 4
Work
Sheets

INSECT PREDICTIONS CHART

Name of organism	Number of body parts	Number of legs	Number of wings	Antennae present?	Is it an insect?

Name _____   Date _____

INSECT DRAWING

Many insects have them, but not all:
- ✓ *2 or 4 wings* (or no wings)
- ✓ *simple eyes* (in addition to the compound eyes listed)

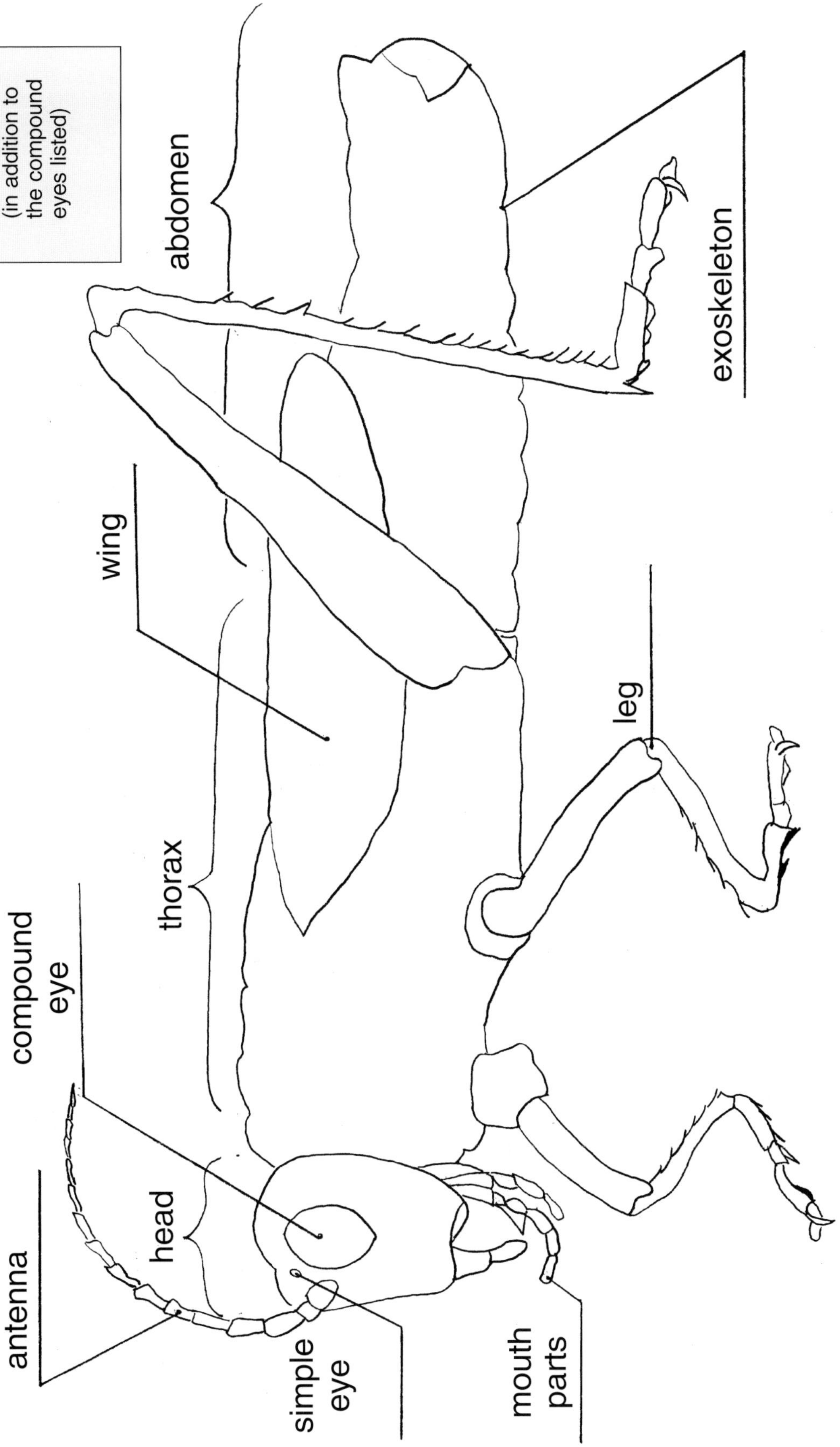

abdomen

exoskeleton

wing

leg

thorax

compound eye

head

antenna

simple eye

mouth parts

All insects are covered by a hard exoskeleton, or skeleton covering the outside of their bodies like armor.

Chapter 4

267

INSECT DRAWING

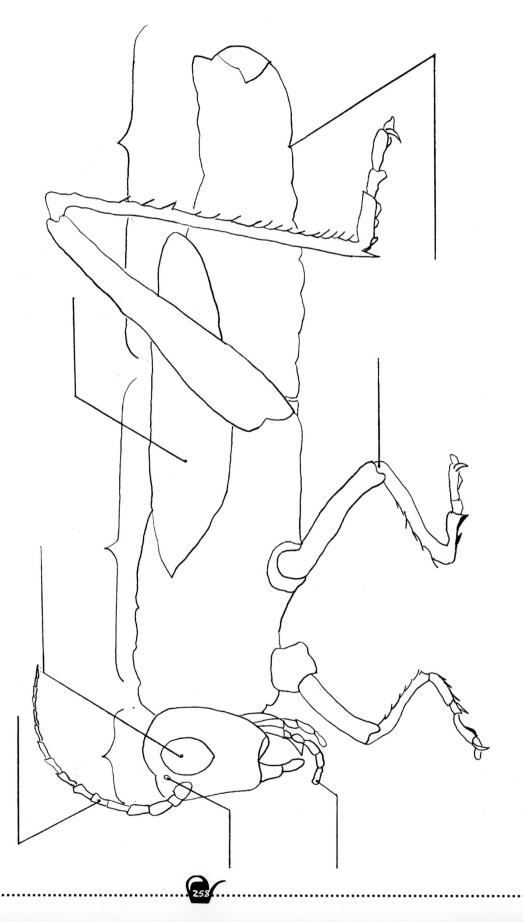

INSECT PREDICTIONS

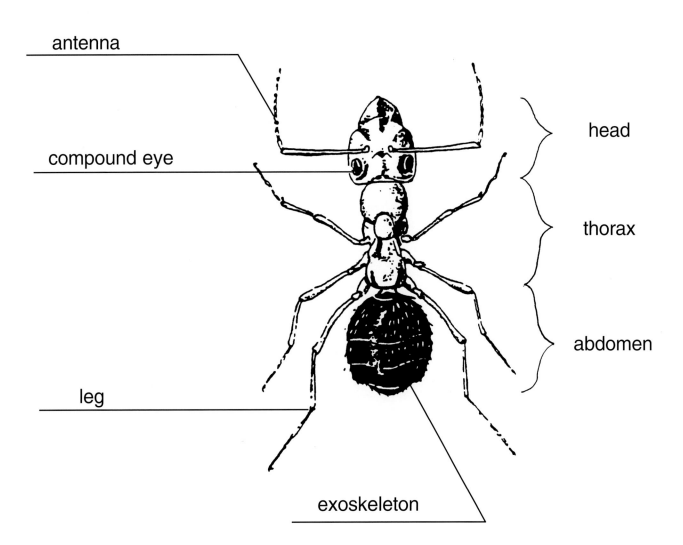

antenna

compound eye

head

thorax

abdomen

leg

exoskeleton

INSECT PREDICTIONS

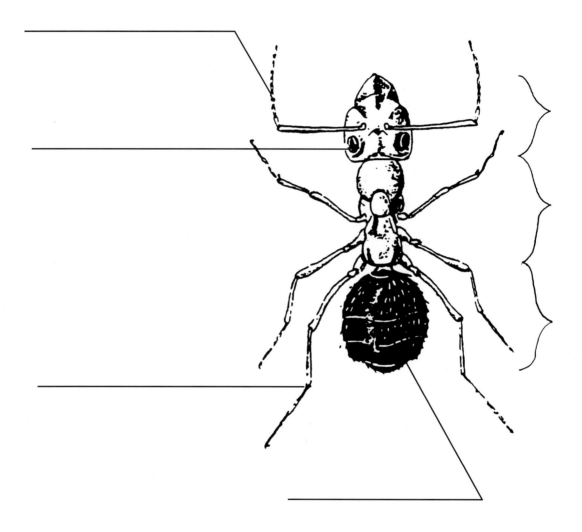

INSECT TEMPLATES

Name _____ Date _____

Insect Nets

Making a Net

You will need:

✔ Hose clip
✔ Broomstick handle cut in half
✔ ⅛-inch gauge wire
✔ Muslin material
✔ Netting
✔ X-Acto knife

Preparation and sewing

1. Use an X-Acto knife to make a cut near the uncut top edge of the broomstick. This will help the wire to fit into place snugly.

2. Bend the ⅛-inch gauge wire to form a circle, bending down the edges to form a 90-degree angle. This will serve as a frame for the net.

3. Cut a piece of muslin to 22 by 36 inches. Fold the muslin in half to make it measure 22 by 18 inches.

4. Measure 4 inches from the top of the muslin and mark the point A. At the bottom, measure 11 inches from the centerfold and mark this point B. Make a diagonal cut from point A to point B. The top part of the material should now measure 18 inches wide, and the bottom portion should measure 11 inches (see diagram).

5. Fold a 14- by 22-inch piece of netting in half to make it 14 by 11 inches.

6. Measure an 11-inch width from the centerfold and mark at this point C. Next, measure 12 inches in length and mark this point D. At the top, cut the material lengthwise from point C to D. The material should measure 11 inches at the top and 8 inches at the bottom. Now, make a rounded bottom by cutting the netting to form a semicircle (see diagram).

7. You should now have two pieces, a muslin piece and a netting piece.

8. Sew the bottom of the muslin piece (11-inch end) to the top of the netting piece (11-inch end).

9. Sew the open sides together to form a net. Be sure to leave the straight, unsewn edge of the muslin piece open to serve as an opening for the net.

10. Fold the open muslin edge down 2 inches. Fold it down 2 more inches to form a casing. Sew along the edge of the casing, leaving enough room to insert and house the wire.

11. Insert the wire through the casing. Place the ends of the wire in the broomstick grooves and clamp the wire with the hose clip.

12. Hand sew the wire opening closed.

Insect Nets

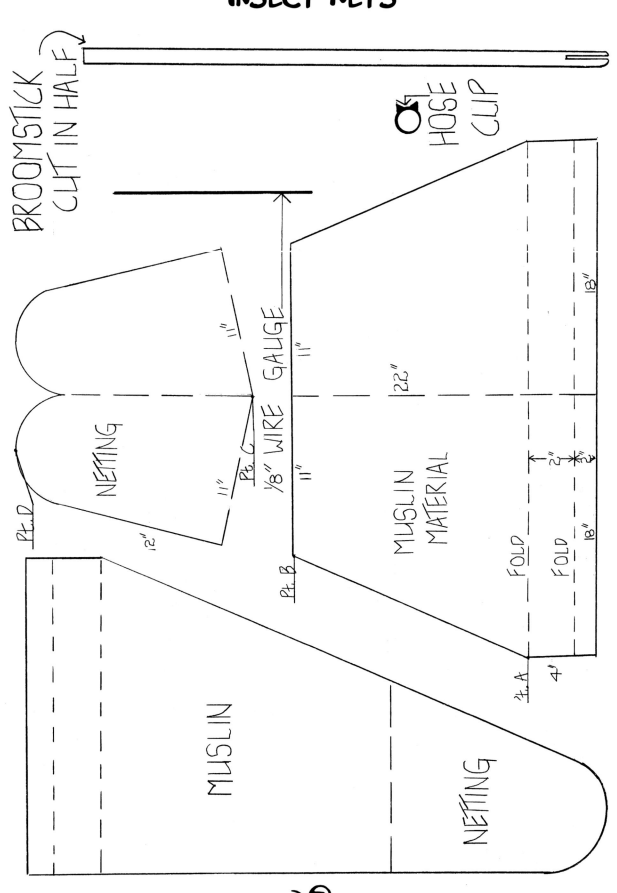

BROOMSTICK CUT IN HALF

HOSE CLIP

NETTING

Pt. D

12"

Pt. C

11"

11"

11"

⅛" WIRE GAUGE

Pt. B

11"

22"

MUSLIN MATERIAL

FOLD

FOLD

2"

2"

18"

18"

Pt. A

4"

MUSLIN

NETTING

Chapter 4

Name _____ Date _____

By Land or Sea

observations

Type of habitat	Name of insect	Number found

Was there variation in the insects you collected from different habitats? Explain._____

_____

_____

_____

_____

Energy Credit Pieces

Name _____ Date _____

Fungi Finds

Food	Location	Light or Dark	Moist or Dry	Did it grow fungi?	Draw it here

1. Which food attracted the most fungal growth? Why do you think this is so? _____

2. What conditions were best for fungal growth? Why? _____

3. Why is it so important to put food in the refrigerator instead of leaving it out? _____

266

Name _____ Date _____

LIKIN' THOSE LICHENS

Chapter 5
Work
Sheets

DIFFERENT STROKES, DIFFERENT FOLKS

Place to grow flowers used in flower designs	Place to watch birds
Place for children to play	Place to play basketball
Place to grow vegetables	Place to talk with friends
Place to store garden tools	Place to read
Place for a small pond of fish	Place to throw a baseball
Place for composting	Place to practice soccer
Place to put a hammock	Place to throw a football
Place to barbecue	Place to grow fruit trees
Place to sit in the sun	Place to grow shrubs
Place for swimming	Place to grow plants from seed
Place to eat with the family	

SITE MAP SYMBOLS

NOISE

PROPERTY LINE

PL

ELECTRICITY

E

TELEPHONE

T

NORTH WINDS

SOUTHERLY
BREEZES

Chapter 5

Site Map Symbols

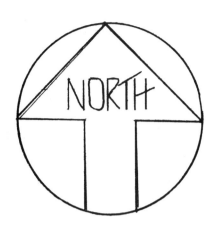

EXISTING TREE

EXISTING SHRUB

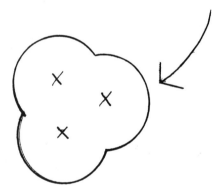

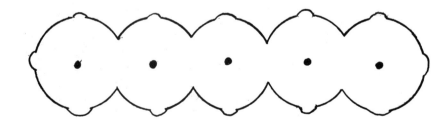

EXISTING HEDGE

SCREENING NEEDED

SITE MAP SYMBOLS

SLOPE →

LOW SPOT

KEEP VIEW OPEN

SUNNY

SITE MAP SURVEY

Be sure to check off ✓ each question after you have transferred all the information to your graph paper.

____ Which way is north? (Stand at the lower right-hand corner of the site and draw an arrow pointing to north.)				
____ Are there any buildings on the property?			Yes	No
____ Are trees and shrubs located on the property?			Yes	No

What kinds of trees?

_____

_____

_____

What kinds of shrubs?

_____   _____

_____   _____

_____   _____

____ Are there any sunny areas?			Yes	No
____ Are there any shady areas?			Yes	No
____ From which direction do the winds blow?	North	South	East	West
____ From where do the gentle summer breezes come?	North	South	East	West
____ Are there low spots on the property?			Yes	No
____ Does water stay in this spot for a long time, or does it seep into the soil quickly?	Runs off	Seeps	Stays	

____ Is there a slope or is it flat?   Slope   Flat

____ Do any overhead telephone lines or other utility lines cross the space?   Yes   No

____ Are there good views to keep? *(such as mountain scenery, beautiful blooming plants, play area, etc.)*   Yes   No

____ Do any views need to be hidden? *(such as utility areas, trash can bins, busy/noisy street, etc.)*   Yes   No

ONE-LEGGED TABLE

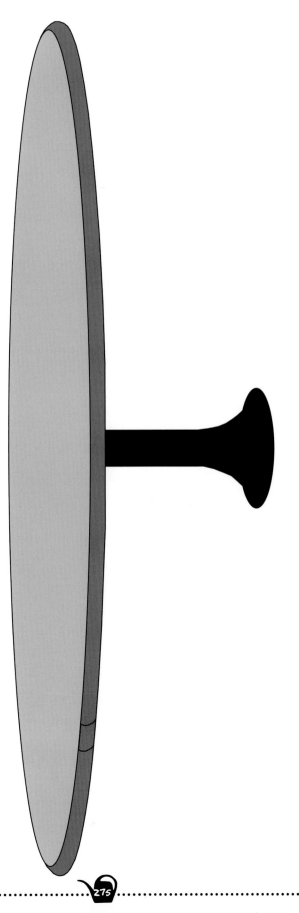

ONE-LEGGED TABLE

Name _____ Date _____

BUTTERFLY SYMMETRY

DOES IT FIT?

DOES IT FIT?

DOES IT FIT?

DOES IT FIT?

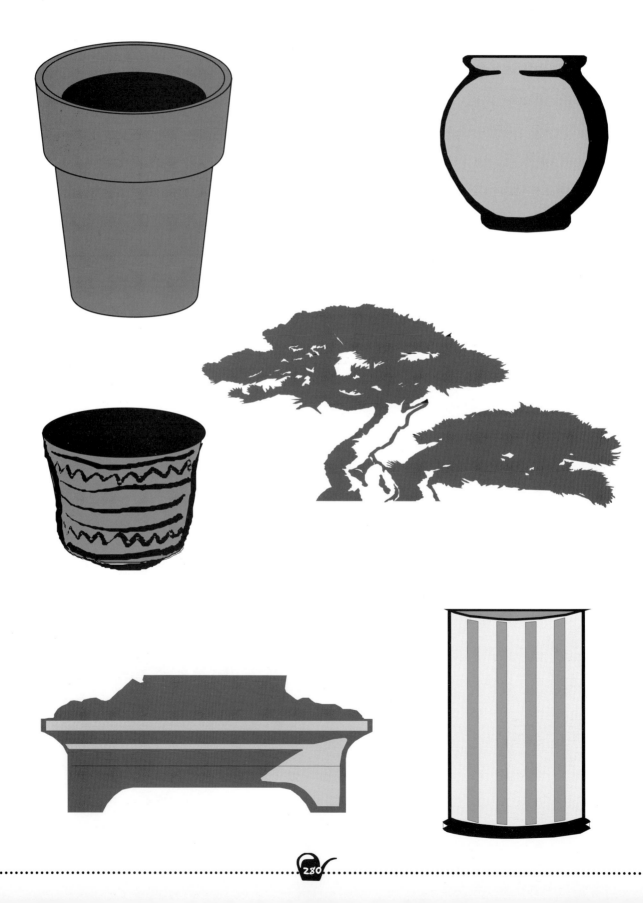

DOES IT FIT? ANSWER KEY

DOES IT FIT? ANSWER KEY

Name _____   Date _____

TREE SHAPE ID PAGE

Columnar

Irregular

Mound or spreading

Oval

Prostrate

Pyramidal

Round

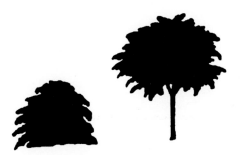

Rounded

V-shaped

MY TREE FRIEND

has a/an _____

shape.

Seed, Sod and Plugs Interview

What is your job? _____

What is sod? _____

How long do you have to wait to have a lawn when sod is used? _____
_____

How often and how long each time do you have to water the sod? _____
_____

What types of turf grass seed do you sell? _____
_____

How long does it take before a lawn comes up when you plant with grass seeds? _____
_____

How often and how long each time do you have to water the seeds? _____
_____

What are plugs? _____

How long before the lawn fills in when you use plugs? _____

How often and how long each time do you have to water the plugs? _____
_____

What type of grass works best in this area? _____

Which grass has the FEWEST disease and pest problems? _____

Which type of grass needs to be mowed most often? _____

Are there any new types of grasses?   Yes No   (If yes, list them on the back).

Inch of Water

Question
Do irrigation systems sprinkle the water equally across the lawn?

Hypothesis
The pans will fill in _____ seconds / minutes. (circle one)
                                  (fill in blank)

I think / do not think the pans will have the same amount of water.
  (circle one)

Other things that will happen are: _____

_____

Experiment
Pan Readings

5 minutes	_____	10 minutes	_____
15 minutes	_____	20 minutes	_____
25 minutes	_____	30 minutes	_____

Weather conditions today (circle all that apply)

Rainy   Windy   Cloudy   Partly Cloudy   Sunny

Results
What happened? Why?

_____

_____

_____

Chapter 6 Work Sheets

Name _____ Date _____

DR. FRUIT

Name of fruit _____

Scientific name _____

Drawing of fruit	*Drawing of plant*	*Drawing of seeds*

Climate fruit is grown in _____

How is the fruit harvested? _____
(This means how is the fruit picked.)

How do you eat it? _____
(Fresh, cooked)

What country and continent does it come from? _____

_____

What vitamins does this fruit have in it? _____

Write two interesting facts you found out about this fruit.

1. _____

2. _____

Linnaeus Name It

Linnaeus Name It

Bushel and a Peck

1 pint = 2 cups

1 quart = 2 pints

1 peck = 8 quarts

1 bushel = 4 pecks

◼ pint

◼◼ cup

quart

◼◼ pint

peck

| quart | quart | quart | quart |
| quart | quart | quart | quart |

bushel

| peck | peck |
| peck | peck |

1 peck = _____ quarts

1 quart = _____ pints

2 pecks = _____ quarts

2 quarts = _____ pints

1 bushel = _____ pecks

1 pint = _____ cups

2 bushels = _____ pecks

2 pints = _____ cups

2 pecks = _____ quarts = _____ pints

2 quarts = _____ pints = _____ cups

2 pints = _____ quarts

16 quarts = _____ pecks

8 quarts = _____ pints

4 cups = _____ quarts

Gold leaf Challenge

1   bushel = _____ pints

16   pints = _____ pecks

2   bushels = _____ cups

32   quarts = _____ bushels

1   peck = _____ cups

BUSHEL AND A PECK ANSWER KEY

1 pint = 2 cups

1 quart = 2 pints

1 peck = 8 quarts

1 bushel = 4 pecks

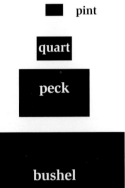

1 peck = 8 quarts	1 quart = 2 pints
2 pecks = 16 quarts	2 quarts = 4 pints
1 bushel = 4 pecks	1 pint = 2 cups
2 bushels = 8 pecks	2 pints = 4 cups

2 pecks = 16 quarts = 32 pints

2 quarts = 4 pints = 8 cups

2 pints = 1 quart	16 quarts = 2 pecks
8 quarts = 16 pints	4 cups = 1 quart

Gold leaf challenge

1	bushel	=	64	pints
16	pints	=	1	pecks
2	bushels	=	256	cups
32	quarts	=	32	bushels
1	peck	=	32	cups

Name _____ Date _____

Fruit Taste Test

Fruit	Color					Texture					Taste					Smell					Total
a	1	2	3	4	5	1	2	3	4	5	1	2	3	4	5	1	2	3	4	5	
b	1	2	3	4	5	1	2	3	4	5	1	2	3	4	5	1	2	3	4	5	
c	1	2	3	4	5	1	2	3	4	5	1	2	3	4	5	1	2	3	4	5	
d	1	2	3	4	5	1	2	3	4	5	1	2	3	4	5	1	2	3	4	5	
e	1	2	3	4	5	1	2	3	4	5	1	2	3	4	5	1	2	3	4	5	

What letter has the highest total? _____

What do you think the fruit is? _____

Name _____ Date _____

Fruit Frenzy!

Guess how many seeds a fruit has, and write the number in the Guess circle. Then, open each fruit and sketch what it looks like in the box. Then count the seeds and write that number in the Actual circle.

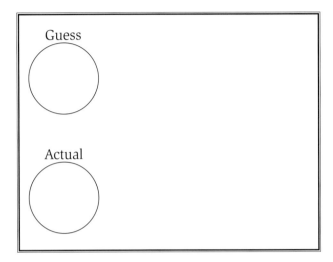

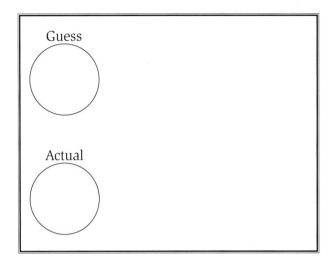

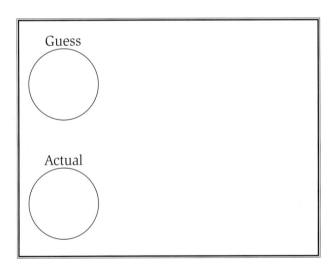

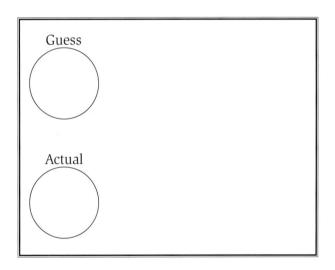

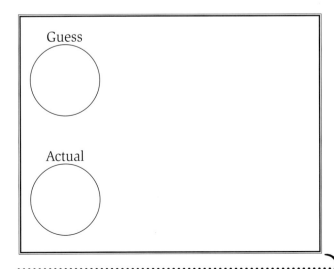

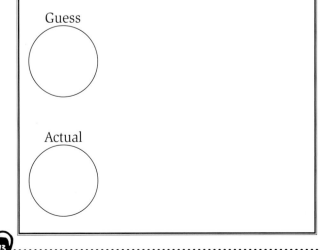

Name _____ Date _____

HARDINESS ZONE MAP

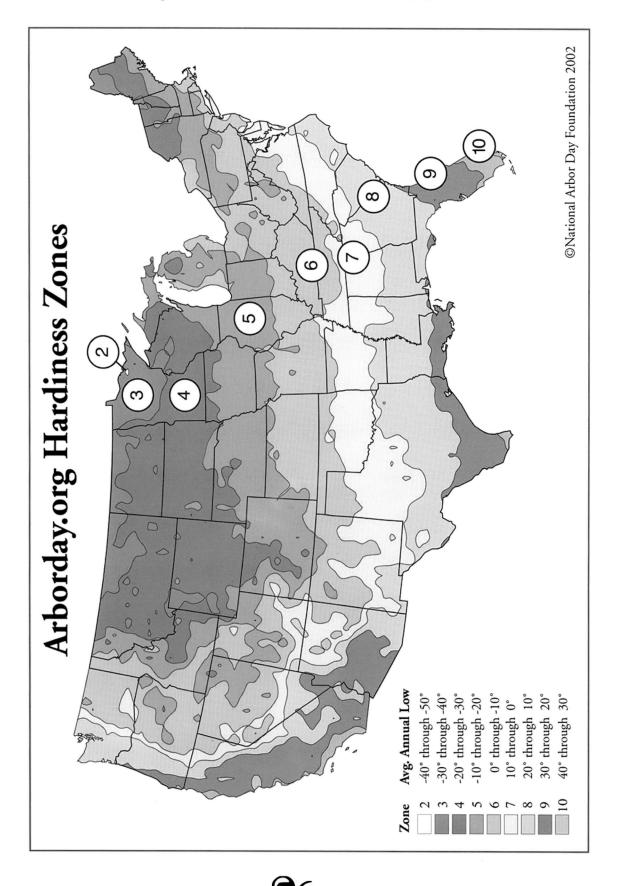

Arborday.org Hardiness Zones

©National Arbor Day Foundation 2002

Zone	Avg. Annual Low
2	-40° through -50°
3	-30° through -40°
4	-20° through -30°
5	-10° through -20°
6	0° through -10°
7	10° through 0°
8	20° through 10°
9	30° through 20°
10	40° through 30°

HARDINESS ZONE MAP

Chapter 7
Work
Sheets

Name _____ Date _____

SITE EVALUATION

You are trying to decide on the best place to put your group's garden. Circle one number for each line. 1 means it's not very good, and 5 is the best.

Location of Site _____

Area has sunlight.	1	2	3	4	5
Area is near a water source.	1	2	3	4	5
Area has good , well-drained soil.	1	2	3	4	5
Area is near where tools are stored.	1	2	3	4	5
Area is close by and easy to get to.	1	2	3	4	5

Add up all of the numbers in the box above and write it in the star.

What was that site's score?

Location of Site _____

Area has sunlight.	1	2	3	4	5
Area is near a water source.	1	2	3	4	5
Area has good , well-drained soil.	1	2	3	4	5
Area is near where tools are stored.	1	2	3	4	5
Area is close by and easy to get to.	1	2	3	4	5

Add up all of the numbers in the box above and write it in the star.

What was that site's score?

Location of Site _____

Area has sunlight.	1	2	3	4	5
Area is near a water source.	1	2	3	4	5
Area has good , well-drained soil.	1	2	3	4	5
Area is near where tools are stored.	1	2	3	4	5
Area is close by and easy to get to.	1	2	3	4	5

Add up all of the numbers in the box above and write it in the star.

What was that site's score?

Which site had the highest score? _____

FALL PLANTING GUIDE

The time to plant vegetables is based on the weather. Plant crops that are susceptible to cold early enough in the fall so that they mature before the first freezing weather.* Cold-hardy crops, which can withstand all but the coldest of weather conditions, are usually planted much later.

If a frost occurs earlier than the average date, some of the less frost-tolerant plants may be damaged, and some of the harvest may be lost. You can minimize this problem by preventing heat from escaping by covering the garden with a light blanket, a clear plastic shower curtain or a row cover that you can buy.

Some crops with special considerations are noted on the chart and explained below:

♣ Garlic is grown by dividing a head into individual cloves and planting each one. Onions can be grown by seed; however, they are usually planted as "sets," or small onions, in late fall to early winter. Potatoes are grown by planting "seed" potatoes, which are sections of large potatoes that have been cut into chunks including an "eye," or node. The new growth will emerge from these nodes.

T Transplants can be grown by either seed or transplant—you may want to do both. Tomatoes are not included in the seed list. They should be grown from transplants in the fall, unless you start them from seed in midsummer. Plant transplants so that the root ball is completely covered with a soil layer no more than $\frac{1}{4}$-inch thick. If the root ball is left exposed, it may wick water into the air away from the plant, and the plant may dry out and die.

* The recommended planting dates can vary greatly depending on where you live. Contact your county Extension office for information to complete your Fall Planting Chart.

Name _____ Date _____

FALL PLANTING CHART

Crop	Recommended Planting Date	Number of Seeds per Paper Towel	Planting Depth	Days to Harvest	Country of Origin
Root Crops					
Beets		9	½ inch	55 to 70	Mediterranean area
Carrots		16	¼ inch	70 to 80	Afghanistan
Garlic ♣		16	1 inch	100 to 200	Pakistan
Onions ♣		16	1 inch	80 to 120	Pakistan
Potatoes ♣		1	4 inches	70 to 90	Chile and Peru
Radishes		16	½ inch	25 to 40	China and Middle Asia
Turnips		9	½ inch	30 to 60	Mediterranean area
Leaf Crops					
Brussels sprouts		1	¼ inch, or T	120 to 150	Mediterranean area
Cabbage		1	¼ inch, or T	60 to 120	Mediterranean area
Chard		4	1 inch	45 to 80	Mediterranean area
Collards		4	½ inch	45 to 80	Mediterranean area
Kohlrabi		1	½ inch	50 to 75	Mediterranean area
Lettuce(leaf)		4	¼ inch, or T	45 to 60	Egypt or Iran
Lettuce(head)		4	½ inch, or T	40 to 90	Egypt or Iran
Mustard greens		4	½ inch	30 to 50	Mediterranean area
Parsley		4	T	20 to 120	Mediterranean area
Spinach		9	½ inch	40 to 60	Iran
Turnip greens		4	½ inch	30 to 60	Mediterranean area
Flower/Fruit Crops					
Beans (bush)		4	1 inch	45 to 60	Mexico, SW U.S.
Beans (pole)		4	1 inch	50 to 70	Mexico, SW U.S.
Broccoli		1	¼ inch, or T	60 to 80	Mediterranean area
Cauliflower		1	¼ inch, or T	60 to 100	Mediterranean area
Cucumbers		2	1 inch	50 to 70	India
Squash	1 plant per 4 squares		1 inch	45 to 90	Mexico, SW U.S.
Tomatoes		1	¼ inch, or T	60 to 80	Andes Mountains in South America

SPRING PLANTING GUIDE

The time to plant vegetables is based on the weather. In the spring, you should plant vegetables that are susceptible to cold after all danger of frosty weather is over.* Plant cold-hardy vegetables before the frost-free date, and early enough for them to mature before the weather gets too hot.

Keep in mind that the last frost date is an average. If a frost occurs later than average, it may damage some plants less able to tolerate cold, and some of the harvest may be lost. You can minimize this problem by keeping heat from escaping from the garden by covering plants with a light blanket, a clear plastic shower curtain or a row cover that you buy.

Some crops with special considerations are noted on the chart and explained below:

♣ Potatoes are propagated vegetatively (not from seeds). Potatoes are grown by planting "seed" potatoes, which are sections of large potatoes that have been cut into chunks including an "eye," or node. The new growth will emerge from these nodes. Shallots can be grown from seeds; however, they are usually planted as "sets," or small mature bulbs, in early winter.

♠ Vine crops are generally grown on raised beds with 7 to 10 feet between each row. You can plant squash, cucumber and small watermelon varieties closer together; dwarf varieties need the least amount of space between plants. You can conserve space between rows by using a trellis, which allows vines and fruits to grow vertically. This method may also discourage diseases.

T Transplants can be grown by either seed or transplant; you may want to do both. Tomatoes are not included in the seed list, because transplants are normally used in spring plantings. Although peppers can be grown from seed, generally they are grown from transplants too. You can plant transplants earlier because the plants are more established and take less time to reach the harvest stage. Tomatoes and peppers benefit if you cover the top of the root ball with 2 to 3 inches of soil. Plant all other transplants so that the root ball is completely covered with a layer of soil no more than $\frac{1}{4}$ inch thick. If you leave the root ball exposed, it may wick water into the air away from the plant, and the plant may dry out and die.

* The recommended planting dates can vary greatly depending on where you live. Contact your county Extension office for information to complete your Spring Planting Chart.

Spring Planting Chart

Crop	Recommended Planting Date	Number of Seeds per Paper Towel	Planting Depth	Days to Harvest	Country of Origin
Root Crops					
Potatoes ♣, (Irish)		1	4 to 6 inches	70 to 90	Chile and Peru
Carrots		16	¼ inch	70 to 80	Chile and Peru
Shallots		4	1 inch	80 to 120	Asia
Radishes		16	½ inch	25 to 40	Chile and Peru
Leaf Crops					
Cabbage, Chinese		1	½ inch	65 to 70	Asia
Lettuce (leaf)		4	¼ inch, or T	45 to 60	Egypt or Iran
Mustard Greens		4	½ inch	30 to 50	Mediterranean area
Parsley		4	½ inch	20 to 120	Mediterranean area
Spinach		9	½ inch	40 to 60	Iran
Turnip greens		4	½ inch	30 to 60	Mediterranean area
Flower/Fruit Crops					
Eggplant		1 plant per 1 square	T	80 to 90	Asia
Muskmelon, ♠ (cantaloupe)		1 plant per 9 squares	½ to 1 inch	90 to 120	Asia and Africa
Cucumbers ♠		1	½ to 1 inch	50 to 70	Asia
Peppers ♣		1 plant per 2 squares	T	80 to 100	South America
Squash (summer)		1 plant per 4 squares	1 inch	50 to 60	North America
Tomatoes		1 plant per 4 squares	T	60 to 80	Andes Mountains in South America
Watermelon ♠		1 plant per 9 squares	1 to 2 inches	80 to 100	Africa
Seed Crops					
Beans, lima (bush)		2	1 inch	65 to 80	Mexico and Central America
Beans, lima (pole)		4	1 inch	75 to 85	Mexico and Central America
Beans, snap (bush)		4	1 inch	45 to 60	Central America
Beans, snap (pole)		4	1 inch	60 to 70	Central America
Corn, sweet		1	2 inches	70 to 90	South America
Peas, English		12	1 to 2 inches	55 to 90	Europe and Asia
Peas, black-eyed (southern)		2	1 to 2 inches	60 to 70	Asia

Some Like It Hot

Copy the cards on this page and the next back to back so the pictures will correspond with the descriptions.

SOME LIKE IT HOT

Copy the cards on this page and the previous back to back so the descriptions will correspond with the pictures.

Asparagus

Sun requirement: Full sun

When to plant: October from transplant

Planting depth: $1\frac{1}{2}$ inches

Spacing: 18 inches between plants
36 inches between rows

Time to germination: 7 to 21 days

Time to harvest: 3 years; late February to early May

Beets

Sun requirement: Full sun; tolerates partial shade

When to plant: 4 to 6 weeks before last frost

Planting depth: $\frac{1}{2}$ to 1 inch

Spacing: 2 inches between plants
12 to 18 inches between rows

Time to germination: 7 to 10 days

Time to harvest: 55 to 65 days

Broccoli

Sun requirement: Full sun

When to plant: 2 weeks before last frost

Planting depth: $\frac{1}{4}$ inch

Spacing: 8 to 12 inches between plants
24 to 30 inches between rows

Time to germination: 3 to 10 days

Time to harvest: 60 days

Cantaloupe

Sun requirement: Full sun

When to plant: Up to 6 weeks after last frost

Planting depth: $\frac{1}{4}$ inch

Spacing: 24 to 36 inches between plants
60 to 96 inches between rows

Time to germination: 6 to 8 days

Time to harvest: 80 to 85 days

SOME LIKE IT HOT

Copy the cards on this page and the next back to back so the pictures will correspond with the descriptions.

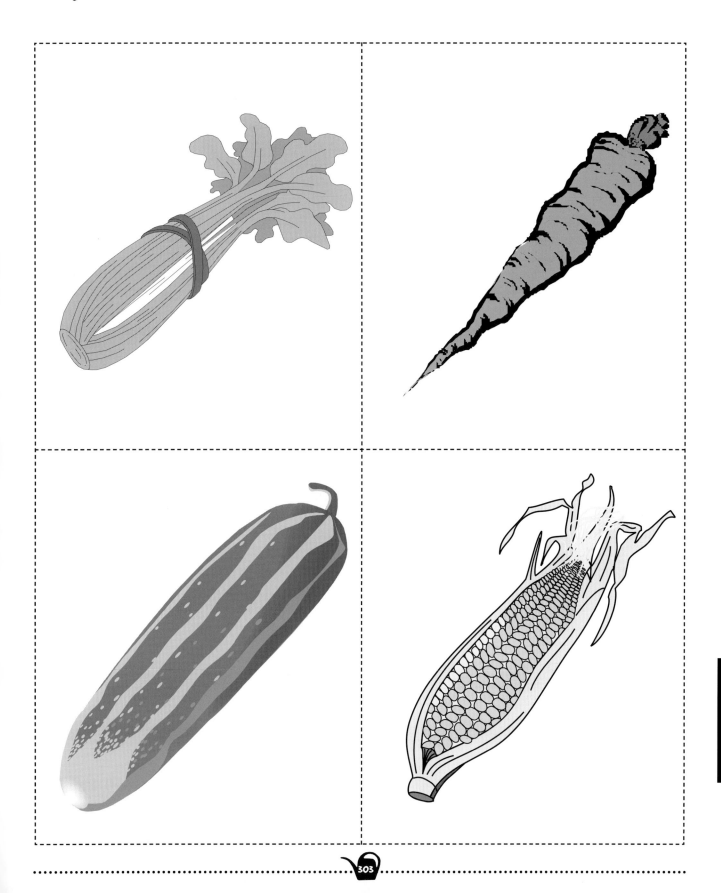

SOME LIKE IT HOT

Copy the cards on this page and the previous back to back so the descriptions will correspond with the pictures.

Carrots

Sun requirement: Full sun; will tolerate partial shade

When to plant: Late winter or early spring

Planting depth: ¼ inch

Spacing: 1 to 2 inches between plants
14 to 24 inches between rows

Time to germination: 10 to 17 days

Time to harvest: 60 to 80 days

Celery

Sun requirement: Full sun

When to plant: Indoors, 12 to 16 weeks before taking outdoors in mid to late spring

Planting depth: ⅛ inch

Spacing: 8 inches between plants
24 to 30 inches between rows

Time to germination: 3 to 4 weeks

Time to harvest: 5 to 6 months

Corn

Sun requirement: Full sun

When to plant: After danger of frost is past and soil temperatures reach 60°F

Planting depth: 1 ½ to 2 inches

Spacing: 8 to 12 inches between plants
24 to 36 inches between rows

Time to germination: 5 to 8 days

Time to harvest: 60 to 90 days

Cucumbers

Sun requirement: Full sun

When to plant: After danger of frost is past and soil has warmed

Planting depth: 1 to 1 ½ inches

Spacing: 12 to 18 inches between plants
14 to 24 inches between rows

Time to germination: 6 to 10 days

Time to harvest: 60 to 80 days

SOME LIKE IT HOT

Copy the cards on this page and the next back to back so the pictures will correspond with the descriptions.

Some Like It Hot

Copy the cards on this page and the previous back to back so the descriptions will correspond with the pictures.

Leaf lettuce

Sun requirement: Full sun, tolerates partial shade

When to plant: Spring - December to January; fall - September

Planting depth: ½ inch

Spacing: 2 to 3 inches between plants

Time to germination: 6 to 8 days

Time to harvest: 60 to 70 days

English peas

Sun requirement: Full sun

When to plant: 6 weeks before last spring frost

Planting depth: 1 to 1 ½ inches

Spacing: 12 to 18 inches between plants 14 to 24 inches between rows

Time to germination: 6 to 10 days

Time to harvest: 60 to 80 days

Onion

Sun requirement: Full sun

When to plant: Late September to mid-November

Planting depth: 1 inch

Spacing: 3 to 4 inches between plants

Time to germination: 7 to 4 days

Time to harvest: 80 days

Peppers

Sun requirement: Full sun

When to plant: 2 weeks after last frost

Planting depth: ⅛ inch

Spacing: 18 to 24 inches between plants 14 to 24 inches between rows

Time to germination: 3 days

Time to harvest: 80 to 95 days

Some Like It Hot

Copy the cards on this page and the next back to back so the pictures will correspond with the descriptions.

Some Like It Hot

Copy the cards on this page and the previous back to back so the descriptions will correspond with the pictures.

Potatoes

Sun requirement: Full sun

When to plant: 6 weeks before last spring frost

Planting depth: 6 inches

Spacing: 9 inches between plants
36 inches between rows

Time to germination: 12 to 14 days

Time to harvest: 13 to 17 weeks

Pumpkins

Sun requirement: Full sun

When to plant: After danger of frost is past

Planting depth: 1 to 1½ inches

Spacing: 6 feet between plants

Time to germination: 5 to 7 days

Time to harvest: 80 days

Yellow squash

Sun requirement: Full sun

When to plant: After danger of frost is past and soil has warmed

Planting depth: 1 inch

Spacing: 6 feet between plants

Time to germination: 3 to 5 days

Time to harvest: When squash is 4 to 6 inches long

Tomatoes

Sun requirement: Full sun

When to plant: Shortly after last frost

Planting depth: 1 to 1½ inches

Spacing: 3 feet between plants

Time to germination: 3 to 5 days

Time to harvest: 65 to 80 days

Name _____ Date _____

Veggie Research

Name of plant _____

Drawing of plant   Drawing of seeds

Season plant is grown _____

How deep should the seed be planted? _____

How many days until plant can be harvested? _____
   (This means how many days after planting can you pick the vegetables growing on the plant?)

How do you eat it? _____
   (Fresh, fried, boiled)

What continent did it come from? _____

What vitamins does this vegetable have in it? _____

Why did you choose to plant this vegetable? _____

_____

Write two interesting facts you found out about this plant.

   1.

   2.

PLANT FACT AND OPINION

Decide if each sentence below is a fact or an opinion. Write an **F** in the blank if it is a **fact** and an **O** if it is an **opinion.**

_____ **1.** All flowers are beautiful.

_____ **2.** Flowers grow to attract pollinators.

_____ **3.** Mulch is sometimes used to keep moisture in the soil.

_____ **4.** Grass clippings make better mulch than shredded newspaper.

_____ **5.** Roses smell better than other flowers.

_____ **6.** Sunflowers grow during the summer.

_____ **7.** Roots grow in the soil and absorb moisture.

_____ **8.** Kids do not like broccoli.

_____ **9.** It is important to have rules in the garden.

_____ **10.** Vegetable gardens should have plenty of sunlight.

_____ **11.** If seeds are planted too deep, they may not grow.

_____ **12.** Tomatoes taste better than green beans.

Write five opinions you have about plants:

1. _____

2. _____

3. _____

4. _____

5. _____

Food Guide Pyramid

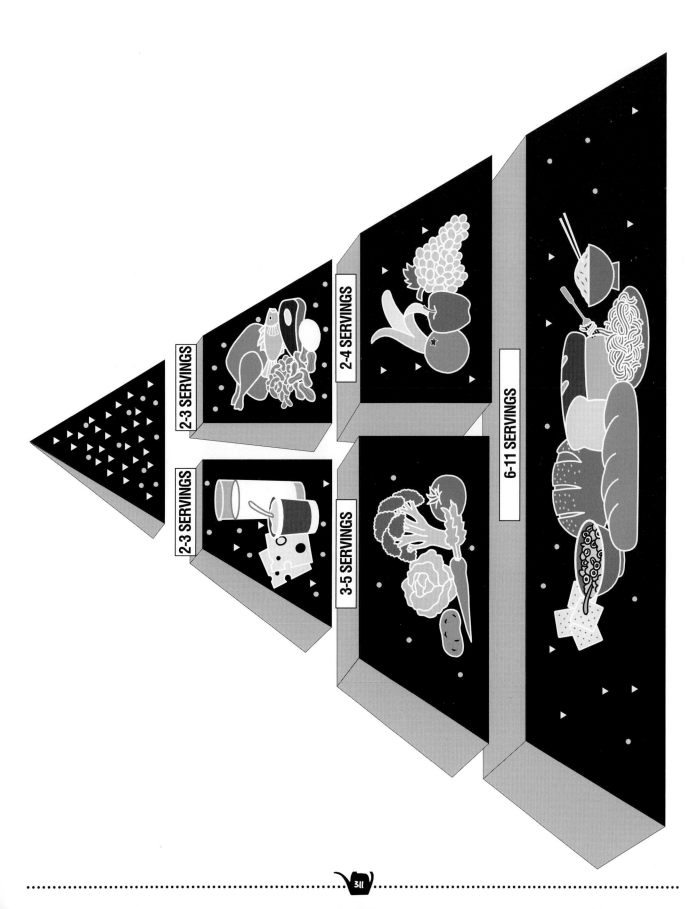

2-3 SERVINGS

2-3 SERVINGS

2-4 SERVINGS

3-5 SERVINGS

6-11 SERVINGS

Name _____ Date _____

LABEL READER

Nutritional information

Serving size:	The amount commonly eaten in one sitting. Be careful: Some products contain more than one serving.
Dietary fiber:	Derived from plants and found in foods containing plant parts. Helps the body digest foods and absorb nutrients; helps lower blood cholesterol.
Vitamin A (retinol):	Helps you see better; helps bones grow and skin develop; helps fight disease.
Vitamin C (ascorbic acid):	Helps fight infections and heals wounds; helps the body absorb iron and calcium.
Calcium:	Promotes strong bones and teeth; needed for blood to coagulate, or thicken; used by muscles and nerves.
Iron:	Needed for hemoglobin (the part of red blood cells that carries oxygen) and myoglobin (the protein in muscle cells that holds oxygen).

Apricots

Calories	60	Total fat	1g
Dietary fiber	1g	Protein	0g
Vitamin A	45%	Vitamin C	20%
Calcium	2%	Iron	2%

Cantaloupe

Calories	50	Total fat	0g
Dietary fiber	1g	Protein	1g
Vitamin A	100%	Vitamin C	80%
Calcium	2%	Iron	2%

Grapefruit

Calories	60	Total fat	0g
Dietary fiber	6g	Protein	1g
Vitamin A	15%	Vitamin C	110%
Calcium	2%	Iron	0%

Kiwifruit

Calories	100	Total fat	1g
Dietary fiber	4g	Protein	2g
Vitamin A	2%	Vitamin C	240%
Calcium	6%	Iron	4%

Mango

Calories	70	Total fat	0.5g
Dietary fiber	1g	Protein	0g
Vitamin A	40%	Vitamin C	15%
Calcium	0%	Iron	0%

Raspberries

Calories	50	Total fat	0g
Dietary fiber	8g	Protein	1g
Vitamin A	0%	Vitamin C	40%
Calcium	2%	Iron	2%

Name _____ Date _____

Food Labeling

Directions: Choose five foods that are found in your home. For each food chosen, use the food label to identify the amount (percent of the daily value, or % DV) of calcium, iron, vitamin A, vitamin C and fiber found in one serving. Then answer the questions below.

Nutrient Amount (%DV)

Food Name	Calcium (Ca)	Iron (Fe)	Vitamin A (A)	Vitamin C (C)	Fiber (Fiber)
1.					
2.					
3.					
4.					
5.					

Questions

1. Which food is highest in calcium? _____

2. Which food is lowest in calcium? _____

3. Which food is highest in iron? _____

4. Which food is lowest in iron? _____

5. Which food is highest in vitamin A? _____

6. Which food is lowest in vitamin A? _____

7. Which food is highest in vitamin C? _____

8. Which food is lowest in vitamin C? _____

9. Which food is highest in fiber? _____

10. Which food is lowest in fiber? _____

Veggie Taste Test

Vegetable	Color	Texture	Taste	Smell	Total
a	1 2 3 4 5	1 2 3 4 5	1 2 3 4 5	1 2 3 4 5	
b	1 2 3 4 5	1 2 3 4 5	1 2 3 4 5	1 2 3 4 5	
c	1 2 3 4 5	1 2 3 4 5	1 2 3 4 5	1 2 3 4 5	
d	1 2 3 4 5	1 2 3 4 5	1 2 3 4 5	1 2 3 4 5	
e	1 2 3 4 5	1 2 3 4 5	1 2 3 4 5	1 2 3 4 5	

What letter has the highest total? _____

What do you think the vegetable is? _____

Chapter 8
Work
Sheets

Name _____   Date _____

Know Your JMG Friends

Write on each line the names of two people in the group. Use every gardener's name at least once. Share what you have learned with your JMG group.

Someone who:

1. Has planted a seed _____

2. Is wearing tennis shoes _____

3. Has a loose tooth _____

4. Has been to another country _____

5. Has red hair _____

6. Likes to sing _____

7. Has a brother _____

8. Is in the fourth grade _____

9. Has pierced ears _____

10. Has a garden at home _____

11. Has a pet fish _____

12. Has a collection _____

13. Has read a book this week _____

14. Plays softball/baseball _____

15. Has brown eyes _____

16. Has gone fishing _____

17. Has attended summer camp _____

18. Has seen a caterpillar in the garden _____

19. Is wearing a T-shirt _____

20. Knows ballet _____

21. Has eaten five servings of fruit and vegetables today _____

22. Can name five parts of a plant _____

23. Lives in an apartment _____

24. Rides a bus to school _____

25. Is wearing a bracelet _____

Name _____ Date _____

OFFICIAL JMG GROUP FINGERPRINT CARD

Name_____

JMG'er Taking Fingerprints _____

Date _____

Right Thumb	Right Index	Right Middle	Right Ring	Right Little

Left Thumb	Left Index	Left Middle	Left Ring	Left Little

How Would You Feel?

Ignore me	Be friendly to me
Laugh at me	Agree with me
Listen to me	Disagree with me
Ask me questions	Make me do all the work
Boss me around	Don't look at me

Feeling Bee

anxious   kind   creative   cry   lonely   confused   praised

exhausted   different   calm   content   angry   smart   challenged

happy   special   loved   guilty   frightened   puzzled   rich

honest   excited   scared   sad   triumphant   super   grateful

poor   insecure   helpless   encouraged   negative   mad   respected

bored   positive   upset   surprised   lazy   joyful   shy

miserable   frustrated   ashamed   proud   afraid   nosy   jealous

explode   silly   relieved   hurt   undecided   yucky   envious

shocked   uncomfortable   responsible   worried

COOPERATION COUNTDOWN

1.	**6.**
2.	**7.**
3.	**8.**
4.	**9.**
5.	**10.**

Name _____ Date _____

WHO'S ON OUR TEAM?

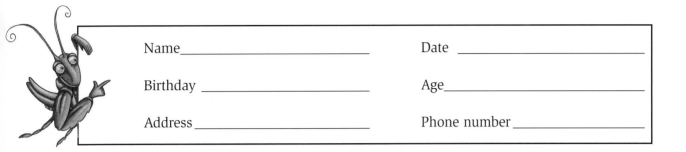

Name_____   Date _____

Birthday _____   Age_____

Address _____   Phone number _____

1. How tall are you?_____

2. What would you like to be doing 10 years from now? _____
Twenty years from now? _____

3. How do you spend your time after school and on weekends? _____
_____

4. Of all the things you do in your free time, what do you like to do best? _____
_____

5. What do you like the most about adults? _____
_____

6. What qualities do you admire in your friends?_____
_____

7. What are your favorite sports, hobbies and crafts? _____

8. What are your favorite television shows? Why? _____
_____

9. What magazines do you like to read?_____

10. Why do you think your friends like you?_____

11. What is your favorite time of day? _____

12. What are things that bother you? _____

Name _____ Date _____

MY JMG TARGETS FOR THIS WEEK

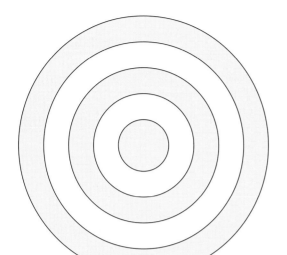
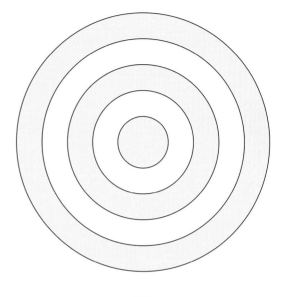
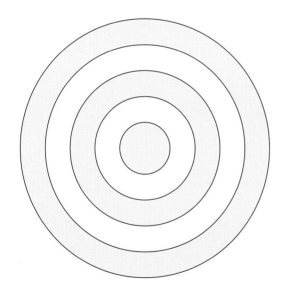
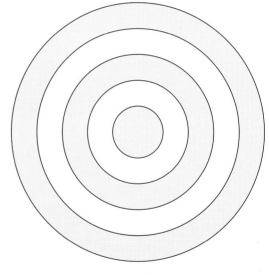
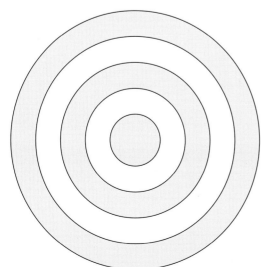
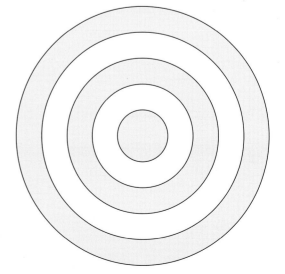

CLASS/CLUB CHRONICLE

DATE: _____

Dear _____ ,

The most exciting thing that our group did in class/JMG club this week was _____

_____

_____.

My favorite group leadership/community service project was_____

_____

_____.

Some interesting and funny things that happened this week were _____

_____

_____

_____.

Next week our group plans to _____. I will help
to accomplish this by _____.

_____
My name

Name ____________________ Date ______________

My Growing Season

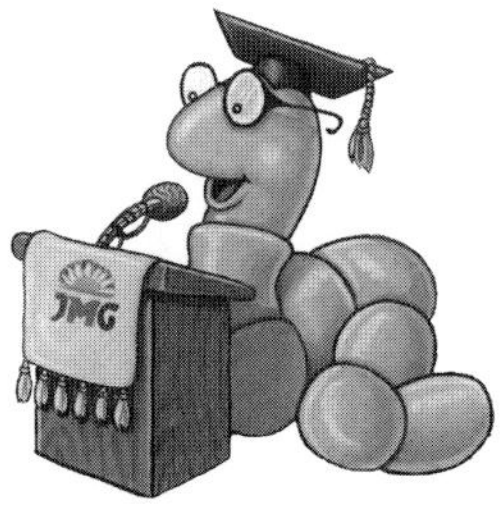

The coming months can be a growing season for me. I would like to improve in

____

____

____

____

____

Watch me grow and blossom in this area: ______________________________

Here is my goal for the area I want to improve in: ______________________

____

Here is my plan of action or how I plan to reach my goal: ________________

____

____.

Here are some people I would like to have help me to reach my goal:

______________, ______________, ______________.

Here are some things they could help with:

1. ____
2. ____
3. ____

Subjects and Career Cards

computer programmer	author
lawyer	TV announcer
waitress	artist
astronaut	athlete
nurse	musician
truck driver	secretary
mechanic	veterinarian
welder	scientist
doctor	landscape designer
engineer	jeweler
teacher	hair stylist
actor/actress	model
chemist	pilot
printer	store owner
architect	florist
newspaper reporter	

Name _____   Date _____

MOBILE CAREERS

1. Which of the following works mainly with AUTOMOBILES:
carpenter
pilot
mechanic

2. Which of the following is NOT in the field of CONSTRUCTION:
architect
mechanic
carpenter

3. A college education is NOT required to be a:
chemist
doctor
store clerk

4. Which of the following has to know the MOST about MATH:
pilot
doctor
secretary

5. Which of the following spends the MOST time preparing food:
flight attendant
cook
nurse

6. A college education is usually NEEDED to be a:
mail carrier
lawyer
farmer

7. Which of the following DESIGNS buildings:
architect
principal
engineer

8. Which of the following works closest with a VETERINARIAN:
soldier
farmer
author

9. Which of the following is NOT in the field of TRANSPORTATION:
bus driver
plumber
ship captain

10. Which of the following spends the most time with TAX RECORDS:
accountant
refinery worker
movie director

MOBILE CAREERS

11. Which of the following works closest with a CASHIER:
librarian
bookkeeper
actress

12. Which of the following is in the field of AGRICULTURE:
homemaker
sculptor
rancher

13. Which of the following works closest with an AUTHOR:
game warden
publisher
shrimp boat captain

14. Which of the following is in the field of COMMUNICATION:
telephone operator
athlete
plumber

15. Which of the following works closest with a GEOLOGIST:
landscaper
teacher
surveyor

16. Which of the following is in the field of ENTERTAINMENT:
manufacturer
make-up artist
store manager

17. Which of the following is in the field of GOVERNMENT:
senator
musician
police officer

18. Which of the following spends the MOST time at a DESK:
actress
receptionist
marine biologist

19. Which of the following spends the MOST time OUTDOORS:
landscaper
counselor
barber

20. Which of the following is not in the field of MEDICINE:
pharmacist
X-ray technician
pet store owner

WHo Am I?

I watch my baby sister while my mom cooks dinner.

I pick up my things and put them away.

I hold the flashlight when my dad fixes the car.

I go get papers for my teacher from the office.

I never throw candy wrappers on the ground.

I lend my friend a book she wants to read.

I carry in the grocery bags for my grandma.

CAREER HELPER CARDS

Operating a dump truck

Checking out a customer at a store

Fighting a fire

Designing a building

Teaching school

Arguing a case in court

Acting in a movie

Playing a ball game

Baking bread in a bakery

Roofing a house

Operating on someone

Exploring the ocean or space

Preaching a sermon

Building a bridge

Name _____   Date _____

GROUP OR ALONE

Examples

Alone	Group
Artist	Rock group
Writer	Assembly line
Hunter	Football team

Careers in Which People Work in Groups

Careers in Which People Work Alone

Answer the following questions ALONE.

Did you enjoy working alone or in a group? _____

What are some advantages of working in a group?_____

What are some advantages of working alone? _____

What are some disadvantages of working in a group? _____

What are some disadvantages of working alone? _____

Rhythms

The Choo-Choo Song

From Chapter 1, Plant Growth and Development, page 5

Tomato sat on the railroad track,
Thought he was the boss,
Along came the choo-choo train, (clap)
Tomato sauce.

Avocado sat on the railroad track,
All jolly and rolly,
Along came the choo-choo train, (clap)
Guacamole.

Cucumber sat on the railroad track,
For this there is no excuse,
Along came the choo-choo train, (clap)
Pickle juice.

Other Verses:
Blueberry, huffin' and puffin', (clap) Blueberry muffin
Apple, playing with a spider, (clap) Apple cider
Lemon, where he often stayed, (clap) Lemonade
Strawberry, being such a ham, (clap) Strawberry jam
Orange, silly as a goose, (clap) Orange juice
Grape, Sunning his fat belly, (clap) Grape jelly
Onion, Doing his own thing, (clap) Onion ring
Potato, Wishing he could fly, (clap) French fry

The Choo-Choo Song

Plant Parts Rap

From Chapter 1, Plant Growth and Development, page 8

Plants are our friends, we give them special care.
They feed, they shelter, they give us fresh air.

Without plants in our world, we simply could not live,
Because of all of the awesome gifts that they give.

The tiny plant begins as a seed that germinates.
And from this moment on, here's the journey that it takes.

The roots are in the dirt to help the plant grow
And hold it in place when the winds blow.

Just like a soda straw, they suck up H_2O.
And when the plant gets water, stand back and watch it grow.

Stems hold the plant up, they carry water to
The leaves, flowers, fruit and seeds. . .that's what the stems do.

Leaves grow from the stem. They soak up lots of sun.
When they change it into food, then their job is done.

The food is for the plant—it gives it strength and power.
It helps it to grow and make a nice flower.

Wind, birds, and bees. . .these are a flower's friend.
They help the life cycle to start once again.
The flower makes a fruit with a seed deep inside.
Some are eaten, some are blown, or some just hitch a ride.

Once a fruit is dried and a little seed comes out,
The seed will find the dirt and a new plant will sprout.

Coconut Float

Once a young seed said to its big Mother plant,
"I want to stay with you!" She said, "I'm sorry, seed—you can't."

"You need your own piece of earth, a place where you can grow."
Then the trees began to rustle and strong winds began to blow.

The seed was pulled far away and carried by the winds.
It fell lonely to the ground, but soon it made some friends.

A squirrel scampered by with some seeds in his cheeks.
It buried seeds all over, to hide them for a week.

The squirrel forgot about them and they began to sprout.
Those plants were growing strong when they heard a bird call out.

That bird squawked, "Watch out!"—earlier he'd been eating berries,
And now the bird was dropping droppings his body could no longer carry.

The droppings landed with a "SPLAT" in the open field.
From the seeds in that pile sprouted a plant that grows there still.

Soon a cat trotted by with stickers in its tail.
It stopped and scratched to get them out and on the ground they fell.

Those stickers were seeds that sprouted, now a huge bush grows there.
So if you walk in that area, be sure to take great care.

Another young plant that came nearby traveled far and at slow speed.
A coconut tree dropped a nut on the beach. Yes, a coconut is a seed.

The coconut did not grow on that beach, it got washed out to the ocean.
It traveled across great distances just by riding on wave motion.

The seed was splashing along when it bumped into a boat.
The captain looked up as the nut passed by and said, "Look a coconut float!"

The coconut finally landed on an island; it could no longer wait.
Once it found a good sandy spot, it began to germinate.

Now remember, plants need many things like water, air and light.
If they grow too close together, for those things they have to fight.

If seeds did not travel, they couldn't last very long.
But since they are carried, plants can grow to be healthy and strong.

The Numbers on the Bag

From Chapter 2, Soils and Water, page 29

It's time to fertilize,
you've got to realize
that plants need nutrients, too.
You want plants so strong,
it won't be long
before they'll be needing you.

Add nutrients to the soil,
like manure or fertilizer.
You'll learn plants grow better in the rich soil,
now you're a little bit wiser.
When you use fertilizer
you'll have to figure out
what those three numbers printed on the bag
are all about....

Those three numbers side by side
tell you what's in the bag.
Each number means a certain amount
of nutrients to be had.

Nitrogen is the first number,
a nutrient that plants need.
It helps leaves grow strong
and grass grow long and makes plants stay green.

Phosphorus is for all of us,
the second number on the sack.
It helps plants bloom flowers
and make fruit for us to snack.

Potassium gives the plant some
nutrients so roots can grow.
It's the last number on the bag,
something everyone should know.

Plants need these three nutrients,
different plants need different amounts.
The plants won't just stay alive—they will thrive
and when you're gardening, that's what counts!

The Cycle Song
From Chapter 2, Soils and Water, page 37

The plants in the world just continue to grow,
because of the rain that falls and the water that flows.

The rain from the sky, it never runs out,
the water cycle keeps flowing just like a water spout.

The cycle keeps us wet, all around the nation,
when the rain falls down, it's precipitation.

The rain flows on the soil and ground,
some runs off and some soaks down.

The rain going down is drunk by the roots.
It's carried up to the leaves, the flowers and the fruit.

Once it gets to the leaves, the water starts to fly,
transpiration takes the water from the leaves to the sky.

The water that runs to rivers, oceans and the lakes
doesn't rest for long—there it cannot stay.

It doesn't stop long and take a vacation,
it travels up to the sky—evaporation.

From a liquid to gas and it travels up so high,
then it condenses to a cloud you can see floating by.

Some clouds get so big, they grow gray and tall,
they get so full of water that the rain has to fall.

The rain hits the earth as the water cycle starts again,
life on earth continues as the water cycle spins.

A Fruit's Life Rhyme

From Chapter 6, Fruits and Nuts, page 151

The fruit we get from plants
all start as flowers.
Big or small, short or tall,
all have attracting power.

Flowers attract a visit
from a bird, bug or bee.
They buzz around from flower to flower
all for a nectar fee.

A flower's job is to make a seed
to grow a baby plant.
Without help, it won't do that job;
by itself, the flower just can't.

The pollen from the flower
must be carried to a mother.
It takes a bug to move it there,
or a bird, wind or others.

When the pollen gets to the pistil
it can become a brand-new seed.
How can the seed find a place to grow?
it becomes animal feed!

Seeds can grow a thick coat—
bright colors, reds and blues.
The color covering those little seeds
is yummy, juicy fruit.

The fruit can be eaten
or just fall to the ground.
Either way it ends up in the soil,
to the new home it's found.

Then it sprouts to become a new plant
and grows a new flower.
Could be big or small, short or tall,
but will have attracting power.

Junk Food Blues

I had a big hunger, wanted a tasty treat.
Grabbed some soda and chips—started to eat.
I ate the whole bag of chips, drank a can of soda, too.
Now I ache somethin' awful—I got the low-down junk food blues.

Chorus:
I'm tired, my stomach hurts, my head and body ache.
I'm eatin' too much junk food, too many fries and sugar flakes.
Now I want some good food—something my body really needs.
Payin' attention to what I eat—each time before I feed.

Now I forgot my own song, when I fixed today's lunch.
I packed some nachos, cookies and candy bar that crunched.
Same thing happened when I ate, 'cause healthy food I did not choose.
I got that achy, tired feelin'—the low-down junk food blues.

I'm tired, my stomach hurts, my head and body ache.
I'm eatin' too much junk food, too many fries and sugar flakes.
Now I want some good food—something my body really needs.
Payin' attention to what I eat—each time before I feed.

Gotta big game today, playing the Mighty Bears.
Eatin' some candy, lots of sugar, my plan to get prepared.
Wanna be fast and win against this other guy named Fred.
But the candy didn't work, I lost, my face is sweaty and red.

I'm tired, my stomach hurts, my head and body ache.
I'm eatin' too much junk food, too many fries and sugar flakes.
Now I want some good food—something my body really needs.
Payin' attention to what I eat—each time before I feed.

The game was over and they had won, they were happy but I felt sick.
Saw Fred munchin' on some grapes and some orange carrot sticks.
Then I knew it was my fault, I finally got a clue,
'Cause all the junk that I ate before, gave me the low-down junk food blues.

Standardized Test Formatted Reading Passages

ALIEN BUG

"It looks like an alien from another planet!" Octi exclaimed. He and his best friend, Chris, had stopped to make sure his plants were doing all right when they saw it. They always checked to see how their tomato plants were growing before playing basketball during recess. Usually they just stopped to notice that their plants were getting bigger, and sometimes they pulled some weeds that had grown up in their group's garden. Today was different. Today, some kind of creature was crawling over one of the leaves.

Octi thought the spiked insect looked like an alien. Chris just wanted to get rid of it. "I think it may be eating holes in the leaves," Octi told Chris. "Or it might be poisonous."

The two boys went to find a stick to knock the dangerous looking arthropod off the plant. When they returned, it was gone. Chris was relieved to see it was not staying around to cause problems. He and Octi went to play basketball before returning to class.

After the boys were back inside, their teacher asked them how their garden looked. They told Mrs. Dell about the dangerous looking insect and even drew a picture of it. The teacher asked them to show her the insect next time they saw it.

The next day the same alien bug was on their plant again, except this time it wasn't just one insect. More than 20 of the creatures were crawling all over the plant. Chris shouted for his friend to look at a group of the alien bugs on the stem of a leaf. "Look, they are even eating other insects!" He was right. The alien bugs were eating tiny green insects that Chris thought looked like baby insects. Octi ran in for Mrs. Dell as Chris stayed outside trying to thump the alien bugs off their plant.

"Where is the bug spray? We need to kill the alien bugs. They are all over my plant!" Chris was out of breath. Mrs. Dell just said, "I don't think we're going to need any bug spray. Let's go look at these aliens."

Chris took his teacher outside and led her to the plant where Octi had just knocked off another alien bug. "Stop!" Mrs. Dell told Octi, and she picked up one of the creatures he had just thumped to the ground.

"These dangerous looking creatures are really one of a gardener's best friends," she said. "This beneficial insect is really just a young ladybug. It is perfectly harmless."

"But Mrs. Dell, it's eating those baby insects over there!" Chris told her. He pointed out the little green insects that were being gobbled up.

"Those cute little creatures are called aphids," Mrs. Dell said. "And they are sucking the juices from inside the plant's leaves. They can cause a lot of damage to plants."

Now Chris and Octi knew that these alien bugs were helpful because they were helping get rid of the harmful aphids. They wondered how long it would take for the baby ladybugs to grow up and start looking like the ladybugs they were used to seeing.

It wasn't long before the alien looking bugs had grown into the bright red ladybugs. After that, Chris and Octi stopped at their group's garden each day to see how the plants and the ladybugs were doing. Then they played basketball before going back to class.

ALIEN BUG QUESTIONS

1. Why is this story called "Alien Bugs?"

   ○ The story is about bugs from Mars.

   ○ The ladybugs in this story look like aliens.

   ○ The story is about bugs biting aliens.

   ○ The story is about bugs going to space in a space shuttle.

2. What happened AFTER the teacher saw the insects?

   ○ She told the boys the creatures were ladybugs.

   ○ Chris went to get a stick.

   ○ Octi thumped a bug to the ground.

   ○ The boys sprayed the alien bugs.

3. What does the word "arthropod" mean in this story?

   ○ Snake.

   ○ Angry.

   ○ Unhappy.

   ○ Insect.

4. Why did the boys think the insect was dangerous?

   ○ It was making a hissing noise.

   ○ They saw it eating leaves.

   ○ It bit one of the boys.

   ○ It was unusual looking.

5. What does the word "beneficial" mean in this story?

   ○ With wings.

   ○ Harmful.

   ○ Helpful.

   ○ Brightly colored.

6. Which of these events did NOT happen in this story?

   ○ Chris and Octi took a ladybug inside.

   ○ Mrs. Dell told them the alien bug was just a ladybug.

   ○ The boys played basketball after recess.

   ○ The ladybug ate the aphids.

CRACKER BUGS

There may be times before dinner or lunch when you are too hungry to wait for meal time. A Cracker Bugs snack is fun and easy to make. Cracker Bugs are a healthful way to satisfy your hunger.

The first part of this recipe uses raisins. You may already know that raisins come from grapes. But you may not know that you can make your own raisins at home in your own kitchen!

To make raisins, you will need a cluster of grapes. Any type of grapes will work, but be sure they are seedless. Rinse the grapes. Then ask an adult to boil 3 cups of water. Drop the grapes in the water and quickly remove them. This will help prevent mold from growing on your raisins. The grapes should be in the boiling water only for a few seconds. A quick way to separate the grapes from the boiling water is to pour the grapes and water through a sieve. Then allow the grapes to cool.

Place the grapes on a cookie sheet so they do not touch each other, and place them in an oven at its lowest setting. Check the grapes after 2 hours and then every 30 minutes after that. It may take as long as 6 hours before the grapes turn brown and shrink to become raisins. Once they have finished turning into raisins, take the cookie sheet out of the oven and let it cool for 30 minutes.

This recipe also uses peanut butter. You can make your own peanut butter, too. Put 1 cup of roasted peanuts and 1 teaspoon of salt in a blender. Add 4 tablespoons of vegetable oil and ½ cup of sugar. Turn the blender on a high setting until the peanut butter is smooth. If you like crunchy peanut butter, add a small handful of peanuts and blend them for a few more seconds.

Now spread the peanut butter over a cracker. The last step is to sprinkle the raisins over the peanut butter. This makes the snack look like bugs all over the cracker!

CRACKER BUGS QUESTIONS

1. Which of the following steps should happen first?

   ❍ Turn blender on high.

   ❍ Allow grapes to cool for 30 minutes.

   ❍ Rinse grapes

   ❍ Place grapes in oven on lowest setting.

2. What do you need an adult to help with in making raisins?

   ❍ Putting grapes on a cookie sheet.

   ❍ Boiling water.

   ❍ Checking to see if the raisins are done.

   ❍ Letting the grapes cool.

3. What does the word "sieve" mean in this story?

   ❍ A special bowl with tiny holes that allow water to drain through it.

   ❍ A spice used to make raisins taste better.

   ❍ Fresh grapes.

   ❍ A blender.

4. How much salt should be added to the blender?

   ❍ 1 teaspoon.

   ❍ 1 tablespoon.

   ❍ ½ cup.

   ❍ 1 cup.

5. Which ingredient is not used to make peanut butter?

   ❍ Boiling water.

   ❍ Salt.

   ❍ Peanuts.

   ❍ Sugar.

6. Why is this snack called "Cracker Bugs?"

   ❍ It is made with crackers and bugs.

   ❍ The crackers are shaped like bugs.

   ❍ It looks like bugs on a cracker.

   ❍ It is food for pet insects.

THE GREAT FRUIT DEBATE

Every day at the lunch table, students in Mrs. Bishop's class talked about what they had brought to eat that day. One day Melinda told the rest of the group that she had brought only vegetables. She said, "I have carrots, broccoli, cauliflower and tomatoes."

"Tomatoes aren't a vegetable," John said. "They're a fruit."

All through lunch, John and Melinda debated whether a tomato was a fruit or vegetable. They decided to ask their teacher when they returned to the classroom to see who was right.

"Well, both of you are right," answered Mrs. Bishop. She explained that there are different ways to determine whether a food is a fruit or vegetable. You can use a botanical definition or social customs. "Why don't the two of you prepare a report for the class so we can all learn from your debate?" she said.

John and Melinda went to the library together that afternoon after school. John looked up the botanical definitions of a fruit and vegetable. He found that a fruit is the part of the plant that grows from a flower and usually has seeds inside. Vegetables are other parts of the plants, including the roots, stems and leaves.

"See, I was right!" John said. "Tomatoes come from flowers and have seeds inside them just like apples and oranges and grapes—they are all fruits."

"Not so fast, John," said Melinda. "Look what I found." She showed him the book she found on social customs that told about fruits and vegetables. The book said you can tell the difference between a fruit and vegetable depending on how it's grown. Vegetables are grown in 1 year and are planted in rows in fields. Fruits are grown for more than 1 year and usually grow on trees or bushes.

"So this definition says that tomatoes are a vegetable," Melinda said. "They are grown for 1 year in rows in a field."

Melinda also found that even the U.S. government had had to decide if a tomato was a fruit or a vegetable. In the late 1800s, people had to pay more taxes on fruits than on vegetables. At the time tomatoes were considered a fruit. People didn't want to be taxed more for tomatoes, so they argued that tomatoes were a vegetable because they are grown in 1 year in the field. So, in 1893 the Supreme Court decided that tomatoes would be considered a vegetable, and they weren't taxed as much.

"Mrs. Bishop was right—tomatoes can be defined as a fruit or a vegetable," John said. "So can cucumbers, squash and pumpkins. We were both right!"

The next day John and Melinda told the rest of their class what they had learned about fruits and vegetables at the library. They also found out that one person doesn't always have to be right and the other wrong. They were both right. A tomato is called a fruit and a vegetable, depending on where you find your information.

The Great Fruit Debate Questions

1. What is this story mostly about?
   - ❍ How to grow fruits.
   - ❍ Whether something is a fruit or vegetable.
   - ❍ Melinda's lunch.
   - ❍ How to find out new information.

2. Where did John and Melinda get their information?
   - ❍ At the lunch table.
   - ❍ In the classroom.
   - ❍ At the library.
   - ❍ At John's house.

3. What does the word "debate" mean in this story?
   - ❍ Eat.
   - ❍ Agree.
   - ❍ Sing.
   - ❍ Argue.

4. What did John and Melinda do after lunch?
   - ❍ Worked in the garden.
   - ❍ Went to the library.
   - ❍ Talked to their teacher.
   - ❍ Talked with other classmates.

5. What does the word "botanical" mean in this story?
   - ❍ Relating to animals.
   - ❍ Relating to plants.
   - ❍ Dealing with boats.
   - ❍ Strong.

6. What did the students learn by going to the library?
   - ❍ Tomatoes are definitely a vegetable.
   - ❍ Tomatoes are definitely a fruit.
   - ❍ People with two different opinions can both be right.
   - ❍ No one knows what a tomato is.

Mika's Maze

Mrs. Jasell's class was working outside in the school garden. As the students were returning inside, the teacher reminded the class that Science Fair Day was coming up. She also told them that everyone should already have ideas for a project to have enough time to finish before Science Fair Day.

Mika was worried. The Science Fair Day at Stephens Elementary School was just 3 weeks away. Many other students in her class had already begun working on their projects, but Mika still had no idea what she would do.

On Monday she asked her teacher for help in thinking of an idea. Mrs. Jasell was always very helpful and told her, "Try going to the library to find a book on science experiments."

After school she stopped by the library to ask Mr. Winston if there were any books about science experiments. He said so many people were getting ready for the science fair that all those books had been checked out.

Mika felt anxious. She wanted Mrs. Jasell to be proud of her. She also wanted to make a good grade on her project. She needed an idea and she needed one soon.

The next day, her brother told her about the science fair project he did when he was in fourth grade. He had made a maze out of cardboard and taught his pet hamster to find the way out. That gave Mika an idea for a project she could do.

Mika remembered Mrs. Jasell telling her once that plants grow toward light. Her teacher had also told her that she left a plant in a dark room once and that the plant had begun to grow under the door to find the light in the hallway.

Mika decided to make a maze in a box to see if a plant could find its way out just as her brother's hamster did. She found a big shoe box and made two cardboard walls in the middle of the box. She cut a small hole in each wall and another window at the end of the box to let in light. Next, she put a small bean plant at the dark end of the box and closed the lid. She put the box by the window in her living room.

On Thursday she took the lid off of the box to water her plant. She yelled, "It's working!" so loudly that her brother came running in. She showed him how the little bean plant was already beginning to grow toward the hole in the box.

By the time Science Fair Day came, the small bean plant had grown a stem that was several inches long. It had grown through the little window and out of the opening at the end of the box.

Mika had written a report that told how she got the idea and how she made the maze. Her teacher was very impressed by the plant maze. Mika made an A+ on her project. Her teacher said she thought it was very creative.

MIKA'S MAZE QUESTIONS

1. What is this story mostly about?
   ◯ How to make a science fair project.
   ◯ Mika working in the garden.
   ◯ Mika finding an idea and doing a project.
   ◯ Science Fair Day at Stephens Elementary.

2. Where did this story take place?
   ◯ In the playground.
   ◯ At Mika's house.
   ◯ In a grocery store.
   ◯ At Mrs. Jasell's house.

3. What does the word "anxious" mean in this story?
   ◯ Worried.
   ◯ Angry.
   ◯ Unhappy.
   ◯ Mean.

4. What did Mika do after she talked to Mr. Winston?
   ◯ Worked in the garden.
   ◯ Went to the library.
   ◯ Talked to her Mom.
   ◯ Talked to her brother.

5. What does the word "impressed" mean in this story?
   ◯ Happy with.
   ◯ Disappointed in.
   ◯ Upset with.
   ◯ Worried about.

6. Why did Mika make an A+ on her science fair project?
   ◯ The teacher liked Mika.
   ◯ Mika did a good job.
   ◯ The library was out of books.
   ◯ Everyone made a good grade.

THE FIRST DAY MYSTERY

On the first day of school, William got up early. He had his clothes on and was eating a bowl of cereal when his mom woke up.

"I guess you are ready for school to start," she said. He smiled and nodded as milk dripped from his chin.

William was excited because it was his first day of fifth grade. He already knew that his teacher would be Mr. Moore. William was looking forward to being in that class. He had heard the other kids talk about all of the fun things Mr. Moore did with his students. He knew that Mr. Moore's class had a garden outside and that the class grew different kinds of fruits, vegetables and flowers.

William liked to get his hands dirty. He liked to be outside. He was going to like being in Mr. Moore's class.

When he walked into the classroom, he felt nervous. He looked around the room. Each desk had a sticker with a student's name on it. He found his name and sat down. In the middle of his desk he found a small white seed. There was a big question mark written on the chalkboard. William did not know what he was supposed to do.

The whole class was looking around and wondering what the seeds and question marks were for. When the morning bell rang, Mr. Moore walked into the classroom and said, "OK. Let's go!" He took the class outside and showed them their new garden. He told them they would have a guessing contest.

Each student had to plant the seed from his or her desk and try to guess what plant would grow from it. The teacher had drawn lines in the dirt of the garden and everyone had a square of garden space. All the kids began digging little holes in the ground and dropping in their seeds.

The whole class was planting their seeds, except William. He was afraid that Mr. Moore had forgotten about him, because he did not have a space for his seed. Mr. Moore walked up to him and pointed to a part of the garden that was away from the rest of the class. The teacher said, "You will have to plant your seed over there. It's going to need plenty of space to grow." He wondered what kind of plant would need so much space.

William carefully planted the seed. He tried to think of a plant that needed a lot of space to grow. He wrote his guess on a sheet of paper and turned it in to his teacher.

Every few days after that he went outside and sprinkled some water where the seed was planted. In about 10 days, the seed sprouted and a little green plant began to poke out of the ground. William took care of his plant and it grew. Mr. Moore was right. It did need a lot of space. The plant grew vines that spread out in all directions. It was the biggest plant in the whole class. It grew yellow flowers that later become large, round pumpkins. William's guess was right.

The First Day Mystery Questions

1. What is this story mostly about?
   - ❍ William's new teacher.
   - ❍ A large pumpkin plant.
   - ❍ How to plant a seed.
   - ❍ William's mystery on his first day of school.

2. Why was William excited at the beginning of this story?
   - ❍ Mr. Moore was his new teacher.
   - ❍ He liked pumpkin plants.
   - ❍ He woke up before his mother.
   - ❍ He was in fifth grade.

3. What was the class doing outside?
   - ❍ Walking to school.
   - ❍ Watering pumpkin plants.
   - ❍ Picking the flowers.
   - ❍ Planting seeds.

4. What happened right after William walked into the classroom?
   - ❍ He planted a seed.
   - ❍ He sat at his desk.
   - ❍ He ate a bowl of cereal.
   - ❍ He watered his plant.

5. What does the word "sprouted" mean in this story?
   - ❍ Began to grow.
   - ❍ Turned into a pumpkin.
   - ❍ Made a flower.
   - ❍ Buried.

6. How did William feel when his plant grew so big?
   - ❍ Angry.
   - ❍ Proud.
   - ❍ Worried.
   - ❍ Sad.

STARS, STRIPES AND SEEDS

Hannah was having many wonderful dreams. She was sleeping late this morning. Then her mother came in the room and started singing, "Wake up, wake up, the sun is up! The dew is on the buttercup!" Hannah's mother always woke her up with that song.

"Mom! It's summer vacation! I don't have to get up!" cried Hannah.

"Yes, you need to get up. Today is a special day," she said. "Today is the 4th of July!"

Hannah couldn't understand what was so special about the 4th of July. Yesterday was the 3rd of July and her mom didn't come wake her up then.

"Don't you remember? Today is the day that America became a free country," her mother said. "Do you like it when your big brother tells you what to do?"

"No, I don't," Hannah said.

Hannah's mother told her that long ago, that was happening in our country. Before the United States was a country, the king of England was telling the people who lived here exactly what to do. The people here didn't like that. So a group of people met and wrote a document called the Declaration of Independence. It was accepted July 4, 1776. July 4 became the birthday of the United States.

"We have a birthday party to get ready for, and I need your help," said Hannah's mother.

"A party—with decorations and cake and lots of fun? Yippee!" cried Hannah. "What can I do to help?"

"I need you to help me with the decorations, Hannah," her mother said.

Hannah's mother told her they were going to have a party that night. "We will need some nice lanterns outside," she said. "We will make them with watermelons."

Hannah's job was to carve the watermelon as you would a pumpkin for Halloween. She and her mother cut a circle out of the top. Then Hannah used a spoon to remove all the seeds and juicy, red meat from the watermelon.

Next, her mother helped her draw stars on the side of the watermelon. They used a knife to cut stars out of the green rind. Then they put a candle inside the watermelon.

That night at the party they lit the candles. The stars glowed from the light of the candle, and you could still see the green and white stripes on the side of the watermelon. "It looks like our flag!" Hannah said.

"That's right, Hannah," her mother said. "Our flag is made of stars and stripes, too. It is a symbol of our freedom, just like the Declaration of Independence."

STARS, STRIPES AND SEEDS QUESTIONS

1. The main idea of this story is that:

   ○ Watermelons have seeds.

   ○ Hannah had a party.

   ○ July 4th is the day we celebrate our freedom.

   ○ Hannah had to get up early to help with decorations.

2. The word "document" in this story means:

   ○ Story.

   ○ An important paper.

   ○ Song.

   ○ An article.

3. How did Hannah feel about getting up early?

   ○ Excited.

   ○ Angry.

   ○ Sad.

   ○ Curious.

4. Which is a FACT in the story?

   ○ Hannah didn't get up to help her mother.

   ○ Hannah helped clean the house for the party.

   ○ The Declaration of Independence was accepted July 3.

   ○ Hannah took the juicy, red meat out of the watermelon.

5. What is the first thing that Hannah had to do to the watermelon?

   ○ Draw stars on the side of it.

   ○ Dig out the seeds and meat.

   ○ Cut a hole in the top.

   ○ Put a candle inside.

6. What did the watermelon lantern remind Hannah of?

   ○ A pumpkin.

   ○ Our flag.

   ○ A ball.

   ○ A boat.

The Veggie Fair

The end of the school year at Willow Oaks Elementary was exciting. Many of the students in Mrs. Taylor's fifth grade class and other classes were going to compete in the school's annual Veggie Fair. Every June the school held a competition to see who had grown the best tomatoes, peppers, squash and many other vegetables.

Mrs. Taylor called her students "gardeners" because they all liked to grow vegetables and other plants in the class garden. The teacher gave each gardener a partner and assigned them a small section of the garden to take care of. The students could grow anything they wanted. Many chose to grow vegetables so they could compete in the Veggie Fair.

Tanisha and Sam were partners, and they decided to grow tomatoes in their section of the garden. Earlier in the spring, they had transplanted young tomato plants into the garden. They always checked the garden at least three times a week to pull any weeds that had grown and to water the plants if they were dry. They also fertilized their plants and looked for damage caused by insects. They even made a scarecrow to try to keep birds from eating the tomatoes.

On Monday, Sam and Tanisha saw posters in the hallways. They read all about the Veggie Fair and looked forward to having their special tomatoes in the contest.

Willow Oaks Elementary School
Annual Veggie Fair

Date: Friday, June 7
Time: 3:00 - 5:30 p.m.
Place: Cafeteria

Schedule:
    3:00 Classes set out vegetables
    3:30 Fair begins
    4:00 Vegetables are weighed
    4:30 Judging begins
    5:00 Awards are announced

Rules:
1. All vegetables must be grown by students on campus.
2. All vegetables must be labeled with student's name, class and grade level.
3. There will be awards for first, second and third place for each category.

Categories:
    Awards will be given for the largest, heaviest, most colorful and the tastiest of each type of vegetable entered.

Prizes:
    Trophies and a pair of leather gardening gloves will be given for first place winners.
    Second place winners will receive a red ribbon and leather gloves.
    Third place winners will receive a white ribbon.
    All others who enter the Veggie Fair will receive a yellow ribbon.

The Veggie Fair Questions

1. What does the word "annual" mean in this story?

   ○ Night time.

   ○ Once every year.

   ○ Winter.

   ○ Every month.

2. Where does the Veggie Fair take place?

   ○ Cafeteria.

   ○ Garden.

   ○ Parking lot.

   ○ Playground.

3. What does the word "transplanted" mean in this story?

   ○ Pick tomatoes.

   ○ Put plants into the ground.

   ○ Pull weeds.

   ○ Water the plants.

4. What time does the judging begin?

   ○ 4:00.

   ○ 4:30.

   ○ 5:00.

   ○ 5:30.

5. Which of these is NOT a category in the fair?

   ○ Largest.

   ○ Heaviest.

   ○ Longest.

   ○ Most colorful.

6. What prize is awarded for third place?

   ○ Leather gloves.

   ○ Red ribbon.

   ○ White ribbon.

   ○ Vegetable seeds.

EARTHWORM FARM

"The worms will be here tomorrow!" Miss Fuller announced to her class. The class began to cheer. The students were looking forward to the earthworms coming to their room. Miss Fuller had promised that when they finished studying about worms, they could start an earthworm farm in the class.

At first, Kayla thought the earthworms were gross. She thought they were dirty and slimy. Miss Fuller said, "Of course they are dirty. They live in the dirt." The students had been learning about earthworms and how they can help people recycle trash and make it into something useful. Kayla actually began to like the earthworms. She learned that the worms are slimy to keep their skin from drying out.

The students in Miss Fuller's class studied about how worms eat leftover food scraps and turn the scraps into compost. They learned that compost is like dirt that is full of vitamins for plants.

The class already had the worm farm ready for the worms to move in. The students made it out of a big plastic box with little holes in it. They also tore newspaper into small pieces, put it in the bottom of the box, and wet the newspaper. The worms would eat through the newspaper and turn it into compost too. Next they sprinkled some dirt over the newspapers.

The next day, the worms arrived in a small paper bucket. The class was amazed when Miss Fuller said the bucket contained more than 2,000 worms. The students dug a little hole in the dirt and wet newspaper and poured the earthworms in. The worms began to crawl around in their new home.

Miss Fuller told her class that the worms were hungry and that they would eat their first lunch leftovers that day. She asked for someone to be the first worm feeder. Kayla raised her hand and said, "The worms can have my lunch!"

The teacher reminded her that the worms were to help get rid of their leftover food that was trash. She did not want the worms to eat food the students were supposed to eat.

When Kayla had finished eating her lunch, all that was left on her tray was a spoonful of corn, an apple core and a chicken bone. Mrs. Fuller reminded Kayla that no meat or bones should be put in the worm farm, because they would get smelly before the worms could eat them. Kayla buried the rest of her leftovers under the dirt.

Kayla had the job of feeding the earthworms all week. On Friday she checked the spot where she first buried the corn and apple core. The corn was gone and the apple core had earthworms eating all over it. Those worms were hungry!

After feeding the worms for 3 months, Kayla's class noticed that almost all the newspaper had been completely eaten away, too. Mrs. Fuller had the class take some of the compost out of the worm farm and mix it in the dirt around the flowers in their garden. The sunflowers that grew in the garden that year were taller than they had ever been before.

EARTHWORM FARM QUESTIONS

1. What is this story mostly about?
   - ○ Why worms are slimy.
   - ○ How Kayla's class learned about worms.
   - ○ What earthworms eat.
   - ○ How to grow tall sunflowers.

2. What happened before the class sprinkled dirt on top of the newspaper?
   - ○ The class put the worms in the bin.
   - ○ The worms crawled around.
   - ○ The worms ate the corn.
   - ○ The students made the paper wet.

3. What does the word "recycle" mean in this story?
   - ○ Make something useful from trash.
   - ○ Make an earthworm farm.
   - ○ Make the newspaper wet.
   - ○ Throw away trash.

4. Which of these did NOT happen in this story?
   - ○ The class learned about earthworms.
   - ○ The sunflowers grew tall.
   - ○ The worms came to the class in a paper bucket.
   - ○ The worms ate a chicken bone.

5. What does the word "compost" mean in this story?
   - ○ Soil that is good for plants.
   - ○ An earthworm farm.
   - ○ Leftovers.
   - ○ A place to put trash.

6. Why do you think the sunflowers grew so tall?
   - ○ They were growing in a sunny place.
   - ○ Kayla watered them.
   - ○ The compost was put in the garden.
   - ○ The newspaper helped them to grow.

4-H Basic Facts

4-H Basic Facts

Preparing young people to be positive, contributing members of society is one of the most important tasks facing our society today. The 4-H & Youth Development Program of the Texas Agricultural Extension Service has been a key player in youth development since its modest start in 1908. In recent years, between 10 and 15 percent of all Texas youths between the ages of 5 and 19 have enrolled as 4-H members or 4-H Clover Kids each year. Annually, about 50,000 adults volunteer their time, talents and resources in support of the 4-H & Youth Development Program.

Motto   To Make the Best Better

Colors   Green and white. Green symbolizes nature's most common color and represents life, springtime and youth. White symbolizes purity.

Emblem   The 4-H emblem is a four-leaf clover with the letter "H" on each leaf, standing for head, heart, hands and health.

Head
4-H will get the youths thinking. They'll learn how to think as team members and to work with others to accomplish their goals. They will discover the world around them. 4-H offers them a chance to build the knowledge, skills and attitudes they will need to be strong, self-directed, productive adults. They'll find new ways to see the world and to see themselves.

Heart
It can be rough growing up today. To sort out their thoughts, ideas and emotions, youths can talk with 4-H members and leaders about what is important to them. They find that others involved in 4-H feel the same way they do. In 4-H, they develop relationships with other young people and with adults. They form lasting friendships and make cherished memories.

Hands
In 4-H, youths will participate in fun activities and learn skills they can use for the rest of their lives—on the job, at home or with their friends. 4-H'ers work to improve their communities, share their skills and ideas with others, and get hands-on experience for the future. They will learn new skills and explore careers that interest them.

Health
4-H helps youths learn to make healthful choices about exercise and eating. Being healthy means feeling good inside and outside, with school, friends and family. In 4-H, they will learn how to develop a healthy lifestyle, and they will understand the consequences of unhealthy decisions. Their physical and emotional well-being are important and in 4-H they can achieve their fullest potential.

4-H Motto and Pledge
In support of the 4-H Club Motto, To Make the Best Better, I pledge:
My Head to clearer thinking
My Heart to greater loyalty
My Hands to larger service, and
My Health to better living
For my club, my community, my country and my world.

4-H is a group of young people who have a lot of energy, enthusiasm and fun. And they make a big difference in the lives of people they know!

What do 4-H'ers do?

4-H members choose projects that interest them. Texas has many 4-H projects to choose from. Members attend meetings, participate in new learning experiences and may be involved in making presentations and community service projects. They may also participate in 4-H camps, the county fair or trips to other states and countries. Youths can make many good friends, learn important skills and have tons of fun too!

How does someone join 4-H?

Call the local office of the Texas Agricultural Extension Service. It is listed in the telephone book along with other county offices. An Extension agent working with 4-H will be able to guide you to 4-H opportunities in your area.

How much does it cost to join 4-H?

Joining 4-H costs little or nothing. Some projects may require an investment to get started.

Can city dwellers join 4-H?

4-H programs are open to all young people, no matter where they live. Programs are in every county in Texas. If you live in a town or city, you can participate in 4-H activities with pets and small animals, drama, food and nutrition, mini gardens, photography, woodworking, leadership and more!

How old must someone be to join 4-H?

4-H programs are open to all young people from third grade through age 19. A special 4-H Clover Kids program is available for children in kindergarten through the second grade, ages 5 through 8.

What about parents or guardians?

Parents don't have to become 4-H leaders when their children join 4-H, but there are many opportunities for them to help. This help can range from being a project leader to driving members to activities or supplying refreshments for a meeting. Adult volunteers supervise the 4-H activities.

Who sponsors 4-H in Texas?

4-H is an education program provided through the Texas Agricultural Extension Service in partnership with The Texas A&M University System and state, federal and county government in each of the state's 254 counties.

Make a difference in 4-H —
And 4-H will make a difference in you!

Support Materials

Importance and Uses of Plants

	Date	Initials
Group Activities		
Hamburger Plant		
Benefits Mobile		
Know & Show Sombrero		
The Choo-Choo Song		
The Medicine Plant		
Individual Activities		
Plant Product Collage		
Plant Press Sandwich		
Journal		

Plant Classification

	Date	Initials
Group Activities		
Leaf and Seet Sort		
Individual Activities		
Leaf Rubbing Rainbow		
Can You Be-Leaf it?		
JMG Web		

Plant Parts

	Date	Initials
Group Activities		
Plant Parts Rap		
Touch and Tell		
Plant Parts We Eat		
Seed Science		
Flower Dissection		
Individual Activities		
Fantastical Plants		
JMG Rap Performance		
Uncover and Discover		

Plant Needs

	Date	Initials
Group Activities		
P.L.A.N.T. Needs		
What's Not the Same?		
Plant People		
Picture Yourself a Plant		
Individual Activities		
Variable Menu		
2-Liter Terrarium		

Plant Growth

	Date	Initials
Group Activities		
Coconut Float		
Plant Performance		
Topiary Design		
Power Seeds		
Pinwheel Plants		
Individual Activities		
Pinto Plant Parts		
Seed Sock Search		
See the Seed Flee		

Plant Processes

	Date	Initials
Group Activities		
Oxygen Factory		
Gas Gobblers		
Spinning Seeds		
Individual Activities		
Initial Leaves		
Plant Maze		
Upside Down Seed		
Patriotic Plant		
Smothering Stomata		

Propagation

	Date	Initials
Group Activities		
Paper Pots		
Gallon Greenhouse		
Propagation Demonstration		
Individual Activities		
Stick and Grow		
Seed Sponges		
Time to Transplant		
Grow Your Own Pineapple		
JMG Web		
Journal		

Leadership/Service Projects

	Date	Initials
Gifts for Others		
Variable Day Demonstration		
Adopt-a-Spot		
Share What You Know		
JMG Know and Show Sombrero Competition		
Create Your Own		

Terms: Junior Master Gardener, JMG, and associated logo designs are registered service marks of Texas Cooperative Extension, The Texas A&M University System

Soil Color, Texture and Structure

		Date	Initials
Group Activities	Touchy Feely		
	Mud Pies		
	Shake, Rattle and Roll		
	Candy Aggregate		
Individual Activities	Making a List		
	Soil Rainbow		
	Soil Sample		
	Compaction Measurement		
	JMG Web		

Nutrients

		Date	Initials
Group Activities	Nutrient Variable		
	The Numbers on the Bag		
	Bumps Below		
Individual Activities	Nutrient Nets		
	The Numbers on Bug Performance		
	JMG Web		

Soil Improvement

		Date	Initials
Group Activities	Compost Sandwiches		
	Composting Critter Page		
	Compost Sandwich Comp.		
Individual Activities	Planting Trash		
	Pile It Up		
	Journal		
	JMG Web		

Water Cycle and You

		Date	Initials
Group Activities	Earth Apple		
	Cloud Maker		
	The Cycle Song		
	Apple Rings and Banana Chips		
Individual Activities	Water Cycle		
	Transpiration Trap		
	How Watery Are You?		

Water Movement

		Date	Initials
Group Activities	Out of the Spout		
	Where Did It Go?		
	Water Flows, Soil Goes		
Individual Activities	Power Shower		
	Water Works		
	Rain Gauge		

Leadership/Service Projects

	Date	Initials
Help Make Their Bed		
Landfill Visit		
Wastewater Visit		
Make A Difference		
Super Soil Business		
Create Your Own		

Balance and Interactions

		Date	Initials
Group Activities	Nature Class Web		
	The Food Chain Gang		
	Polluting Your Planet		
	Exploding Cactus		
	Garden Weather Station		
Individual Activities	Your Own World		
	Wild Weeds		
	A Bee's Eye View		
	Water Balance		
	Become a Spider		
	JMG Web		

Habitats

		Date	Initials
Group Activities	The Tree Community		
	Gourd Bird House		
	Our Pocket Park		
	Backyard Buddy		
	Visit With A Vet		
Individual Activities	Home Sweet Home		
	Toad Abode		
	Feathered Friend Feeder		
	Boarding House		
	Journal		
	JMG Web		

Hand-In-Hand With Nature

		Date	Initials
Group Activities	On the Move		
	Both Sides of the Fence		
	Weighing Wastes		
	Let's Try Organic		
	Xeriscape		
Individual Activities	More Isn't Better		
	Organic JMG		
	Water, Water, Everywhere		
	Meter Reader		
	JMG Web		

Recycling

		Date	Initials
Group Activities	Vermi-composting		
	Supermowing Machine		
	Grow Cards		
	Know & Show Recycling Sombrero		
Individual Activities	Grow Cards		
	Use It...Don't Lose It		
	Critter Condo		
	Composting Homework		
	Recycle Inventory		
	JMG Web		

Eco-Art

		Date	Initials
Group Activities	Plant Pounding		
	Let's Dye It		
	Nature Windows		
	Garden Folks		
	Nature Masks		
	Mother Nature's Children		
Individual Activities	Seed Jewelry		
	Nature Garland		
	Mystery Boxes		
	Seeds Magnet		
	Recycle Sculpture		
	Garden Folks		

Leadership/Service Projects

		Date	Initials
	JMG Web		
	Winder Wildlife Tree		
	Backyard Habitat Garden		
	Recycled Art Show		
	Create Your Own		

Insect Basics

	Activity	Date	Initials
Group Activities	Insect Predictions & Survey		
	Insect Symmetry		
	The Great Cover-Up		
	Designer Bugs		
	Insect Riddles		
	Secret Smells Game		
Individual Activities	Inspector Insect-a		
	Insect Plaster Casts		
	Symmetry Snacks		
	Camouflage Critters		
	JMG Web		

Insect Life Cycles

	Activity	Date	Initials
Group Activities	All in the Family		
	Ordering Insects		
	Metamorphosis Bracelets		
	Morpho Puppets		
	JMG Web Activity: Journey North		
Individual Activities	To Be Or Not To Be...An Insect		
	My Family Tree		
	Change as You Grow		
	Caterpillar Nursery		
	Insect Island		
	JMG Web		

Insect Collecting

	Activity	Date	Initials
Group Activities	Suck-A-Bug!		
	It's a Small World		
	Insect Nets		
	By Land or Sea		
	Ant Lion Farm		
Individual Activities	The Pitfalls of Being an Insect		
	Let's Sweep Up!		
	Scavenger Hunt		
	Insect Night Light		
	Insect Collection		
	JMG Web		

Insect/Plant Interactions

	Activity	Date	Initials
Group Activities	Chew On This!		
	School Yard Survey		
	Pollinator Puppet Show		
	The Bartering System		
	The Lone Bee		
	Designer Plants and Insects		
Individual Activities	Sign Language		
	Good Gall-y!		
	Favorite Colors		
	JMG Web		

Insect Management

	Activity	Date	Initials
Group Activities	Garden Friends and Foes		
	Don't Bug Me!		
	Who Goes There?		
	Critter Creations		
Individual Activities	Attractor Factors		
	Who Goes There?		
	Beneficials Abound		

Plant Diseases

	Activity	Date	Initials
Group Activities	Exploratory Fungi		
	Yeast Bread		
	Lacy Leaves		
	Likin' Those Lichens		
Individual Activities	Prescription for Prevention		
	There's a Fungus Among Us		
	Fun With Fungi		
	Fungus in Your Food		
	Mushroom Prints		
	Prescription for Prevention		
	There's a Fungus Among Us		
	JMG Web		

Leadership/Service Projects

Activity	Date	Initials
Collect and Share		
Butterfly Garden		
Butterfly Release		
Create Your Own		

Terms: Junior Master Gardener, JMG, and associated logo designs are registered service marks of Texas Cooperative Extension, The Texas A&M University System

Design Process

		Date	Initials
Group Activities	Rooms		
	People and Places		
	Money Trees		
	Site Map		
Individual Activities	Interview With a Client		
	Check Out the Site		
	Sun Watch		
	Journal		
	JMG Web		

Design Principles

		Date	Initials
Group Activities	Nature Wheels		
	Texture Collection		
	Same Sides		
	Does It Fit?		
Individual Activities	Potato Vase		
	Texture Rubs		
	Color Wheel Complement		
	Monochrome Mixture		
	Color Moods		
	JMG Web		

Identification and Selection

		Date	Initials
Group Activities	Tearing Trees		
	How Tall is that Tree?		
	Learning Your ABPS		
	Great Green Grass		
Individual Activities	Is It Once or Always?		
	Leaf Book		
	Superstars		
	My Tree Book		
	Pine I.D.		
	JMG Web		

Installation

		Date	Initials
Group Activities	Arbor Day		
	"Do It Right"		
	Seed, Sod and Plugs		
	Make Your Bed		
Individual Activities	Room To Grow		
	JMG Web		

Caring For Your Landscape

		Date	Initials
Group Activities	An Inch of Water		
	Pruning Places		
	More Mulch, More Moist		
	Queen Bud		
	Dead Heads		
Individual Activities	An Inch of Water		
	Clean Cut		
	Keep It Clean		
	Hey Bud! Let's Get Growing!		
	Just Weed It		
	Hole In One		

Leadership/Service Projects

	Date	Initials
Plant a Bed		
Neighborhood or School Tree Book		
Annual Business		
Wildflower Meadow		
Create Your Own		

Terms: Junior Master Gardener, JMG, and associated logo designs are registered service marks of Texas Cooperative Extension, The Texas A&M University System

Facts and History

		Date	Initials
Group Activities	Dr. Fruit		
	Linnaeus' World Wide Names		
	Botanical Wood Prints		
	A Bushel and a Peck		
	Fruit and Veggie Lab		
Individual Activities	Mr. Appleseed		
	Prized Peanuts		
	Pomanders		
	Global Fruit		
	JMG Web		

Growth and Development

		Date	Initials
Group Activities	A Fruit's Life Rhyme		
	Fruit Frenzy		
	The Zones		
	Just Chill		
	Fruit Factory		
Individual Activities	Making Peanuts		
	Ripening Wrap		
	Designer Apples		
	Avocado Seed Soak		
	Attractive Snacks		
	Journal		
	JMG Web		

Products

		Date	Initials
Group Activities	Snooty Fruit		
	Apple-ing Appearance		
	Taste Test		
	JMG Jam		
	Johnny's Appleslop		
Individual Activities	Jammin' Juice		
	Grape Bake		
	A Better Butter		
	Journal		
	JMG Web		

Leadership/Service Projects

	Date	Initials
Share and Care Fruit Basket		
Create Your Own		

Junior Master Gardener — Level 1 - Chapter Seven — Vegetable and Herbs

Planning the Garden

	Date	Initials
Group Activities		
Home Sweet Home		
Make Your Pick		
Small and Large		
Rules are Rules		
Schedule It		
Some Like It Hot		
Individual Activities		
Garden Design		
Journal		
JMG Web		

Growing Techniques

	Date	Initials
Group Activities		
Cylinder Gardening		
Paper Towel Gardening		
Tender Transplants		
Weed Mats		
Season Extenders		
Individual Activities		
Creative Crazy Containers		
Zip and Grow		
Radish Carpet		
JMG Web		

Harvesting

	Date	Initials
Group Activities		
Garden to the Table		
Beauty Contest		
Seed Bank		
Individual Activities		
Seed Saving		
Watermelon Thump		
JMG Web		

Nutrition In The Garden

	Date	Initials
Group Activities		
The Pyramid		
Food Safety		
Label Reader		
Veggie Taste Test		
Junk Food Blues		
Individual Activities		
Food Journal		
Junk Food Blues Performance		
What Are You Eating?		
Making the Menu		

Vegetable Products

	Date	Initials
Group Activities		
Garden Veggie Casserole		
Veggie Pizza		
Party Confetti Salad		
Cultural Cooking		
Garden Sponges		
Vegetable Prints		
Individual Activities		
Interview with A Grocer		
Veggie Critters		
Plant Detective		
Peanut Butter Celery		

Herbal Products

	Date	Initials
Group Activities		
Touch and Smell		
Herbal Vinegar		
Herbal Bath Salts		
Herb Sachets		
Individual Activities		
Ice Cube Seasonings		
Rosemary BBQ Brush		
Herbal Butter		
Mint Tea		

Leadership/Service Projects

	Date	Initials
JMG Cookbook		
Cafeteria Consultants		
Veggie Fair		
Plant a Row		
Pyramid Presentation		
Harvest Fest		
Create Your Own		

Self-Esteem

	Date	Initials
Group Activities		
Who Are You?		
What Are You Like?		
Know Your JMG Friends		
Good JMG'ers Wanted Posters		
How Would You Feel?		
Feeling Bee		
Individual Activities		
My Autobiography		
Advertising Myself		

Relating To Others

	Date	Initials
Group Activities		
Where's My Fruit?		
Let's Build It		
JMG Cooperation Roster		
Musical Chairs with a Twist		
Over and Under		
Cooperation Countdown		
Individual Activities		
Cooperation Collage		
Let's Find Out		

Communication Skills

	Date	Initials
Group Activities		
Garden Shed		
Who's On Our Team?		
Can You Follow Me?		
Plant A Seed		
Individual Activities		
Cheer Cards		
Let Me Hear Your Body		

Decision Making/Goal Setting

	Date	Initials
Group Activities		
Goal Search		
Right On Target		
The Class/Club Chronicle		
Watch Me Grow		
What Are Your Plans?		
Individual Activities		
Great Days or 4-H Record Book		

Planning and Problem-Solving

	Date	Initials
Group Activities		
Making A Machine		
Create A Costume		
Pass It On		
Either/Or		
Let's Make a Case Out of It		
It's In the Bag		
Individual Activities		
Plan and Eat		
Time Marches On		

Responsible Behavior

	Date	Initials
Group Activities		
Shared Responsibility		
Consequences		
Touchdown		
Don't Stamp Me		
Individual Activities		
Who's Responsible		
Proceed With Caution		

Career Awareness

	Date	Initials
Group Activities		
Careers and School		
Career Teams		
When I Grow Up		
Dream House		
All For One		
How I Work Best		
Individual Activities		
Way Back When...		
Career Book		

Leadership/Service Projects

	Date	Initials
Group Activities		
JMG Web		
Career Display		
Job Shadow		
Learning to Share		
Individual Activities		
Create Your Own		

Recycle Treasures

Things to Save for JMG Activities

- ♣ **Broom sticks - Insect Nets**
- ♣ **Pillow Case - Insect Nets**
    Wire coat hangers – Insect Nets
- ♣ **Window screens – Grow Cards**
- ♣ **Old picture frames – Grow Cards**
- ♣ **Film canisters – Suck a Bug**
- ♣ **Poster board – Nature Masks**
- ♣ **Newspapers – Grow Cards, Know and Show Sombreros**

- ♣ **Old nylons – Plant People**
- ♣ **2 liter bottles – Critter Condo**
- ♣ **Natural materials – nuts, acorns, seeds, sticks, leaves - Nature Mask**

- ♣ **Misc. craft supplies – buttons, styrofoam peanuts, popsicle sticks**
- ♣ **Harvest seed from beds and gardens**

(DATE)

Dear Parents,

(YOUR SCHOOL NAME) is starting a Junior Master Gardener(JMG) program that will help our children grow and learn through a "hands-on" learning experiences and activities. The JMG program provides a positive learning experience for youth to develop leadership, responsibility and community pride through organized gardening activities. The JMG program combines a unique gardening based curriculum and web based instruction, community service, character education and service-based learning, into a fun and exciting certification program for youth. This program is designed to incorporate science, math, language arts, geography and other subject area disciplines into the "hands-on" gardening based activities. JMG curriculum is correlated to academic standards and has research supporting how the program improves academic success, nutrition, self-esteem, and leadership development. (YOUR SCHOOL NAME) needs your help to make the JMG program a success! Here are some ways you can become involved.

I am willing to:

_____ Serve on a (YOUR SCHOOL NAME) Junior Master Gardener Garden committee. This group will be made up of administrators, teacher, parents, and students.

_____ Assist in building garden beds, fences, arbors, and other structures.

_____ Donate money or gardening equipment and/or supplies for use in the garden.

_____ Volunteer my time to assist children in the garden or classroom.

_____ Assist by contacting businesses and community members for support through donations and gifts for the gardens.

Parent_____ Child_____

My child's teacher is _____.

Sample parent solicitation letter created by T. Ledbetter, teacher

Acknowledgments

Junior Master Gardener Project Team

Lisa A. Whittlesey
JMG Coordinator, Extension
Program Specialist-Horticultural
Sciences, The Texas A&M
University System

Randy Seagraves
JMG Curriculum Coordinator,
Extension Program Specialist-
Horticultural Sciences,
The Texas A&M
University System

Douglas F. Welsh
State Master Gardener
Coordinator, Professor and
Extension Horticulturist,
The Texas A&M
University System

Gayle Hall
Associate Professor and
Extension 4-H and Youth
Development Specialist,
The Texas A&M
University System

Shelby Touchy
Harris County Pilot Site
Coordinator

Jayne M. Zajicek
Professor and Associate
Department Head, Horticultural
Sciences, Texas A&M University

David C. Hicks
Director of Development, Texas
A&M Foundation
Former Executive Director, Texas
4-H Foundation

Junior Master Gardener Publishing Team

Editor: Diane Bowen
Assistant Publications Editor and Extension Communications Specialist,
The Texas A&M University System

Page Designer: Michelle Mikeska
Assistant Graphic Designer and Extension Communications Specialist,
The Texas A&M University System

Lead Illustrations: Jackson Price
Communications Specialist, Texas Transportation Institute

Illustrators: Roxy Pike
Former Graphic Designer, The Texas A&M University System

Octavio Tierranegra
Assistant Graphic Designer and Extension Communications Specialist,
The Texas A&M University System

Peripheral materials for the Junior Master Gardener program have been developed by Ann Cole, David Lipe, Judy Winn and Gale Norman of Agricultural Communications, The Texas A&M University System.

Authors

Randy Seagraves
Lisa Whittlesey
Cynthia Klemmer
  Research Assistant, Department of Horticultural
  Sciences, Texas A&M University
Carolyn Walton Robinson,
  Graduate Assistant, Department of Horticultural
  Sciences, Texas A&M University
Gayle Hall

Shelley Siegenthaler Genzer,
  Extension Assistant-Horticulture/Better Living for
  Texans Program, The Texas A&M University System
Cheryl Lewis,
  Teaching Assistant, Department of Horticultural
  Sciences, Texas A&M University
Shari Grahmann,
  Student worker

Reviewers

Douglas F. Welsh

Sam Cotner – Head, Department of Horticultural Sciences, Texas A&M University

Joseph Novak – Senior Lecturer, Department of Horticultural Sciences, Texas A&M University

Sam E. Feagley – Professor and Extension State Soil Environmental Specialist

Debra B. Reed – Assistant Professor and Extension Nutrition Specialist

Jenna D. Anding – Assistant Professor and Extension Nutrition Specialist

Larry Stein – Professor and Extension Horticulturist

Jayne M. Zajicek

Luis Cisneros – Assistant Professor, Department of Horticultural Sciences, Texas A&M University

Al Wagner – Associate Department Head and Extension Program Leader for Horticultural Sciences

Frank Daniello – Professor and Extension Horticulturist (Vegetables)

John Jackman – Professor and Extension Entomologist

Glen Graves – Master Gardener, Harris County Cylinder Gardening Coordinator

Pete Teel – Professor and Associate Head for Academics, Department of Entomology, Texas A&M University

Cheryl Mapston – District Extension Director, Family and Consumer Sciences

Contributing Photographers

Plant Growth and Development:
University Photographic Services

Soils and Water:
University Photographic Services

Ecology and Environmental Horticulture:
Thomas Eisner, Cornell University
University Photographic Services

Insects and Diseases:
Sam Cotner
Joseph Novak
Texas A&M University Entomology Department
John Jackman
Bastiaan Drees – Professor and Extension Entomologist

Pete Teel
Entomology Website –
    http://EntoCentennial.tamu.edu

Landscape Horticulture:
Douglas F. Welsh

Fruits and Nuts:
University Photographic Services

Vegetables and Herbs:
Sam Cotner
Frank Daniello
Joseph Novak
Al Wagner

Life Skills and Exploration:
University Photographic Services

Junior Master Gardener State Steering Committee

Kate Siegal – Youth Volunteer
Cory Wells – Youth Volunteer
Cheryl Supak – Extension Program Leader, Better Living for Texans, Brazos County
Maureen Riebel – Volunteer
Stanley Young – County Extension Agent-Agriculture, Lubbock County
Deborah Benge-Frost – County Extension Agent-Horticulture, Ector County
Bill Kutac – Volunteer
Kim Fuller – Texas Department of Agriculture
Douglas F. Welsh – Professor and Extension Horticulturist
Nancy Wells – Volunteer
Vernon Mullens – Master Gardener, Bexar County
Caren Walton – Bryan Independent School District
Monty Dozier – Extension Program Specialist-Conservation
Debbie Wicke Korenek – Volunteer, Wharton County
Eloise Taylor – Master Gardener, Midland County
Marty Baker – Extension Horticulturist
William Johnson – County Extension Agent-Agriculture, Galveston County
Vince Mannino – County Extension Agent-Horticulture, Jefferson County
Rebecca Parker – County Extension Agent-Agriculture, Denton County
Michael Merchant – Associate Professor and Extension Urban Entomologist
Joanne Witschorke – Agri-Food Masters
Dianna Irvin – Master Gardener, Hopkins County
Darlene Locke – County Extension Agent-Agriculture, Aransas County

Models for Handbook Photographs

Travis Redmond
Matthew Broussard
Patrick Clayton
Yesina Palacios
Megan James

Bobby Malone
Jessica Gold
Kellee Shearer
Alex Sewell
Kristie Sewell

Joyce Johnson
Ann Marie Bettencourt
Deepika Chona
Yvette Esquivel
Bob Esquivel

Octi Esquivel
Kory Davis
Kevin Williams
Taylor Whittlesey

Musical Performances at Pilot Sites

Ruthie Foster – Full Circle Productions
Cyd Cassone – Full Circle Productions
Cheryl Lewis

Pilot Sites

Southwood Valley Elementary School
Galaxy Program
(College Station, Texas)
Starlet Licona – Principal
Sally McKnight – Teacher
Beverly Hetland – Teacher
Gerald McDaniel – Teacher
Mandy Moree – Teacher
Kathy Johnson – Teacher

Owens Elementary School
Cy-Fair School District
(Houston, TX)
Melissa Ehrhardt – Principal
Sherri Steed – Teacher
Elizabeth Villareal – Teacher
Sue Cornelius – Volunteer
The Third Grade Team

Bethune Academy,
(Aldine, Texas)
Nicole Thompson
Monica Donaldson
C. J. Thompson
Joyce Evans
Merilyn Wylie
Robert Roach
Paulette Dukerich
Meagon Bartley
Daniel Miller
Denise Gaudino
Reba Athey
Anette Easley
Elaine Wilkins
Linda Busch

El Centro de Corazon
(Houston, Texas)
Tatiana Guerrero
The Rusk School Health
    Promotion Project
    Mercedes Gonzales
Karen Autrey – Teacher

West Houston Charter School
(Houston, Texas)
Joy Greico – Superintendent

Cloverleaf 4–H Club
Doug Shores – County Extension
    Agent-4-H, Harris County

Clerical and Office Support

Gail Griffin – Staff Assistant, Texas 4-H
    Youth Development Foundation
Lenae Huebner – Development Relations
    Coordinator, Mays College of Business
    Former 4-H Executive Secretary
Sue Ferguson – 4-H Staff Assistant

Shawna Faris – Student Worker
Lenora Sebesta – Administrative Assistant
Dorothy See – Administrative Assistant
Myrna Hill – 4-H Administrative Secretary
Judy Bell Woodward – Intern Volunteer
Rita Newman – Intern Volunteer

Special Thanks to

College Station Independent School District, for allowing Randy Seagraves to work on this project
Mary Frances Cole, President of the Board of Trustees, Texas 4-H Youth Development Foundation
Martha Couch, Professor and Assistant Extension Director for 4-H and Youth
R. Daniel Lineberger, for assisting with the JMG Website design and implementation
Philip Pearce, Executive Director, Texas 4-H Foundation
Martha Cason, Teacher and Master Gardener, Travis County
Bill Adams, County Extension Agent-Horticulture, Harris County
Tom LeRoy, formerly County Extension Agent-Agriculture, Harris County and currently County Extension Agent-
    Horticulture, Montgomery County
Doris Trotter, Master Gardener, Bexar County
Aggie Master Gardeners
Brazos County Master Gardeners
Harris County Master Gardeners
Elizabeth Easterling for contributing chapter overview charts.

Funding for this project was received from Houston Endowment, Inc.